CREATIVITY AND HCI: FROM EXPERIENCE TO DESIGN IN EDUCATION

IFIP – The International Federation for Information Processing

IFIP was founded in 1960 under the auspices of UNESCO, following the First World Computer Congress held in Paris the previous year. An umbrella organization for societies working in information processing, IFIP's aim is two-fold: to support information processing within its member countries and to encourage technology transfer to developing nations. As its mission statement clearly states,

> *IFIP's mission is to be the leading, truly international, apolitical organization which encourages and assists in the development, exploitation and application of information technology for the benefit of all people.*

IFIP is a non-profitmaking organization, run almost solely by 2500 volunteers. It operates through a number of technical committees, which organize events and publications. IFIP's events range from an international congress to local seminars, but the most important are:

• The IFIP World Computer Congress, held every second year;
• Open conferences;
• Working conferences.

The flagship event is the IFIP World Computer Congress, at which both invited and contributed papers are presented. Contributed papers are rigorously refereed and the rejection rate is high.

As with the Congress, participation in the open conferences is open to all and papers may be invited or submitted. Again, submitted papers are stringently refereed.

The working conferences are structured differently. They are usually run by a working group and attendance is small and by invitation only. Their purpose is to create an atmosphere conducive to innovation and development. Refereeing is less rigorous and papers are subjected to extensive group discussion.

Publications arising from IFIP events vary. The papers presented at the IFIP World Computer Congress and at open conferences are published as conference proceedings, while the results of the working conferences are often published as collections of selected and edited papers.

Any national society whose primary activity is in information may apply to become a full member of IFIP, although full membership is restricted to one society per country. Full members are entitled to vote at the annual General Assembly, National societies preferring a less committed involvement may apply for associate or corresponding membership. Associate members enjoy the same benefits as full members, but without voting rights. Corresponding members are not represented in IFIP bodies. Affiliated membership is open to non-national societies, and individual and honorary membership schemes are also offered.

CREATIVITY AND HCI: FROM EXPERIENCE TO DESIGN IN EDUCATION

Selected Contributions from HCIEd 2007,
March 29-30, 2007, Aveiro, Portugal

Edited by

Paula Kotzé
Meraka Institute
South Africa

William Wong
Middlesex University
United Kingdom

Joaquim Jorge
Technical University of Lisboa
Portugal

Alan Dix
Lancaster University
United Kingdom

Paula Alexandra Silva
Universidade de Madeira
Portugal

 Springer

Creativity and HCI: From Experience to Design in Education
Edited by Paula Kotzé, William Wong, Joaquim Jorge, Alan Dix
and Paula Alexandra Silva

p. cm. (IFIP International Federation for Information Processing, a Springer Series in Computer Science)

ISSN: 1571-5736 / 1861-2288 (Internet)
ISBN: 978-1-4419-4704-8
eISBN: 978-0-387-89022-7

Printed on acid-free paper

9 8 7 6 5 4 3 2 1

springer.com

Table of Contents

Preface - Creativity and HCI: From Experience to Design in Education

Paula Kotzé, William Wong, Joaquim Jorge, Alan Dix and Paula Alexandra Silva
[1] Meraka Institute, Centre for Scientific and Industrial Research,
and School of Computing, University of South Africa,
P O Box 395, Pretoria, 0001, South Africa
Paula.Kotze@meraka.org.za
WWW home page: http://www.meraka.org.za
Interaction Design Centre
[2] School of Computing Science, Middlesex University, The Burroughs,
Hendon, London NW4 4BT UK.
w.wong@mdx.ac.uk
WWW home page: http://www.cs.mdx.ac.uk/research/idc
[3] Department of Computer Science and Engineering,
Instituto Superior Técnico,
Technical University of Lisboa, Av. Rovisco Pais s/n,
Lisboa 1049-001, Portugal
jorgej@ist.utl.pt
WWW home page: http://web.ist.utl.pt/jorgej
[4] Computing Department, InfoLab21, South Drive Lancaster University,
Lancaster, LA1 4WA, UK
alan@hcibook.com
WWW home page: http://www.hcibook.com/alan/
[5] Departamento de Matemática e Engenharias, Universidade da Madeira
Campus Universitário da Penteada, 9000-390 Funchal, Portugal
palexa@gmail.com
WWW home page:
http://dme.uma.pt/pt/people/faculty/Paula.Alexandra.Silva.html

1   Introduction

There was a time when we knew what to teach in our HCI courses ... For the early stages, we had user-centred design, perhaps ethnography or participatory design. As we looked in more detail there were interface guidelines and platform toolkits. Then, to evaluate we had heuristics (only five users needed, good for student groups), cognitive walkthroughs and formal experiments. Above all, we all knew our ISO

Please use the following format when citing this chapter:

Kotzé, P., Wong, W., Jorge, J., Dix, A. and Silva, P.A., 2009, in IFIP International Federation for Information Processing, Volume 289; *Creativity and HCI: From Experience to Design in Education*; Paula Kotzé, William Wong, Joaquim Jorge, Alan Dix, Paula Alexandra Silva; (Boston: Springer), pp. 1–11.

mantra efficiency and effectiveness… and what was that third one? Of course some students still found it hard to 'think user', and it was such a pain trying to mark all that project-based coursework … But we knew what we were doing, and we knew what we were designing for … Computer systems stayed safely behind glass screens and about their only physical influence was when they spat out a floppy disk …

But for several years now feral computers have escaped office desks, and found their way into bedrooms and television sets, mobile phones and smart cards … They even talk to us in our cars and turn on the tap in the bathroom. Users have now even discovered that third part of the ISO mantra, but having done so are never satisfied and expect to enjoy using these things and even have fun! Even the safe world behind the glass screen has gone wild, with Web2.0, and community content … Would the person who user-tested that JavaScript rollover, please stand up?

Of course, we can teach our students about AJAX and mobile usability guidelines, and on our reading lists Nielsen [1] is silently being dropped in favour of Csikszentmihalyi [2]. If we are especially adventurous we may even swap the odd lecture with a product designer. As for our students, when they hit the workplace they might manage a whole three or four years before the next wave of technology hits them, and they find themselves moving rapidly into management and seeking to recruit a fresh group of graduates who might just understand the latest acronym technology and interface fad.

If we are to equip our students for their future working lives we need to give them not merely the knowledge of current technology and practice, but the means to adapt and engage with whatever comes their way. They will clearly need fundamental understanding of people both cognitively and socially and to be able to learn new technologies as they emerge. However, they also need to apply these basic understandings to create innovative solutions to as yet unthought-of problems.

This volume comprises papers selected and developed from HCIEd 2007, the Second International Working Conference of Human-Computer Interaction Educators. All the papers in the volume has been subjected to two rounds of strict peer-review, and the final selection of papers in this volume reflects the best work presented and developed from the lesson learnt at HCIEd 2007.

The HCIEd series of conferences started off as a series of workshops run by the British Computer Society's Human-Computer Interaction (BCS HCI) Specialist Group's Education and Practice Sub-Group. For a number of years it had focused on revising the HCI syllabus in response to the changing technology environment, characterised by, for example, mobile computing, ubiquitous technology and an aging population. In parallel with this, Working Group (WG) 13.1 on Education in HCI and HCI Curricula of the International Federation for Information Processing (IFIP), with whom the BCS HCI Group is affiliated through Technical Committee (TC) 13, was running a series of workshops, mainly in Europe, focussing on HCI curricula and ways and means to teach HCI in order to 'experience HCI'. While curricula and syllabus issues are still on both groups' agendas, learning to create, learning to find innovative solutions and designs, so that we can further influence and make a significant impact on society, is becoming an increasingly important focus. In 2006 these two groups combined forces by deciding to jointly take these workshops to an international level, expanding the horizons and thinking about the teaching and learning of creativity and invention in HCI. The result of this cooperation was HCIEd 2006 in Limerick, Ireland, co-organised with the additional support of the EU CONVIVIO European Network for Human-Centered Design of Interactive Technologies. The paper by Wong et al. [3] in this volume describes the lessons learnt from HCIEd 2006 and serves as historical introduction to the rest of the papers in the volume. HCIEd 2007 was held in Aveiro, Portugal during March 2007, with the additional support of EPCG (Eurographics Portuguese Chapter) and IEETA (Instituto de Engenharia Electrónica e Telemática de Aveiro).

Fig. 1. *Racing the LEGO robots along the tracks*   **Fig. 2.** *Trying out the home-made "toothpaste"*

The theme of HCIEd 2007 was *Creativity[3]: Experiencing to Educate and Design* seeking to encourage participants to think about the need for both creative teaching and also teaching for creativity. While it has been argued that creativity is an innate human quality, it is also true that expanding our experiences of creativity and increasing our repertoire of design solutions can substantially improve our ability to develop innovative HCI design solutions.

Creativity, education and design are big issues. The goal of HCIEd 2007 was to explore and extend the reach of these concepts in HCI education, focusing on the creation of vivid and compelling learning experiences. It sought to forge a better understanding of creative processes and abilities and to nurture creative, free-thinking mindsets.

As befits a conference focused on creativity, the conference format encouraged creative thinking, from carefully chosen pens and conference bags, to playing with LEGO robots and making toothpaste during a visit to Fábrica da Ciência (http://www.ua.pt/fabrica/), a hands-on science museum (Fig. 1 and 2). (Even the conference dinner broke new ground featuring a live demonstration of cooking as a design activity. A professional cook, a macrobiotic cook and a house wife (Fig. 3) were given identical ingredients and were asked to prepare the participants' desserts during the main course of dinner. Some of the results can be seen in Fig. 4. Whilst the ingredients were exactly the same, the results were as different as can be, just as in any design process!

Fig. 3. *The chefs - upon learning of their task*   **Fig. 4.** *The variety of desserts (design solutions) that emerged from the same ingredients*

This is not mere frivolity. To address novel and changing environments, user needs and technology, we need our students to think and act innovatively and creatively. However, to teach innovation and creativity, we need innovative and creative methods, and it would be foolish to think that we can develop and reflect upon such practices if we do not create for ourselves environments and activities stimulating creativity.

The papers in this volume in various ways grapple with these issues: how we can encourage creativity, how we can promote rich design and how we can apply this not just to the mechanics, but also to the experience of interaction. In themselves they certainly exhibit this creativity both in addressing new aspects of HCI education and also in interrogating more traditional themes in new ways.

2   Design and Trans/Multi Disciplinarity

Design was one of the HCIEd 2007 themes and art of a broader agenda of trans-disciplinarity. A number of papers in this volume deal with the meeting of technology design as encountered (largely) in computing science backgrounds and other forms of more aesthetic-focused design practices such as industrial design, graphic design and architecture, whilst some stretch further still and seek to include inspiration from cinematography, arts and crafts (van der Veer [4]) and even placing HCI within widening spheres that eventually lead to the 'meta-disciplines' of philosophy, art, mathematics and science (Bongers and van der Veer [5]).

The word 'design' is perhaps becoming increasingly problematic. In software engineering 'design' is one the standard stages meaning the 'design' of code to meet an objective, in HCI 'design' is also a common stage referring to the more behavioural aspects influencing the user … itself part of the broader process of interaction design. However, increasingly when we say 'design' or 'designer' in HCI the image is of mainly industrial/graphic design or possibly experience design.

Give this caveat, several authors have embedded elements of 'design' (meaning industrial/graphic) practice within a computing syllabus including Greenberg [6], who describes the user of various practices as part of a studio-based approach including the use of sketch books (drawing on Buxton's inspiration [7]); and Kotzé and Purgathofer [8], who use components of good design garnered form several sources.

In contrast Leblanc [9] comes from an environmental design context and has been seeking ways to instil trans-disciplinary thinking in her students. Rather than adopting a syncretistic approach, instead multidisciplinary teams were encouraged to establish a common knowledgebase while addressing real-life problems, and given the intellectual means to do this by short intensive block of different disciplines, but focused around a common topic. The power of concrete examples or problems to enable cross-disciplinary thinking is a theme that can be found from project-focused work in primary schools to scenario-based approaches in research projects. The eschewing of a simplistic homologisation of disciplines is perhaps pertinent for more specialised HCI courses where we may risk loosing deeper disciplinary understanding.

In HCI, while we embrace the strengths and lessons to be learnt from other disciplines, it is important to note the strengths that have emerged in our own area over the last 25 years, that we must both hold on to ourselves and offer to others. In particular, Kotzé and Purgathofer [8] remind us that the user and human focus, which we take for granted in HCI, is rare both in other areas of computer science, and also in most traditional 'design'. Within design teams both technological and aesthetic, our students need to be prepared to stand up for utility and fitness for purpose rather than conceptual purity and delighting the end-users or impressing the design community. We have much to learn, but also much to give.

While the authors in this book and most likely you, the reader, may take the value of cross-disciplinary work for granted, this is often not the case within the broader disciplinary areas within which we work, and van der Veer's [4] account of the end of their innovative course underlines the political fragility of cross-disciplinary work within many academic institutions.

3   Creativity, Constraints and Problem Solving

As already noted, creativity was a hot topic at HCIEd 2007 and amongst the papers in this volume. In their report on HCIEd 2006 in Limerick, Wong et al. list a number of questions addressed by the papers in that conference. This included:

- 'Nature vs. nurture: can creative invention be taught?'
- 'What tools and methods are there to help students learn to develop creative solutions?'

Many of the papers in this volume address these issues offering explicit ways to teach and support creativity and innovation.

A common problem is that students (and indeed designers) are blinkered by standard solutions to problems rather than finding novel ones, or become personally committed to early designs; Larusdottir [10] describes her students getting 'locked' into designs at prototype stage.

To avoid this, various authors force their students into novel or unfamiliar situations. Greenberg [6] poses design briefs for his students in a 'personally unfamiliar interaction area'; Oestreicher [11] uses challenging examples of bad design ('mind shakers') to stimulate students to 'break away from traditional ways of thinking'; Bongers and van der Veer [5] have students design for unusual application areas including a musical glove and 'interactive architectural forms'; and Sas and Dix [12] use unusual technology to prompt students to explore new application areas.

Paradoxically, while creativity is often about breaking bounds, also much of the literature on creativity emphasises the importance of various forms of constraint. Not surprisingly this also figures in many of the papers in this volume. Oestreicher [11] mentions the importance of a 'constrained design space' and how 'restraining can force the students into lateral thinking'; this is implicit also in many of the design briefs used by other authors. Sas and Dix [12] not only constrain the technology, but also encourage students to explicitly explore the nature of the constraints imposed by the technology. Even during the mundane task of note taking, Read et al. [13] report on constraining students to three electronic worksheets in order to prevent unlimited scribbled notes. In contrast, Greenberg [6] has (verbally) reported that he forces his students to produce 10 initial ideas in order to avoid early fixation … different kinds of constraint are important at different stages of education and design.

As well as constraints on the design itself, often creativity is encouraged by quite structured process. We see this in many papers including Greenberg's [6] structured studio sessions and Leblanc's [9] structured ideation/creativity sessions that make use of linguistically inspired techniques, categorisation and scenarios. These structured creativity techniques are themselves often inspired by theoretical understanding of creativity. For example, Kotzé and Purgathofer [8] use Laseau's twin funnels [14] of elaboration and reduction to structure their understanding of the role of techniques such as sketches and prototypes; Wesson [15] draw on various techniques such as BadIdeas [16]; Rapid Contextual Design [17]; and Beckhaus' seven factors to support teaching creative design [18]; and Sas and Dix [12] use an explicit representation of the design space to explicate the way their technology-focused brief encourages innovation.

These theoretical understandings are important as they help protect us from over-simplistic and dualistic characterisations of creativity: right brain vs. left brain, divergent vs. convergent, open vs. structured. In Csikszentmihalyi's [2] studies of 'creative' people, one of the observations was that many of them were extreme on many of the scales of personality and cognitive type ... but it was not because that they were all on one extreme, nor even that different individuals were on different extremes, but that single individuals, exhibited both extremes. As educators it is not so much that we want to take all those over-focused computer scientists and teach them to be more open-minded like arts students, but that we want to show them how to think divergently *without losing* structured attention, and to teach those with more divergent minds *also* to apply more analytic methods.

4   Education, Assessment and Evaluation

Of course the whole of this volume is about HCI education, so not surprisingly there are interesting lessons for general HCI education beyond those specifically about creativity or trans-disciplinarity.

Several papers mention that HCI is still seen as somehow 'soft' or 'woolly' by both students and fellow staff (e.g. Read et al. [13]) even though students are 'not always very successful at mastering it' (Chambel et al. [19]). We still clearly have a big education job here not just teaching techniques, but educating about HCI itself to our students and colleagues. It is interesting to note that several paper present examples of their best student work (e.g. Bongers and van der Veer [5] and Fonseca et al. [20]), and of course we want to show how good students can be when taught effectively. Oestreicher's [11] use of bad examples to motivate students is one approach to educating students, but perhaps also we ought to collect bad examples of our students work in order to say 'yes you do have something to learn' ... and maybe we should collect examples of systems our colleagues produce!

As with the teaching of creativity, theoretical approaches were evident, for example, Oestreicher [11] reviews several models including Bloom's taxonomy [21] and the 'Pyramid of Competence' [22], both of which emphasise higher level understanding and application of knowledge leading to meta-cognitive skills, not just mere rote learning. Fonseca et al.'s [20] focus on conceptual design also picks up this need for reflective application for both good interaction design and creative design. Another high-level skill is the need for clear problem framing, an issue raised by Leblanc [9] quoting Csikszentmihalyi [2] 'how you define a problem usually carries with it an explanation of what caused it', but is implicit in several others. However, worryingly Larusdottir [10] found that 73% of students reported they did not understand the requirements fully when they were half way through their project period. At best, this may simply reflect the fact that usability requirements often only become clear as we engineer solutions ... but probably also means that we have some way to go in teaching students how to understand problems.

While we all recognise the importance of teaching students about accessibility, Chambel et al. [19] raised the issue of accessibility of our teaching – how do you teach blind students. In fact there are several practicing usability professionals and academics who are blind and yet have not only learnt HCI, but teach it as well. This issue also affected the work reported by Read et al. [13] in that the CRaSH system could not be deployed more widely because it was too visual and therefore did not meet accessibility standards within the institution. With, very welcome, accessibility legislation in many countries, this may become an increasing issue for any form of practice-based user-interface research where even early prototypes may need to be designed to full accessibility standards if they are to be used in deployed, albeit experimental, applications.

Issues of collaboration and sharing are mentioned in several papers. Group based projects are common and Larusdottir [10] found that project and team management were one of the crucial success factors for student projects. As well as collaboration with groups or teams, more general sharing is often encouraged: Read et al.'s [13] CRaSH system is explicitly built to facilitate on this, and Greenberg [6] seeks to encourage 'ideas exchange' even though 'conventional courses call this cheating'. The latter also reminds us again of disciplinary conflicts and also problems of assessment ... how do we design project work that is both meaningful, and also assessable!

Assessment is particularly difficult for creativity or innovation. Wesson [15] uses a variant of 'functional creativity' (borrowed from the engineering domain) assessing whether the product produced exhibits novelty (is it original or innovative), relevance and effectiveness (does it do what it is supposed to do) and is germinal (does it lead to new metaphors and/or designs). Assessing these aspects is still bound to be very subjective and Greenberg [6] in his talk at HCIEd 2007 said that his criterion for an 'A' grade was if the work 'knocked his socks off'!

Koukouletsos et al.'s [23] paper is rare in that it reports a rigorous comparative study of techniques for teaching usability: patterns vs. guidelines. The complexity of usability and the complexity of learning mean that theoretical understanding, shared personal experiences and hard empirical evidence are all needed. However, evaluation of education is fraught with methodological problems, not least for meta-cognitive skills such as creativity, where one would argue that the true value lies in long-term change of mindset, not necessarily short-term outcomes. It is hard enough to assess the creativity of a single product or process; how are we to assess the success of education for creativity?

5   Experience and Change

As described previously, the HCI Educators conference in Aveiro was an Experience (capital intentional!). We all know that user experience has become an important issue of what we teach in HCI and throughout this volume there are instances that indicate the importance of experience in learning about HCI. Kotzé and Purgathofer [8] say that 'students must experience design to enable them to learn effectively' and Leblanc [9] talk about the importance of students being immersed in each discipline they study. Education is experience design!

However, what constitutes a good 'experience' is maybe itself changing. Van der Veer [4] notes that users of the iPod 'enjoy uncertainty', and it is perhaps notable that while the complexity of the web has grown, the 'lost in hyperspace' issues that dominated hypertext and early web usability is now forgotten – not forgotten because it has been solved, but forgotten because nobody cares anymore. Is this simply cyber-culture or a deeper cognitive shift? On television programmes the average length of shots has halved in the last 15 years – do our professional practices need to change as the 30 second attention span generation grows up and becomes our students and the designers of tomorrow?

Van de Veer also paints a picture of change users who are increasingly savvy in the use of technology but ignorant of its mechanisms. This may point the way to better metaphors and designs to enable users to make sense of increasingly complex functionality, or may mean we have to increasingly design more 'intelligent' interfaces that do the right things for users even if the users have no idea how they behave ... an 'I'm feeling lucky' button on your car's satellite navigation system?

Whichever way the future moves, it is clear that our students need more than a set of rules optimised for 1980s GUIs or even 2008 smart phones. Instead they need the means to adapt and change to a changing world, to be deeply versed on the fundamentals of human behaviour and technical possibilities, but also ready to invent, innovate and create. And our job is to prepare them for that.

References

1. J. Nielsen, Useit.com: Jakob Nielsen's Website, (cited 10 May 2008); http://www.useit.com/ (Nielsen Norman Group, Fremont, 2008).
2. M. Csikszentmihalyi, *Creativity, Flow and the Psychology of Discovery and Invention* (HarperCollins Publishers Inc., 1997).
3. W. Wong, P. Kotzé, J. Read, L. Bannon, and E. Hvannberg, From inventivity in Limerick to creativity in Aveiro: Lessons learnt, in: *Creativity and HCI: From Experience to Design in Education - Selected Contributions from HCIEd 2007 (this book)*, edited by P. Kotzé, W. Wong, J. Jorge, A. Dix, and P.A. Silva, IFIP Series, (Springer, 2008), pp. 19-29.
4. G.C. van der Veer, Between the ivory tower and babylon –Teaching interaction design in the 21st century, in: *Creativity and HCI: From Experience to Design in Education - Selected Contributions from HCIEd 2007 (this book)*, edited by P. Kotzé, W. Wong, J. Jorge, A. Dix, and P.A. Silva, IFIP Series, (Springer, 2008), pp. 150-165.
5. B. Bongers and G. van der Veer, HCI and design research education, in: *Creativity and HCI: From Experience to Design in Education - Selected Contributions from HCIEd 2007 (this book)*, edited by P. Kotzé, W. Wong, J. Jorge, A. Dix, and P.A. Silva, IFIP Series, (Springer, 2008), pp. 97-112.

6. S. Greenberg, Embedding a design studio course in a conventional computer science program, in: *Creativity and HCI: From Experience to Design in Education - Selected Contributions from HCIEd 2007 (this book)*, edited by P. Kotzé, W. Wong, J. Jorge, A. Dix, and P.A. Silva, IFIP Series, (Springer, 2008), pp. 30-46.
7. B. Buxton, *Sketching User Expereinces - Getting teh Design Right and the Right Design* (Morgan Kaufman, San Francisco, 2007).
8. P. Kotzé and P. Purgathofer, Designing design exercises – From theory to creativity and real-world use, in: *Creativity and HCI: From Experience to Design in Education - Selected Contributions from HCIEd 2007 (this book)*, edited by P. Kotzé, W. Wong, J. Jorge, A. Dix, and P.A. Silva, IFIP Series, (Springer, 2008), pp. 47-66.
9. T. Leblanc, Transdisciplinary Design Approach, in: *Creativity and HCI: From Experience to Design in Education - Selected Contributions from HCIEd 2007 (this book)*, edited by P. Kotzé, W. Wong, J. Jorge, A. Dix, and P.A. Silva, IFIP Series, (Springer, 2008), pp. 113-129.
10. M.K. Larusdottir, A case study - Hindrances and success factors in student projects, in: *Creativity and HCI: From Experience to Design in Education - Selected Contributions from HCIEd 2007 (this book)*, edited by P. Kotzé, W. Wong, J. Jorge, A. Dix, and P.A. Silva, IFIP Series, (Springer, 2008), pp. 196-209.
11. L. Oestreicher, Teaching human-computer interaction from real world examples – Furnishing creativity? in: *Creativity and HCI: From Experience to Design in Education - Selected Contributions from HCIEd 2007 (this book)*, edited by P. Kotzé, W. Wong, J. Jorge, A. Dix, and P.A. Silva, IFIP Series, (Springer, 2008), pp. 67-84.
12. C. Sas and A. Dix, Enhancing creativity in interaction design: Alternative design brief, in: *Creativity and HCI: From Experience to Design in Education - Selected Contributions from HCIEd 2007 (this book)*, edited by P. Kotzé, W. Wong, J. Jorge, A. Dix, and P.A. Silva, IFIP Series, (Springer, 2008), pp. 182-195.
13. J.C. Read, M. Horton, G. Sim, and E. Mazzone, CRaSh-ing into HCI, in: *Creativity and HCI: From Experience to Design in Education - Selected Contributions from HCIEd 2007 (this book)*, edited by P. Kotzé, W. Wong, J. Jorge, A. Dix, and P.A. Silva, IFIP Series, (Springer, 2008), pp. 225-235.
14. P. Laseau, *Graphic Thinking for Architects & Designers* (Wiley, 2000).
15. J. Wesson, Teaching creative interface design: Possibilities and pitfalls, in: *Creativity and HCI: From Experience to Design in Education - Selected Contributions from HCIEd 2007 (this book)*, edited by P. Kotzé, W. Wong, J. Jorge, A. Dix, and P.A. Silva, IFIP Series, (Springer, 2008), pp.
16. A. Dix, T. Ormerod, M. Twidale, C. Sas, P.A.G. da Silva, and L. McKnight, Why bad ideas are a good idea, in: *Inventivity: Teaching Theory, Design and innovation in HCI, Proceedings of of HCIEd2006-1 First Joint BCS/IFIP WG13.1/ICS/ EU CONVIVIO HCI Educators' Workshop, 23-24 March 2006, Limerick, Ireland*, edited by E.T. Hvannberg, J.C. Read, L. Bannon, P. Kotzé, and W. Wong, (University of Limerick, Limerick, 2006), pp. 9 - 14.
17. M.K. Larusdottir, Using Rapid Contextual Design at Reykjavik University, in: *Inventivity: Teaching Theory, Design and innovation in HCI, Proceedings of of HCIEd2006-1 First Joint BCS/IFIP WG13.1/ICS/ EU CONVIVIO HCI Educators' Workshop, 23-24 March 2006, Limerick, Ireland*, edited by E.T. Hvannberg, J.C. Read, L. Bannon, P. Kotzé, and W. Wong, (University of Limerick, Limerick, 2006), pp. 35 -39.

18. S. Beckhaus, Seven Factors to foster creativity in university HCI projects, in: *Inventivity: Teaching Theory, Design and innovation in HCI, Proceedings of of HCIEd2006-1 First Joint BCS/IFIP WG13.1/ICS/ EU CONVIVIO HCI Educators' Workshop, 23-24 March 2006, Limerick, Ireland*, edited by E.T. Hvannberg, J.C. Read, L. Bannon, P. Kotzé, and W. Wong, (University of Limerick, Limerick, 2006), pp. 91 - 95.

19. T. Chambel, P. Antunes, C. Duarte, L. Carriço, and N. Guimarães, Reflections on teaching human computer interaction to blind students, in: *Creativity and HCI: From Experience to Design in Education - Selected Contributions from HCIEd 2007 (this book)*, edited by P. Kotzé, W. Wong, J. Jorge, A. Dix, and P.A. Silva, IFIP Series, (Springer, 2008), pp. 130-149.

20. M.J. Fonseca, J.A. Jorge, M.R. Gomes, D. Gonçalves, and M. Vala, Conceptual design and prototyping to explore creativity, in: *Creativity and HCI: From Experience to Design in Education - Selected Contributions from HCIEd 2007 (this book)*, edited by P. Kotzé, W. Wong, J. Jorge, A. Dix, and P.A. Silva, IFIP Series, (Springer, 2008), pp. 210-224.

21. K. Baumann, Design education methods – Examples and findings in: Proceedings CONVIVIO Faculty Forum: Teaching Design for HCI (Graz, Austria, CONVIVIO, 2006).

22. P. Kotzé, K. Renaud, and J. Van Biljon, Don't do this. Pitfalls in using anti-patterns in teaching human-computer interaction principles, *Computer & Education*, **50**, 979 – 1008 (2008).

23. K. Koukouletsos, B. Khazaei, A. Dearden, and M. Ozcan, Teaching usability principles with patterns and guidelines, in: *Creativity and HCI: From Experience to Design in Education - Selected Contributions from HCIEd 2007 (this book)*, edited by P. Kotzé, W. Wong, J. Jorge, A. Dix, and P.A. Silva, IFIP Series, (Springer, 2008), pp. 166-181.

From Inventivity in Limerick to Creativity in Aveiro: Lessons Learnt

William Wong, Paula Kotzé, Janet Read, Liam Bannon and
Ebba Hvannberg
[1] Interaction Design Centre
School of Computing Science, Middlesex University, The Burroughs,
Hendon, London NW4 4BT UK
w.wong@mdx.ac.uk
WWW home page: http://www.cs.mdx.ac.uk/research/idc
[2] Meraka Institute, Centre for Scientific and Industrial Research,
and School of Computing, University of South Africa,
P O Box 395, Pretoria, 0001, South Africa
Paula.Kotze@meraka.org.za
WWW home page: http://www.meraka.org.za
[3] School of Computing, Engineering and Physical Sciences,
University of Central Lancashire,
Preston, PR1 2HE, United Kingdom
jcread@uclan.ac.uk
WWW home page: http://www.uclan.ac.UK
[4] Interaction Design Centre, Department of Computer Science and
Information Systems, University of Limerick, Ireland,
Liam.Bannon@ul.ie
WWW home page: http://www.ul.ie/~cscw/liam.html
[5] Computer Science, University of Iceland,
VR-II, Hjardarhaga 2-6, 107 Reykjavik, Iceland
ebba@hi.is
WWW home page: http://www.hi.is/~ebba/

Abstract. In this introductory chapter, we describe the key lessons from an earlier HCI Educators' conference, held in Limerick in 2006, the outcomes of which led to the theme of HCIEd 2007 – Creativity: Experiencing to Educate and Design. The paper discusses the lessons leant around four key questions: nature vs. nurture: can creative invention be taught; what tools and methods are there to help students learn to develop creative solutions; how do we train educators in creative invention; and what are the stumbling blocks to 'inventivity'?

Please use the following format when citing this chapter:

Wong, W., Kotzé, P., Read, J., Bannon, L. and Hvannberg, E., 2009, in IFIP International Federation for Information Processing, Volume 289; *Creativity and HCI: From Experience to Design in Education*; Paula Kotzé, William Wong, Joaquim Jorge, Alan Dix, Paula Alexandra Silva; (Boston: Springer), pp. 12–22.

1 Introduction

In this paper, we describe the key lessons from an earlier HCI Educators' conference, held in Limerick in 2006, on 'inventivity' – a term coined to highlight the confluence of inventiveness and creativity. There is a distinction between being creative and being artistic. HCI education, in terms of creative inventiveness, is not just about artistically pleasing user interfaces, but also about solutions that are innovative. We can know much about creativity and inventiveness. However, to be able to teach and train students so that they can be creatively inventive, we believe that it would be helpful if educators themselves have personally experienced this. With this in mind, we organised the follow-up conference HCIEd 2007 Creativity: Experiencing to Educate and Design.

Inventivity was coined to refer to the notion of inventing creative and innovative solutions. This term was also intended to mean that such solutions be more than 'creative', artistic or appealing interfaces as designed by artistic or 'creative types' of people. It was also intended to reflect the creativeness of the solutions that had to be invented. One reason for emphasising this aspect at the conference was that, in HCI design it is easy to mis-interpret the focus of HCI design solutions – which should not address just visualisation and interaction design, but also address how that visualisation and interaction creatively represents and simplifies the complexities in work that people engage in.

The recent focus on usability as the more tangible aspect of HCI has made the public, software developers and academics very aware of the problems caused by software with poor interfaces. While this is a good thing, it has perhaps also skewed our education of students in HCI as, resulting from this emphasis: most HCI courses have a significant focus on training our students to evaluate usability. This has led to the creation of a new industry in usability evaluation services. Although much more research is still needed for methods that improve usability, and that a better understanding and classification of usability problems can assist in the design of future products, such an approach, we believe, misses the other problem of a lack of methods for inventing better solutions and designs. If we have better solutions in the first place, there will be a lesser need to make limited improvements to software that has been delivered. In the Limerick conference, the emphasis was on understanding what is involved in inventing creative and innovative solutions, and therefore, how we might be able to teach this to our students.

One other assumption made during this conference was that human nature is such that we are creatures of habit and therefore we tend to follow the path of least resistance. This suggests that the more familiar we are with a particular way of working, the more likely we will stay with this approach, especially when we are under pressure to deliver an outcome. A person familiar with heuristic usability evaluation will most likely use that approach most frequently. Hence, if we as educators can develop such a familiarity amongst our students with the process and methods of inventing creative solutions, then they are also more likely to practise inventing creative solutions when in industry. It is against such a backdrop that we organised the conference on 'inventivity', and we used it to investigate the issues that helped or impeded teaching 'inventivity'.

Some of the issues that arose from the Limerick workshop concerning how we teach and educate our students 'inventivity', include:

a) Nature vs. nurture: can creative invention be taught?
b) What tools and methods are there to help students learn to develop creative solutions?
c) How do we train educators in creative invention?
d) What are the stumbling blocks to 'inventivity'?

We will briefly report on these areas next.

2   Nature vs. Nurture: Can Creative Invention be Taught?

Understanding the nature of creativity and inventiveness and therefore how it can be fostered, was the theme of a number of papers presented at the workshop [1-3]. Alexander and de Villiers [2] suggested that prior knowledge, insight, personal development and practice, collectively influences creative ability. This was nicely summarised as partly talent, partly solid skills, understanding of the problem and requirements, planning and implementation issues, and the theories that apply to the problem and the solution.

Computer science and information systems students are taught structured methods to analyse, decompose, and to develop systems. Such rigid structures can hamper creativity, which is generally a much less structured activity. The challenge for educators then is to move from these highly organised structures, to organised, but yet creative, structures that can facilitate creative invention (see Fig. 1 and Fig. 2).

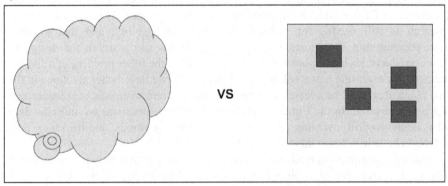

Fig. 1. *Fuzzy creative processes (left) vs. structured development processes (right).*

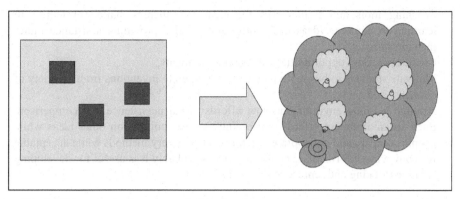

Fig. 2. *From structured processes (left box) to structures that facilitate creative invention (right clouds).*

Questions that emanate from this consideration include: Can computer science and information science students be creative? How might we influence the thinking of students and the capabilities they might use? It would seem that the answer to both these questions is 'yes', by perhaps, structuring creative processes and by giving students the needed knowledge, theory and skills to define the direction and boundaries of the invention. Wong [3] explains that part of the prior knowledge should be an understanding that invention occurs at different levels of innovation. According to Altshuler [4], this ranges from minor improvements to new concepts, and to true discoveries. Each level within this range of invention is informed by different understanding of the problem and guided by different levels of knowledge outside the problem domain.

Beckhaus suggests that to nurture creative invention, "Inventivity needs creativity ... [and creativity needs] space to develop" [1]. This is also echoed by Giovanella [5] as he reflects on his experiences in encouraging creativity in his teaching, writing: creativity cannot be forced into a restricted time window of a lecture session - it needs time and space for social interaction. Together with Wong [3], these authors provide some further suggestions for nurturing creativity within the classrooms. These suggestions include:

1. There needs to be an expectation of inventiveness in the curriculum. This would then set clear goals for how space and resources can be used so that creativity can evolve. This, when coupled with assessment, will also be a source of motivation for students to take the effort to think creatively beyond the basic deliverables. This idea of using assessments - e.g. short weekly quizzes - to motivate students to remain engaged in the process of nurturing inventivity, is also suggested by Read, Kelly and Sim [6];
2. The need for more realistic settings that reflect the complexity and serendipity of the real world and by specifying development tasks and processes that include phases for creative thinking, so that students develop a sound understanding of the domain;

3. Teaching tools and frameworks for creativity, thereby build confidence in learning to combine ideas differently, and by also providing assistance rather than interference;
4. Create classroom opportunities for 'eureka' moments;
5. Motivate students to be creative by exposing them to inventions from a variety of domains; and
6. Arrange learning environments that affords visual persistence and comparison. Such an environment affords scaffolding as ideas build upon other ideas while people compare and collaborate. Lecture-style delivery methods while acceptable for conveying information about creativity is probably less useful for developing creative thinking and representation skills.

3   What Tools and Methods are there to Help Students Learn and Develop Creative Solutions?

From the Limerick conference, it would seem that there are many tools that exist or have been developed or modified by participants at the conference to assist in teaching creativity. Dix and his colleagues [7] proposed the Bad Ideas Toolkit to help in the process of creativity. Using systematic methods to critically review bad ideas from different perspectives provides a way of training students to explore and to understand the extent and the constraints of the design space. These methods create new opportunities to make good the bad ideas, avoid design fixation, and to reduce any emotional attachments ("Hey, that's my baby you are talking about...!"), which then allow the students the freedom to re-consider or criticise earlier design decisions. Along similar lines of critique, based on the notion that 'creativity is an individual characteristic, and innovation is a social activity' Giovannella [5], proposed the use of an on-line repository, or 'lab-diary', for public brainstorming of ideas about the problem and the design concept. This lab diary would be used as a classroom tool and technique for stimulating the socialisation and sharing of ideas, resources and knowledge. Harrison and Tatar [8] described how their students were also encouraged to keep a 'design journal', not of class notes, but of design ideas and observations, and in keeping the diary, noting how their ideas develop over time. The diaries allowed the students to systematically record their reflections and insights, which could then be shared and discussed with teammates.

Lennon and Bannon [9] report using the worksheets to collate, organise and present photos and artefacts. These worksheets are then displayed on a wall in the classroom or project room to create a persistent visual environment where the key elements of the domain are continuously in view. The use of worksheets in this way allows discussions to take place within the context of the domain, reminding the students of the issues, highlighting important factors, and providing an arena for 'seeing' new relationships. The worksheet method so described was found to be a very simple technique that helped students gain insights about the problem and the environment in which the solution must succeed.

Experiences with a number of methods for generating ideas were also described. Larusdottir [10] described her experiences in using Rapid Contextual Design (RCD) and her reflections about how new ideas were generated through the process. The contextual interviews, the affinity diagrams, and the development and use of personas and scenarios, helped the students understand the context and the nature of the problem. One of the activities in the RCD, the data walk, was used to identify missing information and highlight incorrect assumptions. A second activity, the visioning process, was used to sketch and visualise the proposed solutions, and develop paper prototypes from which to evaluate solutions. Ciolfi and Cooke [11] suggest 'cooperative evaluation' as another technique one should have in the toolset. Through the cooperative nature of the evaluation, partners think aloud in a process of co-discovery of the problems. The record of the evaluation then provides a source of reflection and insight to designers about what is good or bad with regard to the 'bigger picture'. While much can be done mechanistically, the philosophy adopted was to use this method to focus on creative thinking at each stage of the process in a cooperative manner.

'More than a method' is a suite of methods and techniques that are tightly coupled into a Project-Based Learning approach [8]. 'More than a method' emphasizes familiarity with a variety of functionally overlapping tools where their use can be orchestrated together at appropriate phases of development and idea generation. These methods include the design journal (discussed earlier), the morphological box that shows different combinations of all possible solutions, the use of sketching and representation techniques, project planning, scenarios-based design, and other methods employed with a user-centred design approach. These are similar approaches adopted by other participants at the conference [12-14].

However, good methods or even the adoption of user-centred design alone cannot compensate for a lack of creativity skills. We need to learn how to "look" for creative solutions. The methods give us new or better ways of "seeing" the problem and opportunities for framing the solution. This is what we need to teach our students: how to use them to think more creatively.

One approach suggested by Kotzé et al. [15], is to adapt the more structured software engineering methods that use patterns and anti-patterns to illustrate HCI principles. Another hybrid approach, XpnUE, has been suggested by Obendorf et al. [16]. This method fuses eXtreme Programming with usability engineering to support rapid prototyping within the framework of Contextual Design.

Flowing through these various methods are three basic themes that on the surface appear to have little to do with creative invention, but are in effect crucial aspects of 'inventivity':

1. Understanding the problem, its scope and the constraints they present;
2. Sketching, modelling, and prototyping, as techniques to visualise, represent, and explore the solution space; and
3. The need for critique and reflection using tools like the design log and on-line forums for public discussion among team members and reflection in order to gain deeper insights that can lead to creative solutions.

It appears that while methods can be compiled in a sensible manner, their use should be orchestrated in a way that would foster creativity, so that students should learn to use them to avoid thinking in a rut and learn to develop creative alternative solutions.

4   How do we Train Educators in Creative Invention?

How does one teach what one has not grasped? Students learn best from those who are masters of what they teach. While we as educators can learn about creativity, how do we experience it and become masters of creativity ourselves?

In addition to knowing about and understanding the process of creative invention and having knowledge of the methods that can help in the process as discussed above, perhaps we as educators should also practice what we preach to master the art. Wesson [17], and Wooley and Gill [13] both cite the "Six Golden Rules to Shake the Students' Minds" that arose from the 1999 IFIP WG 13.1 Workshop [18]. These 'rules' were intended for students to experience design in HCI in addition to learning the theory related to HCI and its practical applications. These 'rules' are:

1. Read thought-provoking literature.
2. Observe real users using real tools.
3. Analyse the findings in the observation.
4. Mix the results from the analysis with theory.
5. Redesign the artefact.
6. Iterate the observation phases.

These 'rules' were postulated as a guide to stimulate thinking among our students (although the workshop's focus was distance learning students, the ideas apply just as well to all students), to challenge their assumptions, and to think creatively about developing solutions.

Although the Six Golden Rules apply equally well to faculty, there are a number of other suggestions that can help develop creativity amongst educators. They include:

1. *Be inspired, observe, and practise*: The need for "... space to develop" [1] creativity and inventiveness. We need space to challenge ourselves; one method might be to read thought provoking books as suggested by the Six Golden Rules. For example, being inspired by seeing examples of creative inventions in 'Humble Masterpieces: 100 Everyday marvels of design' [19], and then considering how simple inventions such as the teabag, the compact disc, the bar code, have changed our lives, might widen our creative thinking. Educators should also regularly practise observation and being actually involved in observation and research, reflecting upon what we observe from the perspective of creative problem solving. What we are suggesting here is that as educators, we need to develop expertise and familiarity with the toolsets and how we use them.

2. *Experiential learning*: Sas [20] provides another perspective that, although intended to apply to students, can equally apply to faculty. Viewing design as being both about craftsmanship, and about being a profession, is useful. While the knowledge and the formal aspects of design can be taught (methods, frameworks, theories and concepts), much of what a good designer knows and does, needs to be learnt experientially. Some designers learnt this through an (formal or informal) apprenticeship process, by watching and learning by example and mentoring. If educators want to develop the skilfulness of creative design and invention, some degree of apprenticeship will be useful. Sas also suggests that constructivism, where understanding is constructed by personal

experience, and reflecting on these experiences, and experiential learning (concrete experience, reflection, abstract conceptualisation and active experimentation) should be encouraged within the context of situated learning, within a community of practice.

3. *Be part of a community of practice*: Perhaps this underlies the need for a community of practice in 'inventivity' among educators, to practise and to experience first hand, to mentor and to apprentice, to hone and to refine, our expertise in creative inventiveness. Such an approach underlies the organisation of the HCIEd 2007 Creativity: Experiencing to Educate and Design Conference. Thus, we as educators need to create the space to learn the knowledge, to develop the skills of creative invention, and learn to see opportunities for creative interventions.

5   Stumbling Blocks to 'Inventivity'?

Quite naturally, a lack of attention to the issues raised earlier in this paper, can present problems to learning, teaching and being good at inventivity. Edwards, Wright and Petrie [21] asked the question, "Why is HCI education failing?". The paper provides some evidence of failure, and suggested some answers why. The reasons they cite have provided some insight to the stumbling blocks we face in teaching inventivity, and in being good at it. Some of these stumbling blocks are not as obvious as we might think they should be. We briefly describe some of these stumbling blocks.

1. *It's all common sense*: Anyone with some common sense should be able to design an interface or design an adequate solution.
2. *HCI is 'soft'*: I.e. no hard programming nor difficult maths, and that design is also 'soft', as there are no 'right' answers, and HCI design is therefore easy.
3. *Being creative and being artistic*: We sometimes confuse being creative with being artistic. 'Creative types' are seen to create and design attractive and aesthetically pleasing interfaces. Creative invention is about devising innovative solutions that work, not just pretty or artistic interfaces, although this plays a significant role in the design of engaging software. Similarly, being able to create software, as all programmers do, is not the same as being able to think creatively to devise new concepts and innovative solutions that can be programmed. Hence developing a piece of software that works is quite different from designing software that works in an innovative way.

6   Conclusion: Where to Next?

As educators, how do we progress the teaching and experiential learning of creative invention? In this chapter we have outlined a number of issues. In this concluding section, we summarise some lessons we have learnt that we hope will guide our future efforts:

1. Nature vs. nurture: While some of us are more creative and inventive than others, as educators we can use what is known about creative invention to develop the classroom environments to encourage and to nurture its growth.
2. Tools and methods: We should adapt and re-purpose existing tools and methods, and orchestrate them in a way that would foster creativity so that they help us understand and scope the problem; visualise and explore the solution space; and critique and reflect in order to gain the insights that can lead to creative solutions.
3. How do we train educators in creativity? Just as we would train our students: inspire them, teach them to observe, and practise it in order to experience it.
4. Humans are creatures of habit. Make creative and inventive thinking part of our routine problem solving and design behaviour. Develop our skills in using a suite of creativity tools and techniques for analysis to see the problem and constraints in different ways, and for visualisation and design in order to quickly see how the designs would address the problem.
5. While good designs will arise from good intentions and ideas, not all good intentions and good ideas lead to good designs. We need to recognise this so that we avoid discarding good ideas because of a poor implementation.
6. User-centred design approaches do not necessarily lead to good designs either. UCD helps us focus on the user and the context of their work, which we can then build upon to deliberately and consciously devise creative and inventive solutions.
7. Lecture style teaching is acceptable for learning about creativity, but is not suitable for developing creativity skills in the classroom.
8. Creative invention is more than artistic creativity and the creation of visually attractive interfaces. It is about finding inventive solutions to problems.
9. Stumbling blocks to *inventivity* are often not obvious.

In closing, to teach creativity and inventivity, we as educators need to experience it ourselves – a key issue in the planning and organisation of HCIEd 2007. As educators, we too, need to be good at it.

References

1. S. Beckhaus, Seven Factors to foster creativity in university HCI projects, in: *Inventivity: Teaching Theory, Design and innovation in HCI, Proceedings of of HCIEd2006-1 First Joint BCS/IFIP WG13.1/ICS/ EU CONVIVIO HCI Educators' Workshop, 23-24 March 2006, Limerick, Ireland*, edited by E.T. Hvannberg, J.C. Read, L. Bannon, P. Kotzé, and W. Wong, (University of Limerick, Limerick, 2006), pp. 91 - 95.
2. P.M. Alexander and C. de Villiers, Four facets of inventivity: Prior knowledge, insight, personal development and practice, in: *Inventivity: Teaching Theory, Design and Innovation in HCI, Proceedings of of HCIEd2006-1 First Joint BCS/IFIP WG13.1/ICS/ EU CONVIVIO HCI Educators' Workshop, 23-24 March 2006, Limerick, Ireland*, edited by E.T. Hvannberg, J.C. Read, L. Bannon, P. Kotzé, and W. Wong, (University of Limerick, Limerick, 2006), pp. 15-19.
3. B.L.W. Wong, Inventivity in HCI Education, in: *Inventivity: Teaching Theory, Design and innovation in HCI, Proceedings of of HCIEd2006-1 First Joint BCS/IFIP WG13.1/ICS/ EU*

CONVIVIO HCI Educators' Workshop, 23-24 March 2006, Limerick, Ireland, edited by E.T. Hvannberg, J.C. Read, L. Bannon, P. Kotzé, and W. Wong, (University of Limerick, Limerick, 2006), pp. 67-72.

4. G. Altshuller, L. Shulyak, and S. Rodman, *40 Principles: TRIZ Keys to Technical Innovation* (Technical Innovation Center, Cambridge, MA, 1997).

5. C. Giovannella, Design, technology, scientific and humanistic cultures: Filling the gap, in: *Inventivity: Teaching Theory, Design and Innovation in HCI, Proceedings of of HCIEd2006-1 First Joint BCS/IFIP WG13.1/ICS/ EU CONVIVIO HCI Educators' Workshop, 23-24 March 2006, Limerick, Ireland*, edited by E.T. Hvannberg, J.C. Read, L. Bannon, P. Kotzé, and W. Wong, (University of Limerick, Limerick, 2006), pp. 21-28.

6. J.C. Read, S.R. Kelly, and G. Sim, 'In it to win it - at it to get it': Low-tech interactions for motivation and learning in HCI, in: *Inventivity: Teaching Theory, Design and innovation in HCI, Proceedings of of HCIEd2006-1 First Joint BCS/IFIP WG13.1/ICS/ EU CONVIVIO HCI Educators' Workshop, 23-24 March 2006, Limerick, Ireland*, edited by E.T. Hvannberg, J.C. Read, L. Bannon, P. Kotzé, and W. Wong, (University of Limerick, Limerick, 2008), pp. 123-126.

7. A. Dix, T. Ormerod, M. Twidale, C. Sas, P.A.G. da Silva, and L. McKnight, Why bad ideas are a good idea, in: *Inventivity: Teaching Theory, Design and innovation in HCI, Proceedings of of HCIEd2006-1 First Joint BCS/IFIP WG13.1/ICS/ EU CONVIVIO HCI Educators' Workshop, 23-24 March 2006, Limerick, Ireland*, edited by E.T. Hvannberg, J.C. Read, L. Bannon, P. Kotzé, and W. Wong, (University of Limerick, Limerick, 2006), pp. 9 - 14.

8. S. Harrison and D. Tatar, More than a method, in Inventivity: Teaching theory, design and innovation, in: *Inventivity: Teaching Theory, Design and innovation in HCI, Proceedings of of HCIEd2006-1 First Joint BCS/IFIP WG13.1/ICS/ EU CONVIVIO HCI Educators' Workshop, 23-24 March 2006, Limerick, Ireland*, edited by, Limerick, 2006), pp. 61-66.

9. M. Lennon and L.J. Bannon, Worksheets in practice: Gathering artefacts for reflection in interaction design education, in: *Inventivity: Teaching Theory, Design and Innovation in HCI, Proceedings of of HCIEd2006-1 First Joint BCS/IFIP WG13.1/ICS/ EU CONVIVIO HCI Educators' Workshop, 23-24 March 2006, Limerick, Ireland*, edited by E.T. Hvannberg, J.C. Read, L. Bannon, P. Kotzé, and W. Wong, Limerick, 2006), pp. 29-34.

10. M.K. Larusdottir, Using Rapid Contextual Design at Reykjavik University, in: *Inventivity: Teaching Theory, Design and innovation in HCI, Proceedings of of HCIEd2006-1 First Joint BCS/IFIP WG13.1/ICS/ EU CONVIVIO HCI Educators' Workshop, 23-24 March 2006, Limerick, Ireland*, edited by E.T. Hvannberg, J.C. Read, L. Bannon, P. Kotzé, and W. Wong, (University of Limerick, Limerick, 2006), pp. 35 -39.

11. L. Ciolfi and M. Cooke, HCI for interaction designers: Communicating "the bigger picture", in: *Inventivity: Teaching Theory, Design and Innovation in HCI, Proceedings of of HCIEd2006-1 First Joint BCS/IFIP WG13.1/ICS/ EU CONVIVIO HCI Educators' Workshop, 23-24 March 2006, Limerick, Ireland*, edited by E.T. Hvannberg, J.C. Read, L. Bannon, P. Kotzé, and W. Wong, Limerick, 2006), pp. 47-51.

12. Y. Sundblad, User oriented cooperative interaction design: a multidisciplinary project course, in: *Inventivity: Teaching Theory, Design and innovation in HCI, Proceedings of of HCIEd2006-1 First Joint BCS/IFIP WG13.1/ICS/ EU CONVIVIO HCI Educators' Workshop, 23-24 March 2006, Limerick, Ireland*, edited by E.T. Hvannberg, J.C. Read, L. Bannon, P. Kotzé, and W. Wong, (University of Limerick, Limerick, 2006), pp. 81-84.

13. A. Woolley and S. Gill, Information ergonomics lectures for creative prototyping, in: *Inventivity: Teaching Theory, Design and innovation in HCI, Proceedings of of HCIEd2006-1 First Joint BCS/IFIP WG13.1/ICS/ EU CONVIVIO HCI Educators' Workshop, 23-24 March 2006, Limerick, Ireland*, edited by E.T. Hvannberg, J.C. Read, L. Bannon, P. Kotzé, and W. Wong, (University of Limerick, Limerick, 2006), pp. 41-46.

14. J. Lores, T. Granollers, and C. Aguilo, An undergraduate teaching experience in HCI at the University of Lleida, in: *Inventivity: Teaching Theory, Design and innovation in HCI, Proceedings of of HCIEd2006-1 First Joint BCS/IFIP WG13.1/ICS/ EU CONVIVIO HCI Educators' Workshop, 23-24 March 2006, Limerick, Ireland*, edited by E.T. Hvannberg, J.C. Read, L. Bannon, P. Kotzé, and W. Wong, (University of Limerick, Limerick, 2006), pp. 85-90.

15. P. Kotzé, K. Renaud, K. Kouloulestsos, B. Khazaei, and A. Dearden, Patterns, anti-patterns and guidelines - effective aids to teaching HCI principles? in: *Inventivity: Teaching theory, design and innovation in HCI, Proceedings of of HCIEd2006-1 First Joint BCS/IFIP WG13.1/ICS/ EU CONVIVIO HCI Educators' Workshop, 23-24 March 2006, Limerick, Ireland*, edited by E.T. Hvannberg, J.C. Read, L. Bannon, P. Kotzé, and W. Wong, (University of Limerick, Limerick, 2006), pp. 109-114.

16. H. Obendorf, A. Schmolitzky, and M. Fink, XPnUE - Defining and teaching a fusion of eXtreme Programming and Usability Engineering, in: *Inventivity: Teaching theory, design and innovation in HCI, Proceedings of of HCIEd2006-1 First Joint BCS/IFIP WG13.1/ICS/ EU CONVIVIO HCI Educators' Workshop, 23-24 March 2006, Limerick, Ireland*, edited by E.T. Hvannberg, J.C. Read, L. Bannon, P. Kotzé, and W. Wong, (University of Limerick, Limerick, 2006), pp. 103-108.

17. J. Wesson, Teaching HCI from an interative design perspective, in: *Inventivity: Teaching theory, design and innovation in HCI, Proceedings of of HCIEd2006-1 First Joint BCS/IFIP WG13.1/ICS/ EU CONVIVIO HCI Educators' Workshop, 23-24 March 2006, Limerick, Ireland*, edited by E.T. Hvannberg, J.C. Read, L. Bannon, P. Kotzé, and W. Wong, (University of Limerick, Limerick, 2006), pp. 109-114.

18. P. Kotzé and L. Oestreicher, Teaching human-computer interaction: Qualitative support for an alternative approach, in: *Usability: Gaining a Competitive Edge, IFIP World Computer Congress*, edited by, (Kluwer Academic Publishers, Boston, 2002), pp. 267 - 281.

19. P. Antonelli, *Humble Masterpieces: 100 Everyday Marvels of Design* (Thames and Hudson Ltd, 2006).

20. C. Sas, Learning approaches for teaching interaction design, in: *Inventivity: Teaching theory, design and innovation in HCI, Proceedings of of HCIEd2006-1 First Joint BCS/IFIP WG13.1/ICS/ EU CONVIVIO HCI Educators' Workshop, 23-24 March 2006, Limerick, Ireland*, edited by E.T. Hvannberg, J.C. Read, L. Bannon, P. Kotzé, and W. Wong, (University of Limerick, Limerick, 2006), pp. 53-59.

21. A.D.N. Edwards, P. Wright, and H. Petrie, HCI Education: We are failing - why? in: *Inventivity: Teaching theory, design and innovation in HCI, Proceedings of of HCIEd2006-1 First Joint BCS/IFIP WG13.1/ICS/ EU CONVIVIO HCI Educators' Workshop, 23-24 March 2006, Limerick, Ireland*, edited by E.T. Hvannberg, J.C. Read, L. Bannon, P. Kotzé, and W. Wong, (University of Limerick, Limerick, 2006), pp. 127-129.

Embedding a Design Studio Course in a Conventional Computer Science Program

Saul Greenberg
Department of Computer Science, University of Calgary
Calgary, Alberta Canada T2N 1N4
WWW home page: http://www.cpsc.ucalgary.ca/~saul/

Abstract. Within undergraduate Computer Science, Human Computer Interaction is often considered a blend of user-centered requirements analysis, design, implementation and evaluation. While most are teachable within the constraints of a conventional undergraduate lecture course, design is much more difficult to pass on. We know that design-oriented programs (e.g., arts, industrial design, and architecture) teach design practice as arising from the culture of a design studio. The problem is: how can we pass on the best practices of design studios within traditional programs that follow a standard lecture/tutorial format? My solution was to create a design studio atmosphere within a lecture/tutorial time-frame. Over the semester, students are introduced to four quite different state-of-the-art interaction domains, each chosen to minimize students' pre-conceived notions of what comprises a 'standard' design within these domains. They are given substantial freedom to design projects within these domains. They are required to sketch out their ideas and publicly show these sketches to other classmates for critique. Idea exchange is encouraged, where classmates can use parts of each other's ideas in their own work (conventional courses call this 'cheating'). Many lectures are replaced by studio work where students develop their designs during class time. Thus students and instructors see each other's work as it is being develop, they share tricks and techniques, and they engage in on-going commentaries. Students demonstrate final projects publicly within a design critique setting. Finally, every student has to create learning and professional portfolios illustrating their work using a mix of paper and electronic mediums.

Please use the following format when citing this chapter:

Greenberg, S., 2009, in IFIP International Federation for Information Processing, Volume 289; *Creativity and HCI: From Experience to Design in Education*; Paula Kotzé, William Wong, Joaquim Jorge, Alan Dix, Paula Alexandra Silva; (Boston: Springer), pp. 23–41.

1   Introduction

Human Computer Interaction (HCI) undergraduate education is expanding far beyond what it used to be. Teaching HCI was once constrained to a single class module or (if lucky) a single junior or senior-level course within computer science or psychology curriculum. Now, HCI programs are emerging that are centered on training students to become HCI professionals. Such programs are often inter-disciplinary, where they train students through a balanced pedagogy including design, engineering, evaluation, requirements engineering, and business practices.

While these programs point the way, the reality is that they are few and far between. Most are offered as post-graduate professional programs at prestigious institutes (e.g., CMU's Human-Computer Interaction Institute; Stanford's D-School Institute of Design). A few institutions have similar offerings available at the undergraduate level, usually as specialized interaction design programs outside of Computer Science departments (e.g., University of Queensland's Information Environments program [1]; Simon Fraser University's School of Interactive Arts and Technology). Most programs, whether undergraduate or graduate, are tailored to students who want to be HCI professionals or information architects. They do not help the vast masses of computer science students who plan to be software engineers but who could still benefit from strong HCI training.

Thus for most computer scientists, HCI is taught as a mix of user-centered requirements analysis, design, implementation and evaluation within the constraints of a conventional undergraduate lecture course. While many of these topics are amenable to the lecture setting [2], the subject of design is much more difficult to handle in a lecture setting. Quoting Reimer and Douglas [3]:

> Traditionally, HCI design has been taught as an abstract process of iterative user-centered design with a recommended set of design aids such as task analysis, GOMS, guidelines, heuristic evaluation and usability testing. During a typical HCI course there might be an occasional practice exercise for the student to evaluate and even improve, for example, an interface with poor usability. Adding a team-based final project to design, implement and evaluate a working interface provides more experience in actual HCI design, but still falls short of teaching the student good design of a real-world artifact while engaging in a real-world design process. In these courses we leave it to faith that students will be able to make the transition from theory to practice. [3, p.192].

Indeed, the whole process of generating and developing interesting design ideas within an HCI course structure is often at odds with usability and evaluation criteria. For example, creative design in HCI is often taught 'by example': students are introduced to many interesting and novel interaction techniques generated by others (e.g., I teach a long module on information visualization methods to encourage students to design interfaces using these methods [2]). Yet in my experiences, students who apply some of these novel methods to their initial project ideas tend to put them aside in favor of a traditional interface. This is because the many usability principles they are taught suggest that people will fare better with interfaces that are familiar to them, e.g., through positive transfer and learnability. As well, students consider unusual interfaces as 'riskier' than conventional interfaces in terms of how they would fair in a usability evaluation – and many instructors use usability evaluation as a criterion of design competence. For example, I have seen quite a few students suggest initial designs based upon information visualization techniques, and then discard these designs because they were concerned they would not do as well as, say, a traditional database table interface. And they are probably correct, for relatively small factors in novel designs – factors that could perhaps be corrected over time – could have a profound effect on people's performance. Thus students tend to follow safe conventional designs rather than push the design envelope.

The question is: how can we engage computer science students in the practice of design by creating an environment that is conducive to it? The answer may seem obvious. We know that design-oriented programs (e.g., arts, industrial design, and architecture) teach design practice as arising from the culture of a design studio [4], and this practice can apply to HCI as well [5,6,7]. In related work, Reimer and Douglas [3] nicely summarize the design studio pedagogical model as: learning by doing through an experiential pedagogy and by using teachers as resources; integration of theoretical knowledge; creating realistic artifacts through a professional design process where these artifacts are the primary basis of assessment; and primary teaching through a design critique – *aka* design crit. They also elaborate several important properties of the studio environment that helps realize this pedagogy. These include specialized studio rooms that are inhabited by the student peer group for substantial periods of time. In turn, the studio becomes a place where students do their on-going designs, where students constantly see each other's work, where they communicate to each other, and where they share practices. This leads to a communal design input, design reflection, and on-going design critique.

Given that the design studio is key to nurturing design pedagogy, the real problem facing computer science educators is: how can we pass on the best practices of design studios within traditional programs that follow a standard lecture/tutorial format and classroom constraints?

This paper describes my solution to this problem: how to create a design studio atmosphere for computer science students within a traditional lecture/tutorial timeframe and limited workroom availability. Of course, others have also tackled this problem either in courses or by proposing design methodologies [e.g., 1, 3, 8, 5; see also other publications in this book], but each in their own way. Indeed, a recent ACM CHI Workshop had as its theme the question of how one supports a design studio culture in HCI [6]. I don't argue that the course described below is 'better'. Rather, it complements and overlaps other approaches, where it adds to the richness of possibilities that course designers can choose from.

The purpose of my studio course is to have students experience the 'best practices' of design. In parallel, they learn several emerging areas within Human Computer Interaction, and become well versed with tools that let them develop prototypes within those areas. The gist of the course is summarized below.

- The course repackages the standard Computer Science lecture/tutorial time slots into a single 'studio' time slot.
- It creates a temporary studio by having all classes in a computer-equipped classroom, with at least one computer per student.

- Over the semester, students are introduced to four quite different state-of-the-art interaction domains. Each domain is chosen to minimize students' pre-conceived notions of what comprises a 'standard' design within these domains.
- They are given substantial freedom to propose design projects within these domains.
- They are required to sketch out a multitude of ideas, and publicly show chosen sketches to other classmates for critique.
- Idea exchange is encouraged, where classmates can use parts of each other's ideas in their own work (conventional courses call this 'cheating').
- Many lectures are replaced by studio work, where students develop their designs during class time. Thus students and instructors see each other's work as it is being develop, they share tricks and techniques, and they engage in on-going commentaries.
- Students quickly learn and use specialized software toolkits that let them rapidly prototype and implement their design ideas within each domain.
- Students demonstrate final projects publicly within a design crit setting.
- Every student has to create a portfolio illustrating their work using a variety of formats (e.g., paper, poster, video, web).

Details are described below. I begin by describing the basic course structure. I then elaborate on the primary pedagogical artifacts used in this course: the design projects, the sketchbook, and the portfolio. I close by summarizing student outcomes that I have seen after teaching this course for several years.

2   Course Structure

Making a design studio concept work within the constraints of a conventional computer science program structure is challenging but quite doable. I begin with a discussion of how I created and scheduled the studio and class size, and then move onto the life cycle of student projects that formed the student design activity. The context is that this is the student's second course in HCI; the first has already provided the basic background to HCI [2].

2.1   Scheduling

The first issue is scheduling: how can we get sufficient continuous contact time, where all students are working together? At our university, a normal course is typically taught by the instructor through either three 50 minute or two 75 minute lectures per week. These lectures are augmented by two 50 minute tutorial sessions – often scheduled at odd times of the day so as not to conflict with other lectures – and usually run by the teaching assistant. Following conventional practice would restrict the 'studio' time to just the tutorial sessions, which is clearly insufficient. What I did was schedule a 75 minute and 50 tutorial back to back (with a short 15 minute break in-between), thus forming two 2½ hour slots per week as the studio time. While administrators thought it odd that I would request the two together, the primary challenge was to find a 2½ hour block of time that did not conflict with other courses that students would likely want to take.

Of course, 5 hours of studio time per week is still far short of the much longer studio times scheduled in design disciplines (e.g., the introductory design studio course in our industrial design department is 4 hours / day where 4 days a week is not unusual). Still, 5 hours is much better than the standard computer science tutorial time offerings.

2.2 The Studio

The second issue is how to create a physical design studio. This is more challenging, for there were no dedicated facilities at my disposal that I could take over for exclusive student use. Instead, I booked one of our instructional computer workrooms (normally open to all computer science students to do their assignments, where a teaching assistant may give an occasional presentation) for use as our pseudo-studio. This again required just a bit of scheduling. Consequently, all contact hours were spent in a computer workroom. Thus during the 2½ hour classes, each student had their own computer, and no outside students were allowed in the room. Students also tended to linger after class (or come to it before class) to continue their work.

This room was already instrumented with a screen and projector connected to a single computer. I set up additional wiring (just a second long monitor cable) so that I could quickly plug the projector into any student's workstation as well. This meant that, at any time, any student could project his or her work to the class.

2.3 Numbers

The third issue is student numbers. Normally, class attendance is open-ended, and it would be easy to admit too many students to make a studio-based approach unworkable. I set a cap of 15 students. This sufficed to form a critical mass, but was sufficiently small to encourage cross-student interaction and to make sure that all students could demonstrate their work within the 2½ hour studio blocks. A class population of 15 was also considered large enough not to 'raise eyebrows' at the administration level.

2.4 Design Projects

The heart of the course is a series of 4 design projects, each within a different interaction domain (see section 3). While students were encouraged to consult with one another, each student had to design, implement and demonstrate their own individual project. Each would be graded independently on their project design.

An issue is how to get students to think about these projects as design exercises. To set the scene, students were given fairly open ended project exercises within new and unfamiliar interaction domains. They were encouraged to be highly imaginative in what they created – artistic, speculative, and entertainment projects were valued as much as a project oriented toward work productivity. For example, the project description below is for designing within the domain of single display groupware.

> You have been hired to create a demonstration of a single display groupware (SDG) system that allows 2 to 4 people to interact over a single display using multiple mice and (optionally) multiple keyboards. Your demonstration should illustrate at least one object that gracefully reacts to multiple people using it simultaneously, which in turn is embedded in an application that exploits it. You have complete freedom of your design, as long as you can show that the SDG object and its containing application are useful for its intended audience, and that its design is somewhat impressive.

2.5   Software as New Media

As will be detailed in section 3, each design project required students to work with different specialized media, which in turn allowed them to rapidly develop prototypes in different design domains. This new media came in the form of state of the art software toolkits. I pre-installed all specialized software and toolkits on the computer lab computers, so that students did not have to waste time configuring the system. I also recognized that while many students would continue to work in this studio space outside of class time, many would also work at home. Thus I made sure that all software was available for download, and instructed them on how to transport their own software between home and work. As well, they could optionally install this software on their own laptops and use that as their primary machine.

As a cautionary tale, installing non-conventional software on department computers was no easy matter. At our site, computers are 'locked down' for security purposes, where they restrict how software can be installed and how they are used. Yet much of the new software pushed the security limits of our department computers. Our technical support people had to go out of their way to make the software work, and I had to do extensive testing to make sure the software worked as it should. In contrast, students found it trivial to install the software on their home machines, as these rarely have the same level of security management.

2.6   Project Design Cycle

Students then went through the following cycle for each of the 4 project domains.
1. Week 1, 1st class: *background and example of the design interaction area.* Through a lecture, students were introduced to the interaction area. The lecture typically provided conceptual foundations to the area, and then walked through many, many examples of designs produced within this area. Designs were illustrated by photos, videos, and running demonstrations. The student's homework was to come up with their own ideas of a design within this area, where they had to produce a variety of sketches (see section 4 - Sketchbook).
2. Week 1, 2nd class: *sketch presentation and toolkit introduction.* At the beginning of class, I passed around a digital camera. Each student was asked to select and take a photo of their 'best' idea in the sketchbook. I then projected these sketches,

and each student was given about five minutes to explain their sketch. Every student had at least two other students critique their idea - we seeded this by asking observing students to say the best and worst thing about the design, and suggestions for improving it. To encourage idea sharing, I told students to copy design features that they liked into their own sketchpad (with attribution), which they could then use in their own designs. The second part of the class was an introduction to the toolkit. This was a hands-on tutorial where we walked students through a simple 'hello world' style example. Students were lock-stepped; all had to master a step before we went on. Thus at the end of the class, students had seen each other's ideas, and had a basic understanding of the toolkit capabilities. The students' homework was to modify their design based on what they had seen others do, and to leverage both the opportunities and limitations of the toolkit.

3. Week 2, 3rd class: *hands-on in-depth toolkit laboratory, and design elaborations.* The tutorial on the toolkit continued, where more sophisticated examples were demonstrated. Again, all students worked through these examples in lock-step. Afterwards, students were asked to describe their design changes. This sometimes happened in a public setting, or by breaking students up into small discussion groups, or one-on-one with the instructor and/or teaching assistant, or a mix of all approaches. If time allowed, students started programming their design. The students' homework was to work on their design and implementation.

4. Week 2, 4th class to Week 3, 6th class: *design elaboration and implementation.* Students worked on their designs in class. While many were also programming their systems outside the class, they had to have a working copy that they could bring into class to continue their work. During this time, students were encouraged to show their on-going work to the instructor and teaching assistant (who were constantly walking around) and to other students, and more importantly to engage in discussion and critique. They were also encouraged to share technical 'tricks' with one another, i.e., on how they mastered the new media through the toolkit. This usually happened when one person was showing their work to others, who would then ask how they managed to implement a particular feature. When that feature looked generally valuable, we would plug the projector into that student's computer, who would then show the class how to do it. The students' homework was to continue the design, and to begin developing their web-based and paper-based portfolio description of their design (section 5 Portfolio).

5. Week 4, 7th class: *demonstrations.* Students would demonstrate their final system to the entire class within a design crit structure. Each student would typically start with the portfolio entry on the web site, then move onto a live demonstration. At the same time, the paper-based portfolio entry would be passed around. After the demonstration, all students were expected to participate in the 'crit' of the work, emphasizing its positive aspects and potential flaws, and how to improve the design.

Interspersed between classes were other events to encourage design skills. These included rapid-fire design exercises where students (sometimes in groups) would have to create a design that solved a specific problem. It also included discussions, applications and examples of best practices, e.g., in the use of a sketchbook, in portfolio construction, in lateral thinking, in rapid prototyping methods.

3   Selecting Design Domains

Over the semester, students have to sketch (section 4), design and implement, demonstrate and record via a portfolio (section 5) four projects, each in quite different areas of interaction design, following a particular design process (section 3). I choose project areas around the following criteria, which I believe makes them well-suited for beginning computer science designers.

3.1   Novel Interaction Paradigms, rather than User-centered Problems.

Projects are centered on particular interaction paradigms, rather than user-oriented problems. This may seem at odds with an HCI course. However, recall that this is a second HCI course; in the first course, students had already experienced the pedagogy of developing a system based upon a user-centered requirements analysis [2]. By having projects fashioned around a novel interaction paradigm, I believe that students would be more willing to pursue risky designs as a way of exploring that interaction space. At the same time, students would be introduced to an emerging area of HCI.

3.2   Personally Unfamiliar Interaction Area.

I choose interaction paradigms that are emerging but not yet in every-day common usage. Thus students likely have little prior exposure to commercial systems in the project area. My expectation is that students are much more likely to come up with their own novel design, as they cannot fall back on standard solutions that they see in routine use.

3.3   Engaging and Futuristic.

To motivate students, each interaction paradigm has to be in an engaging area, i.e., as an emerging paradigm in HCI and/or as a research area. Motivation is very important: when undergraduate students believe they are working at the frontiers of computer science, they can do amazing things.

3.4   Availability of Rapid Development Tools within that Area.

I strongly believe that students are heavily influenced by their development tools. The offerings of software toolkits are akin to media in the arts: glazes in pottery, paints in painting, wood and tools in woodcrafts. Students learn to think in terms of the affordances of the media, where the media suggests solutions to particular problems. I further argue about the importance of toolkits in fostering creativity in greater detail in [9].

Thus I select interaction areas with the proviso that rapid prototyping and development tools are readily available. These tools must be in the form where they are easily and quickly learnt. While computer science students are gifted programmers, I did not want them to spend their time and effort working on low-level implementation details, figuring out complex APIs, or untangling cryptic documentation. Instead, I wanted to give students tools as media, whereby simple design ideas are actually simple to do, and hard design ideas are possible [9]. As a consequence of working with this media, students could spend their time thinking about the design rather than programming, and could also rapidly iterate over their designs as they reflected on it, and as others critiqued its early versions.

3.5   Tools Work within a Familiar and Rich Programming Environment.

Related to the above, I wanted to select tools that worked (as much as possible) within students' existing programming environments and development paradigms. Again, this is because I wanted students to concentrate on their designs rather than spend time learning a new programming language or IDE. Similarly, I wanted them to develop systems within a commercial quality programming environment so they would have standard high-quality development tools available, such as debuggers and structured programming editors.

3.6   Example Domains

To illustrate how this works in practice, I chose the following four interaction domains last year. Within this domain set, student prototyping and implementation was supported by rapid prototyping tools created in our own laboratory[1].

Single display groupware is a domain where multiple people can work together over a single display using multiple mice and keyboards. We gave students the SDG Toolkit [10,11], which makes it extremely easy to capture input from multiple mice and keyboards, to create multi-user aware widgets, and to draw multiple cursors on the display.

Physical user interfaces is a domain where people interact with computer-controlled devices: tangible media, ambient displays, sensor-driven ubiquitous computing environments, and so on. We gave students Phidgets hardware (available at http://www.phidgets.com/) and our version of the Phidgets Toolkit [12,13]. The Phidgets toolkit makes it very easy to capture data from the input devices, and to control output devices. Phidget hardware at their disposal included servo motors, RFID tag readers, environmental sensors (heat, light, motion…), controls (switches, buttons, sliders), LEDs, and so on.

Distortion-oriented information visualization is a domain where people interactively explore visualizations presented in a distorted space (e.g., fisheye

---

[1] All tools are available at http://grouplab.cpsc.ucalgary.ca/cookbook/, including documentation and tutorials, and all work within C# and Microsoft Visual Studio.

views). We gave students the Elastic Presentation Space (EPS) toolkit, a framework for designing such distorted visualizations [14]. It is a mathematical toolkit: one sets properties of a mathematical space (such as lenses, their shapes, their extents and so on), gives it a point in that space, and gets back where that point is located in the new distorted space. Thus students can experiment with quite different ways of mapping and visualizing information within a distorted space.

Groupware affording small group casual interaction over rich media is a domain where small groups of collaborators engage with one another in a public virtual space. We gave students the Community Bar as a groupware platform [15], and the Media Item Toolkit to actually develop a groupware media item within that platform [16]. Students create interactive multi-media items whose contents are broadcast to others. The toolkit is based on the idea of plug-ins: developers build the multimedia groupware component using a well-defined interface, and that component is then inserted into a pre-existing groupware architecture and system. Thus students can experiment with quite different interfaces of interest to the group, where their items lives in ecology of the Community Bar standard offerings as well as items created by other students.

Of course, these projects are just a vehicle where the goal is to train students on best practices in design. We already described in section 2 how students developed their designs as part of the design studio practice. In the next two sections, we turn to two other valuable artifacts supporting design activity: the sketchbook and the portfolio.

4   The Sketchbook

The sketchbook is perhaps the most prevalent best practice artifact found across all design disciplines. Many designers keep a sketchbook with them at all times. They use it to record and elaborate their ideas, to gather other people's ideas or artifacts of interest that may inspire future ideas, to 'doodle' half-formed thoughts, and to share ideas with others by showing [7]. The sketchbook is particularly valuable as it encourages its owners to develop a multitude of ideas and choose between them, rather than to fixate on a single idea. Buxton [7] calls the process of distilling between many ideas as 'getting the right design', whereas the process of developing a particular idea (e.g., through iterative refinement or usability engineering) is 'getting the design right'. The former emphasizes design that chooses between idea alternatives, while the later is the creative engineering that refines a particular idea.

Computer science students do not normally keep sketchbooks, and as a consequence they typically develop the first idea that comes to them. That is, they worry about 'getting the design right' without considering if the basic idea is the best one worthy of pursuit. This is equivalent to the local hill climbing problem in Artificial Intelligence, where local maxima are reached without considering how they would relate to a global maximum. Sketches become a way to investigate other nearby hills (ideas) to see if they can offer better solutions.

To encourage students to develop many ideas, I made the course text an empty sketchbook. I insist they buy a nice one (hard cover, coiled) so they can take pride in it; otherwise (in my experience), they will end up using scraps of paper. Students are expected to fill their sketchbook with their project ideas over the course of the term, and to show these ideas to others on demand. I can ask to see it at any time, where their number of sketches must reflect where they are in particular projects. This stops students from 'cheating' the process by sketch cramming, where they sit down at some late date (e.g., after the project is being done) and just 'brain dump' a bunch of sketches as a single batch.

With the assistance of Coleen Campbell, a teacher and doer of arts and design, and influenced by Bill Buxton's book 'Sketching the User Experiences' [7], I developed a brief instruction manual for the sketchbook; an extract is included in Table 1. In terms of grading, the key deliverables are that students must generate at least ten different sketches demonstrating quite different ideas for a particular project, and then choose one idea and develop ten variations and/or refinements of that idea. Unlike most grading schemes, they are evaluated on quantity, not quality!

Table 1. *The Sketchbook 'Instruction Manual'*

Why a sketchbook	Real progress in developing yourself as an interaction designer will depend on you frequently and habitually sketching out your ideas and their variations, recording other people's ideas you may see, reflecting and choosing between these ideas, and then further developing those ideas that seem promising. The sketchbook records all these. Carrying the sketchbook with you at all times will help you incorporate sketching and reflection into your daily routines.
What is a sketch?	The following list paraphrases Bill Buxton's properties of sketches [7]. − Quick to make. − Timely so they can be provided when needed − Inexpensive, where cost must not inhibit the ability to explore a concept. − Disposable so you can afford to throw it away - the investment is in the concept, not the execution. − Plentiful, where its meaning is within the context of a collection or series − Clear vocabulary where the rendering style signals that it is a sketch − Distinct gestures, where their fluidity gives them a sense of openness and freedom vs. engineering precision and tightness. − Minimal details, including only what is required to render the concept.

Uses	Sketchbooks are useful in many ways. It is a place where you should:
	— Jot down and annotate your own initial ideas - and there is no such thing as a bad idea!
	— Explore and refine ideas both in the large and in the small
	— Develop variations, alternatives and details
	— Refer back to your ideas and reflect on how your thought processes have changed over time
	— Record other good ideas you see elsewhere e.g., in other systems, in your readings, and in your classmates' work.
	— Collect existing material (e.g., pictures from magazines, screen snapshots) and tape them into the sketchbook.
	— Develop your skills, your accuracy and your confidence in sketching out your ideas through regular use
	— Sketches do not have to be pretty, beautiful, or even immediately understandable by others. However, you should be able to explain your sketches and ideas when anyone asks about them.
Best Practices	— Always carry your sketchbook with you everywhere (a 2nd small sketchbook is helpful). Jot down ideas as you think about them.
	— Always have a pencil handy in the coil binder.
	— Use it frequently, e.g., at least several times a day.
	— Fill pages with a series of related drawings about a design idea, or with a single well-composed design idea.
	— Consider alternatives. A series of sketches related to the same interface problem might explore different aspects of the interface. These could include different interface representations, different interaction details, different screens, different levels of details, different contexts of use, and so on. Each page can become a series of studies that will help you develop and reflect on the many ideas you will have.
	— Annotate drawings appropriately, including information such as descriptions for ideas that you cannot draw out well; textual addendums; sources of your ideas (e.g., books, magazines, classmates), creation date, and any other relevant information.
	— Do not erase ideas because they are messy or because you no longer like them. Your sketchbook is a record of all your developing ideas, good and bad, not just of your final work.
	— The sketchbook is for design only - do not use it for other classes just because you do not have any paper.
Sketchbook grading	— I and the teaching assistant will be looking for the following evidence of use.
	— Idea quantity, where you develop many ideas: for each project, we expect a minimum of 10 sketches illustrating 10 quite different ideas and a minimum of 10 refinements / variations for a chosen idea;
	— Regular use, where you habitually use the sketchbook to jot down, annotate, and develop ideas over time – at any instance, we expect your sketches to reflect where you are in your project;
	— Thoughtfulness, where you can explain the development of your ideas within particular sketches;
	— Attribution, where you credit other people's ideas that you are using.

5 The Portfolio

The portfolio is another 'best practice' found within design disciplines. A portfolio serves as a living resume, where designers use them to collect and illustrate their (usually completed) projects. Designers show portfolios to others both to highlight individual achievements, and – as a collection – to suggest the scope, breadth, depth and quality of the professional's design proficiency. Thus a good portfolio will summarize the professional's abilities, strengths and styles. Portfolios can vary greatly: they can be stand-alone artifacts for others to review, or can serve as a conversational prop where designers tell stories about the artifact to peers, employers, and clients.

Sadly, computer science students rarely create portfolios. Instead, they typically describe their ability to others through a skills-oriented resume format: the programming languages they know, the courses they have taken, and related employment history. This is somewhat surprising, for most computer science students – like designers – spend immense effort developing projects as part of their course work. In spite of these creative experiences, computer science students portray themselves to their potential employers as skill-oriented technicians rather than as people well-practiced in the art of invention.

To encourage students to capture their work in a way that can be presented to others, students are required to construct a portfolio as the course progresses. Two types of portfolios are required, as described below.

The *project learning portfolio* captures the essence of each student's project through a variety of media. As each project is completed, each student creates a detailed portfolio documenting and archiving what they have done. It takes two forms, both done for every project. First, the student creates a web site with a project portfolio entry: this web site includes a brief executive summary, then a visual summary of what they did (captured as annotated screen snapshots, simple animations and/or storyboards, slide show), downloadable executables so that others can try their system, and an archive of their source code. Second, the student uses more traditional media to create an alternate visual summary. The chosen media varies per project, and covers a range including paper-based posters, booklets, commercial packaging (e.g., a box), and a short self-contained video. The goals of these two portfolio styles is to encourage students to create a stand-alone electronic presence of their work (through the web site), and to give them practice creating portfolio entries with alternate media that can be quickly shown to others. As a side effect, the project portfolios are an easy way for the course instructor to access and review each project after the demonstrations, where details can be explored.

The *professional portfolio* is created at the end of the term. Its intent is to be used as a living resume, where students can bring it to their job interviews and show potential employees and/or clients about the kinds of work they did as well as the scope of their many achievements. The emphasis is that these portfolios must serve as a conversational prop: students should be able to conveniently carry it to a job interview, where its contents are easy to show, browse and discuss as opportunities appear. Thus paper-based portfolios are encouraged, although I also suggest they include electronic medium (e.g., a CD) that they can quickly load into a computer if time and facilities allow for further elaboration and demonstration. These portfolios can come in quite different form factors, although the two main styles are booklets or modest-sized posters held in a portfolio case. I should note that the professional portfolio is rarely a rebundling of the project portfolio entries: students create or remix entries to exploit the form factor and visual effect of their professional portfolio.

In practice, students take great pride in their project and professional portfolios. Many are quite creative in building the portfolio web site, to the point that the web site itself demonstrates the student's skills. Similarly, many pay considerable attention to their professional portfolios. They construct it out of high quality materials, and extend it to include projects outside the course. A variety of students described how they used the portfolios during actual job interviews, and how they believed it made the difference in setting them apart from other applicants.

As with the sketchbook, I developed a brief instruction manual for the portfolio; an extract is included in Table 2.

Table 2. *The Portfolio 'Instruction Manual'*

What is a Portfolio?	— A portfolio is a representative or selective collection of one's work. — Design professionals (e.g., architects, industrial designers, artists) often create professional portfolios, and use these to illustrate their work to potential employers or clients. A portfolio is a living resume. They are an expected part of how professionals in many disciplines portray their achievements. A good *professional portfolio* will contain visual samplings that collectively suggest the scope, breadth, depth and quality of the professional's design proficiency. It summarizes the professional's abilities, strengths and styles. — Some educational programs also have students create *learning portfolios*, where students document their work, sometimes over years. These portfolios are used by instructors to evaluate students, and by students to help them reflect on what they have learnt over that time. — Unlike sketchbooks, portfolios are neat, orderly and professional in appearance. You critically select and craft what goes into it. Because this is a design-oriented portfolio, its contents should be highly visual. Each visual summary should tell its own story with only modest labeling and textual descriptions. It should also serve as a conversation piece letting you talk about your work.
Your Portfolio	— You will create your own learning and professional portfolio — Your learning portfolio will show your projects. You will document your developing abilities as an interaction designer by creating visual summaries of how you solved your exercises and assignments. As the course progresses, you will see what you have accomplished to date. — Near the end of the course, you will use this learning portfolio to seed your professional portfolio. Feel free to add samplings of any other relevant work you have done outside of this course to your professional portfolio. — After the course, you can maintain and modify this portfolio into something that will help you present yourself to future employers.

Learning Objectives	Your portfolio will help you learn the following: — Develop skills creating visual summaries of individual designs by using screen snapshots, story boards, videos, and other techniques. — Demonstrate in these summaries how you have used particular interaction techniques. — Learn how to effectively archive your code and supporting documents so you can easily install and demonstrate your system on any handy machine. — Develop your skills in creating both a professional-looking learning and professional portfolio — Use the portfolio as a personal reference summarizing your course accomplishments.
Be Organized	A professional portfolio can be packaged in many ways: — Keeping all summaries organized but separate will allow you to selectively rearrange your portfolio to fit your need (e.g., for a job interview). — The simplest form sees it as separate summaries collected in some kind of container e.g., an artist's portfolio case. — You can also paste summaries into a large high-quality (but very good looking, maybe even hand-made) booklet. Ideally, pages are removable so you can add and rearrange items as needed.
Styles	For each project, you will create two versions of a learning portfolio entry. The first is an electronic web summary (including code archive), while the second is crafted out of a media form selected from the list below. — *Paper*. Each visual summary (screen snapshots, storyboards, etc) are pasted onto a high-quality mat or backing (e.g. poster cardboard). Poster sizes of at least 16"x20" will give you enough space to create an effective visual summary. Alternatively, you may want to create it as a flip-book of screen-shots showing how the interaction flows over time. — *Packaging*. The visual summary is created as packaging, e.g., a paper box that would contain your software and other materials. — *Video*. Create a video is a very effective way of showing your work. The best videos are short ones focused on showing your design in action. — *Interactive multimedia*. You can create a project summary using a multimedia presentation tool e.g., Powerpoint or Flash. — *Running software*. You will archive the system in your electronic portfolio so that you can demonstrate it as needed. Be aware that this does not suffice by itself: over time, it will become unlikely that your system will run due to changes in operating systems and expectations of installed software. Thus you should see this as a way to supplement your other portfolio activities.

Best Practices	*Hint. Stress visuals over text. A common error is to include overly long text descriptions.*
	− Be creative in your portfolio – it also illustrates your design abilities. Search the web (e.g., try the terms Interface Web Design Portfolio) for examples of how other people have created on-line portfolios.
	− Carefully decide what parts of your projects you want to use in your portfolio summary.
	− Treat portfolio creation as a design exercise. Prototype a few different approaches for each project. Your first idea may not be your best one.
	− Label each summary with a descriptive title and its date of completion. You may include short explanatory annotations and paragraphs, but don't go overboard: this should be a visual summary rather than a textual one.
	− If you are using screen snapshots, make sure they are interesting ones i.e., the screen is populated with meaningful data, and the screens are in an interesting visual state.
	− Use storyboards to show how an interesting interaction sequence progresses over time.
	− Print screens in color.
	− Include screen fragments to embellish your story. For example, a blow-up of a screen portion can show hard-to-see details (and can include annotations); a mini-storyboard of an interaction component can illustrate how a particular interaction technique works.
	− Emphasize any uses of novel interaction techniques.
	− Make sure you can 'disassemble' your portfolio summaries or that you have archived electronic copies of images so that you can regenerate them on paper. In the future, you may want to recreate a portion of your portfolio, perhaps in a more expensive book or some other medium, only to find that you cannot unglue your images from the pages.
Portfolio Grading	Every project requires a learning portfolio entry. You will also create a professional portfolio at the end of the course. Portfolios and contents should impress me with both your vision and how well you have mastered the technical aspects of interaction design. Other grading aspects include:
	− Completeness.
	− Quality (how well the portfolio captures your work and the techniques we have asked you to include in it).
	− Professional appearance (including overall organization).
	− Effectiveness of your code archive.

6   Experiences and Reflection

The border conditions of this course are far from ideal: there are scheduling constraints, no permanent studio space, inadequate student background, insufficient crit time (thus requiring forced discussions), requirements to learn different implementation tools, and so on. Yet the first year I taught this class, I was astounded by the quality and the diversity of the students' projects: they all consistently surpassed my expectations. Successive years proved that this was no accident. Because of this quality, I have featured student's work (with permission, of course) in a variety of publications and web sites, as described below.

Greenberg and Tse [17] is a video that catalogues eight student projects in the area of Single Display Groupware. Examples of what they did include: collaborative activities such as photo selection, viewing and organization; children games for cooperative fashion, multi-person music playing, action games where people work together toward a goal vs. competing with one another, multi-person drawing and sketching tools, and so on. Source code and executables of several of these projects are available at http://grouplab.cpsc.ucalgary.ca/cookbook/index.php/Toolkits/SDGToolkit.

In other papers [18,9], I feature projects students did on physical user interfaces, concentrating on those that emphasized collaboration. The range of systems developed include a variety of status indicators of people's activities, devices that serve as multimedia communication channels, notification displays of asynchronous message arrival and of meetings, tools supporting information exchange, sensor-based systems safeguarding privacy, collaborative games, and interactive art. A comprehensive web site features a video gallery of almost all Phidget projects developed in this class over the years: http://grouplab.cpsc.ucalgary.ca/phidgets/gallery/.

McEwan et. al. [16] briefly described various student groupware projects created using the Community Bar media item toolkit. Example projects include a group-editable list of web pages, an awareness tool that displays motion activity at distant sites, a novel visualization of a video media space history over time, a group editable and browsable photo gallery, a group scheduler, a gossip item for teenage girls, a family shopping list, a document status awareness item that tracks documents being worked on by the group, and a group interface to a mobile robot that allows people to view a physical environment and contact people within it.

The main question is, of course, did students gain the rudimentary best practices typically found in a design discipline? The quality of the results above suggests that they did, at least within the constraints of the course. Perhaps a more relevant question is: did students carry theses best practices with them to their jobs, and did they apply them to design problems? This is a more difficult question to answer, as I have not systematically tracked students after they graduated. However, I do know that several students have gone on to careers as interface developers / experience designers. Some still carry a sketchbook with them years after the course. Most said that they believe bringing their portfolio to the job interview helped clinch that position.

The question of whether students continued these best practices is perhaps the difference between a design studio run within the constraints of a computer science department *vs.* the way it happens in a professional design program. Professional design programs have multiple design studios that run almost every semester. Students are so habituated in the design process that best practices become engrained. In contrast, there is only so much that one can do in a single computer science course containing an abbreviated design studio. Perhaps the most we can expect is that it gives students a flavor of what design is all about.

The ideal solution, of course, is to transform a good portion of Computer Science into a design discipline using the tricks of the trade found in design programs. This is not that far-fetched. While some courses are predominantly about knowledge transfer, a vast number of courses in Computer Science are project based amenable to structured design. Perhaps the greater problem is that Computer Science faculty members need to retrain themselves as designers before this can happen.

I am still trying to improve this course structure. First, I am now formalizing the pedagogy of certain design practices. For example, the most recent version of this course includes a series of sketching modules and exercises: students are taught about various sketching methods (e.g., storyboarding, slide shows, video sketches, etc) [7]. For each sketching method, the student learns the technique by replicating an existing interface, and then applies the technique by designing a new interface with that method. Other areas I plan to formalize in future years include professional methods for designing portfolios, and methods for lateral thinking. Second, because of the short amount of time 'in studio', I want to enhance our in-class 'crits'. I am now applying a series of strategies to encourage critical communication between students about their design. This includes splitting them into teams of 2-4, where they do rapid-fire presentation and critique of each other's designs; early feedback from students said that they often altered their design considerably after these sessions. As another strategy, I assign each person a partner, where the role of the partner is to critique the other person's design as it progresses from class to class. Other possibilities include on-line discussions. Third, I plan to invite design experts into the class for guest lectures, where they can enlighten students about the actual practice of design. Finally, I want to restructure our two HCI courses to incorporate design within both of them. Currently, the first course teaches basic HCI usability engineering process, while this second one concentrates on creativity and design. While it works, it does treat them separately. A better method would be to merge the courses, where design and creativity (using this design studio approach) would be incorporated as a fundamental part of the HCI usability engineering process.

Acknowledgments

I am not a formally trained designer. My early attempts to create a design-studio course relied heavily on advice by others. In particular, I thank my colleague Sheelagh Carpendale at the University of Calgary (a computer scientist and a trained artist who also taught one of the modules in this course), and Colleen Campbell, then a design instructor at Mount Royal College, Calgary. If I've said anything that would make a true designer uncomfortable, I assume all blame in misinterpreting what my colleagues said.

References

1. M. Docherty, P. Sutton, M. Brereton and S. Kaplan, An innovative design and studio-based CS degree, in: *SIGCSE Bulletin*, **33**(1), (ACM Press, March, 2001), pp. 233-237.
2. S. Greenberg, Teaching Human Computer Interaction to Programmers, in: *ACM Interactions* **3**(4), (ACM Press, July-August, 1996), pp. 62-76.
3. Y. Reimer and S. Douglas, Teaching HCI Design with the Studio Approach, in: *Computer Science Education*, **12**(3), (Taylor & Francis, 2003), pp. 191-205.

4. B. Lawson, What Designers Know, (Architectural Press, Elsevier, 2004).
5. T. Winograd, What Can We Teach About Human-Computer Interaction, in: *Proc ACM CHI 1990 Conference on Human Factors in Computing Systems*, (ACM Press, 1990), 443 – 449.
6. E. Blevis, Y. Lim, E. Stolterman, T. Wolf and K. Sato, Supporting design studio culture in HCI. Workshop Overview, in: *Proc ACM CHI 2007 Conference on Human Factors in Computing Systems v.2,* (ACM Press, 2007), pp. 2821-2824.
7. B. Buxton, *Sketching User Experiences: Getting the Design Right and the Right Design.* (Morgan-Kaufmann, 2007).
8. S. Klemmer, B. Hartmann and L. Takayama, How Bodies Matter: Five Themes for Interaction Design, in: *Proc ACM DIS'06 Designing Interactive Systems*, (ACM Press, 2006).
9. S. Greenberg, Toolkits and Interface Creativity, in: *Journal Multimedia Tools and Applications (JMTA),* **32**(2), (Springer, February, 2007), pp. 139-159.
10. E. Tse and S. Greenberg, Rapidly Prototyping Single Display Groupware through the SDGToolkit, in: *Proc Fifth Australasian User Interface Conference, Volume 28 in the CRPIT Conferences in Research and Practice in Information Technology Series*, (Australian Computer Society Inc., Dunedin, NZ January, 2004), pp. 101-110.
11. E. Tse and S. Greenberg, SDG Toolkit, in: *Video Proc ACM CSCW 2004 Conference on Computer Supported Cooperative Work.* (ACM Press, November 6-10, 2004), video and abstract, duration 3:55.
12. S. Greenberg and C. Fitchett, Phidgets: Easy Development of Physical Interfaces through Physical Widgets, in: *Proc ACM UIST Symposium on User Interface Software and Technology,* (ACM Press, 2001), pp. 209-218. Includes video figure.
13. N. Marquardt and S. Greenberg, Distributed Physical Interfaces with Shared Phidgets, in: *Proc. TEI'07 1st International Conference on Tangible and Embedded Interaction.* (Baton Rouge, Louisiana, USA, 2007)
14. M.S.T. Carpendale and C. Montagnese, A Framework for Unifying Presentation Space, in: *Proc ACM UIST Symposium on User Interface Software and Technology.* (ACM Press, 2001), pp. 61-70.
15. G. McEwan and S. Greenberg, Supporting Social Worlds with the Community Bar, in: *Proc ACM Group 2005 Conference*, (ACM Press, 2005).
16. G. McEwan, S. Greenberg, M. Rounding and M. Boyle, Groupware Plug-ins: A Case Study of Extending Collaboration Functionality through Media Items, in: *Proc CollabTech 2006 2nd International Conference on Collaboration Technologies*, (IPSJ SIG Groupware and Network Services, Tsukuba, Japan, July 13-14, 2006), pp. 42-47.
17. S. Greenberg, and E. Tse. SDGToolkit in Action, in: *Video Proc ACM CSCW'06 Conference on Computer Supported Cooperative Work*, (ACM Press, November, 2006) Video and two-page summary, duration 7:14.
18. S. Greenberg, Collaborative Physical User Interfaces, in: *Communication and Collaboration Support Systems*, edited by K. Okada, T. Hoshi and T. Inoue, (IOS Press, Amsterdam, The Netherlands, 2005), pp. 24-42.

Designing Design Exercises – From Theory to Creativity and Real-world Use

Paula Kotzé and Peter Purgathofer
[1] Meraka Institute, Centre for Scientific and Industrial Research,
and School of Computing, University of South Africa,
P O Box 395, Pretoria, 0001, South Africa
Paula.Kotze@meraka.org.za
WWW home page: http://www.meraka.org.za
[2] Design and Assessment of Technologies Institute,
University of Technology Vienna,
Favoritenstraße 9-11, A1040 Vienna, Austria
purg@igw.tuwien.ac.at
WWW home page: http://igw.tuwien.ac.at/

Abstract. This paper discusses a framework for design exercises for interaction design and HCI based on two theoretical frameworks and a set of knowledge transformers. The model scope design exercises on a continuum ranging from creativity to real-world use based on the argument that students must experience design to enable them to learn effectively.

1   Introduction

Interaction design is very much a design discipline, albeit with a different approach than that of scientific and engineering disciplines, schools where it often resides. There is still no agreement (though change is being noticed) in the academic community about what the core elements of an interaction design curriculum might be, or how to approach the teaching of that curriculum [1]. The arts disciplines lean towards advancing interaction design as a creative art, focusing on sensorial elements and a means of personal or brand expression, rather than as an approach to solving product definition and usability issues. On the other end, the more technically inclined disciplines, such as computing, lean towards teaching interaction design from the point of view of exploring and implementing technologies rather than discovering and concentrating on human goals and needs. If one studies current curricula focussing on human-computer interaction (HCI) issues is clear that most focuses on user research and cognitive issues, with less emphasis on the crafts of design (methods and practices). Then again many design programmes in the arts still

Please use the following format when citing this chapter:

Kotzé, P. and Purgathofer, P., 2009, in IFIP International Federation for Information Processing, Volume 289; *Creativity and HCI: From Experience to Design in Education*; Paula Kotzé, William Wong, Joaquim Jorge, Alan Dix, Paula Alexandra Silva; (Boston: Springer), pp. 42–59.

focus on design tools rather than methods and actual use of these methods in real-world situations.

This paper proposes a framework for design exercises for use in the teaching of interaction design aiming at positioning them with regards to both creativity and real-world use. The idea for the framework was conceived during the CONVIVIO Faculty Forum in Austria during December 2006 [2, 3].

The aim of section 2 is to clarify the domain of interaction design, while section 3 highlights the elements or tools of interaction design. Section 4 proposes CTUDE, the framework for design exercises. Section 5 positions design examples presented at the CONVIVIO Faculty Forum within CTUDE, while section 6 concludes.

2   What is Interaction Design

Interaction design is a young field and approach to designing interactive experiences [4]. It is a design discipline aimed at defining the behaviour of artefacts, environments, and systems [1]. According to Preece et al. [5: p.6] interaction design is about 'designing interactive products to support people in their everyday working lives' and interactive experiences that enhance and extend the way people communicate, interact and work. The interactive experiences can be in any medium (such as live events or performances, products, services, etc.) and not necessarily digital media. It involves interactivity. Interactivity is concerned with being part of the action of a system or performance and not merely watching the action passively, which makes it different from animation [4].

As a discipline, interaction design borrows theory and techniques from traditional design disciplines and practices (arts, industrial, communication, etc.), psychology and other social sciences, more scientific and technical disciplines (computing, information sciences, engineering), and also from various interdisciplinary fields. It does, however, not merely borrow, but also synthesise (it is more than a sum of its parts) to create its own unique methods and practices [1, 4, 5].

Interaction designers are involved in all the *interactive aspects* of a product, not only the graphics design of an interface but also with building interactive versions of the designs so that they can be communicated and assessed. They are involved with [1, 5]:

- Defining form: the form of products as they relate to their behaviour and use.
- Anticipating use: how the use of products will mediate human relationships and affect human understanding.
- Exploring dialogue: the dialogue between products, people, and contexts (physical, cultural, historical).

Interaction design is also a perspective that approaches the design of products in several *different ways* [1, 5, 6]:

- Identifying user needs, goals and requirements: forming an understanding of how and why people desire to use products and enable products that are self-aware in terms of behaviour or usage.

- Creating user experiences: aesthetically pleasing, supportive of creativity, rewarding, emotionally fulfilling, fun, satisfying, enjoyable, entertaining, helpful, motivating, etc.
- As gestalts (i.e. more than the sum of its parts), not simply as sets of features and attributes.
- Making sure affordances and seams are clear and malleable.
- By being creative: looking to the future, seeing things as they might be, not necessarily as they are now.

Interaction designers must therefore have a variety of *abilities and skills*. They must be able to [1, 5]:
- Understand the strengths and limitations of both humans (users) and technology.
- Learn new domains quickly.
- Solve problems both analytically and creatively.
- Be able to visualize and simplify complex systems.
- Empathize with users, their needs, and their aspirations, and their experiences.
- Share a passion for making the world a better place through ethical, purposeful, pragmatic, and elegant design solutions.

If we aim to have a successful training programme for interaction designers or HCI experts, we have to make sure our students are equipped with all the necessary skills, also on a practical level. This paper focuses on the development of design exercises that will serve this purpose: exercises on a continuum ranging from pure creative work to real-world applications.

3   The Elements of Interaction Design

Most design disciplines use raw materials. Industrial design, for example, uses simple 3-dimensional shapes such as cubes, spheres, cylinders, etc., while communication design uses basic visual elements such as the line. Interaction designers create products and services that can be digital (e.g. electronic software), analogue (e.g. a karaoke machine), or both (e.g. a mobile phone) [7]. Their design elements are more conceptual, yet powerful. Other design disciplines, however, offer a set of *components* that can be borrowed by interaction designers to support the design of their projects: motion, space, time, appearance, texture, sound [7] and context [8]:
- Motion: Interaction is a sort of communication, and communication is about movement: our vocal cords vibrating as we speak our hands and arms writing or typing as we send e-mail or short messages, sound and data moving between two entities. Interaction designers are concerned with behaviour: the way that products behave in response to the way that people behave. All behaviour can be seen as motion: motion coloured by attitude, culture, personality, and context. [7].
- Space: Space provides a context for motion. Movement happens in some kind of space, even if the boundary of that space is unclear (for example the Internet). Interaction designers work in both 2D and 3D space, whether that space is a

digital screen or the analogue, or the physical space we live in. Interaction design usually involves a combination of physical, analogue and digital space [7].

- Time: All interactions take place over time. Sometimes that time can be near instantaneous, like the time it takes to click a mouse, or it can involve very long durations. Time also creates rhythm and interaction designers can control this rhythm. Interaction designers therefore need an awareness of time [7].
- Appearance: How something looks gives us cues as to how it behaves and how we should interact with it. Appearance is the major source (texture is the other) of what cognitive psychologist James Gibson [9] called affordances, but it was Don Norman's book [10] that spread the term to interaction design and design in general. Affordance is a property, or multiple properties, of an object that provides some indication of how to interact with that object or with a feature on that object. Except to the visually impaired (for who texture often substitutes), appearance also conveys emotional content. Appearance has many variables for designers to alter, for example, proportion, structure, size, shape, weight, colour (hue, value, and saturation), etc. All of these attributes come together to form appearance, and nearly every design has some sort of appearance [7].
- Texture: How an object feels in the hand, i.e. the sensation of an object can provide clues as to how it is to be used as well as when and where. Texture can also convey emotion. Designers can also work with texture variables such as vibration and heat to signify actions [7].
- Sound: Sounds possess many variables that can convey information as well. Sounds are made up of three main components, all of which can be adjusted by a designer: pitch, volume, and timbre or tone quality [7].
- Context: Interaction design is about dialogue with the environment in which it is used. Context is more of a reference element, while the ones listed above are tangible. Designing context, or for context, most likely will speak to reflective emotional responses. Some of the sub-elements of context are: physical environment of use, personas of stakeholders, and culture of use [8].

These components are the interaction designer's toolkit and while interaction designers may not consciously manipulate them, they are the building blocks of interaction design. These elements are mixed and changed and skewed toward learning to master them as ingredients in a designer's kitchen. They should therefore form part of our teaching of interaction design, but they rarely are.

4   Framework for Design Exercises

Various academic institutions with new or established interaction design and HCI programmes are, however, starting to develop an understanding of interaction design and the qualities and skills required of interaction designers [1].

However, teaching students how to develop interactive experiences is not an easy task. There are a myriad of aspects involved that should be considered. Think for a moment how tricky it is to construct a meaningful experience for others. You must first understand your audience, their needs, abilities, interests, and expectations, and how to connect with them. Empathy with users and the ability to conceptualize effective solutions (and then refining them mercilessly) are difficult skills to teach. The same apply to teaching students to be creative and allowing them to experience such skills in giving them the opportunity to 'experience design'.

In the past much teaching attention was focussed on usability, but although usability research is extremely important, it isn't design. Usability identifies problems, but usually doesn't suggest solutions, although the principles of usability can be used to guide design.

Designers all need some basic skills. Interaction designers should be able to draw (sketch) and write well, be at ease with the elements of interaction design (described in section 3), and must be able to communicate excellently with their colleagues and their clients, as well as the users of their designs through their designs.

Although interaction designers seldom code [1] they need to be sensitive to the limitations of the technology they design for. In order to create products, interaction designers will have to communicate coherently with software developers (non-designers). This means understanding code (not necessarily doing the coding themselves) [6].

Increasingly there is also a role for designers to craft systems which in turn enables design, contributing tools, not solutions [6, 11]. There is therefore evidence of designers and developers producing frameworks for others to create with.

The toughest skill to acquire is the combination of creative insight and analytical thinking.

As lecturer, where do you start, how do you define your syllabus and the exercises to equip your students with the practical skills to be successful interaction designers? In this paper we are not going to explicitly focus on the syllabus (although we identify possible shortcomings along the way), but the syllabus should address all the elements of design mentioned in section 3 and all the abilities and skill mentioned in section 2. This paper instead focuses a framework that educators can use to guide them in designing design exercises to enable students to experience design. Since it is generic, it can be adapted to fit design exercises for any syllabus. The issues of what makes a good or bad design exercise, and guidelines to follow in setting up good design exercises are addressed in another paper [2] and will not be repeated here.

4.1   Background

The proposed framework for design exercises is roughly based on two theoretical frameworks: the graphic thinking for architects and designers framework proposed by Laseau [12] and the framework for teaching and learning design proposed by Kotzé et al. [13].

4.1.1 Laseau's Graphic Thinking for Architects and Designers Framework

The first part of our theoretical foundation is based in design theory and practice. Laseau [12] captures a number of interesting aspects of the design process in a simple model, as illustrated in Fig. 1. The model consists of two funnels: an expanding funnel (elaboration) and a contracting funnel (reduction). In this model he balances permanent creativity and idea generation, on the one side, with the reduction resulting from decision-making as main forces in design, on the other side. These two ingredients of design benefit from quite different approaches and methods that can be characterized as sketching and prototyping, respectively.

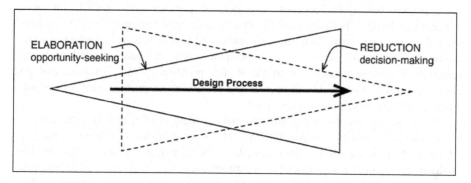

Fig. 1. *Laseau's Model*

In this context, it is necessary to understand sketching as an activity that is not necessarily tied to pen and paper but encompasses any generative design work that share a number of characteristics with pen-and-paper sketching. More specifically, sketches (in any medium) are (among others) quick, inexpensive, plentiful and disposable, and have distinct gesture, constrained resolution and ambiguity [14]. It is obvious that these are properties that prototypes normally don't have.

Buxton [14] draws a separator between sketches and prototypes using a table of opposite concepts, as illustrated in Table 1.

Table 1. *Attributes of Sketches and Prototypes*

Sketch	Prototype
Invite	Attend
Suggest	Describe
Explore	Refine
Question	Answer
Propose	Test
Provoke	Resolve
Tentative, non-committal	Specific Description

It is important to understand that while Buxton's definition of the terms 'sketch' and 'prototype' might collide with their traditional use, it makes much more sense. The 'prototype' is much more restricted in Buxton's classification. In the context of Laseau's model, this table explains why sketching is the primary approach for the expanding funnel of elaboration and opportunity seeking, while prototyping is the ideal method for the contracting funnel of reduction by decision-making. Put differently, it shows that we need to teach two opposite sets of skills to HCI designers in training.

Becoming good in prototyping, on the one hand, is based on skills that are usually subsumed under the term 'problem solving'. Teaching of problem solving skills often makes up the major part of engineering and computing programs. Exercises that let students practice problem solving characteristically have clear and unambiguous objectives, coherent and defined settings and explicit, traceable evaluation criteria. It is understandable that such exercises are preferred by teachers since they are much easier to define and assess and lead to less misapprehension and discussion among the students. Such exercises could be characterized as being relatively 'low-maintenance'. With the design problem 'given', students can go ahead and (taken from Table 1) answer and resolve these problems by testing and refining specific descriptions of a solution.

For sketching, on the other hand, problem solving is of relatively little interest and can even be seen as detrimental. Schön [15] coined the term 'problem setting' as a contrast to problem solving, thus describing the (at that time) missing half of this dualism. To train the skills needed for problem setting, coherent, unambiguous, defined and clear exercises are the exact opposite of what is needed. Students need to work on open and even inconsistent assignments, in undefined and ambiguous contexts. Obviously, this type of exercise is much harder to evaluate, and it is often impossible to publish clear evaluation criteria up-front. Performance in the expanding funnel of Laseau's diagram is often impossible to assess by objective means.

Even when seen as rational activities, problem solving and problem setting require different sets of skills, as e.g. Holt [16] proposes: problem solving as an abstract, symbolic, analytic and verbal activity, versus problem setting as a concrete, holistic, spatial and non-verbal practice.

Still, it is important to see that this is not impossible. Following Laseau, exploration can be conducted systematically. He suggests a number of sketching techniques that are all based on the idea that to change an image enables us to get a new look at them, thereby expanding our thinking [12]. Laseau describes a number of sketching techniques that could be a starting point for the design of exercises, e.g. transforming, structuring and ordering images.

These techniques, however, only work if, as Laseau writes, we are 'comfortable with exploration that is not tightly focused, let the mind wander, and be open to unexpected results' [12: p.115]. This might be the real challenge in any kind of education, as McKim [17: p.45] recognizes: 'For most people, breaking lazy, category-hardened, fear-inducing habits of seeing is an educational task of considerable magnitude'.

4.1.2 Kotzé et al.'s Framework for Teaching and Learning Design

The second part of our theoretical foundation is based in learning theory. People 'learn' by repeated exposure to concepts using one of two major *types of learning*: implicit or explicit [13]:

- *Implicit learning*, or unintended learning or tacit (silent) learning [18, 19], can be seen as a passive process where people, when exposed to information, simply acquire knowledge of the information by means of that exposure, i.e. it is unconscious and always active [19-21]. Invoking implicit knowledge involves the indirect application of the knowledge without the requirement of knowledge declaration [20].

- *Explicit learning,* or intended learning, in contrast, is characterised by people actively seeking out the structure of any information presented to them, i.e. it is intentional and conscious [20-22]. For example, explicit learning would be involved if a designer is instructed to acquire some target knowledge and then to explicitly apply and state the knowledge acquired in the design phase [20].

Kotzé et al. [13] proposes a pyramid of competence model for learning (and consequently teaching) design for HCI based on the models of learning proposed by Gorman [23] and Miller [24]. Both Miller and Gorman communicate the concept of different kinds of knowledge building onto each other, and the acquisition of the knowledge being acquired in a particular sequence over a period of time.

The pyramid of competence model, as illustrated in Fig. 2 identifies four *types of knowledge* in design or technology knowledge transfer [13]:

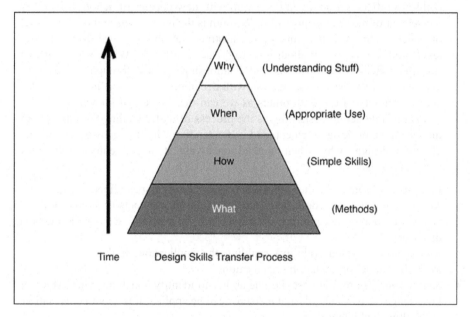

Fig. 2. *Kotzé et al. pyramid of competence model with a link to interaction design skills*

- *Declarative knowledge (what)* refers to the recall of facts and events? Declarative knowledge is composed of chunks, consisting of a number of slots each of which can hold a value (which can also be another chunk) [25]. In the context of interaction design this is the process of learning about design techniques and the elements of interaction design (as mentioned in section 3).
- *Procedural knowledge (how)* that refers to the skill of knowing how to do something. Procedural knowledge is usually encoded as declarative knowledge first and then translated into procedures (algorithms) [26], but can also be learned by feel or intuition. Procedural knowledge therefore consists of productions,

which are condition-action pairs specifying the action to be taken if a particular condition is satisfied [25]. In the context of interaction design this is the process of learning how to use the design elements and design techniques.

- *Judgement knowledge* (*when*) that involves the ability to recognise when knowledge is applicable to a particular instance, i.e. recognising that a problem is similar to one for which a solution is known and knowing when to apply a particular procedure or solution. Judgement knowledge is therefore structured in a way that facilitates problem solving and creativity, and is usually applied by experts in a particular context. Whereas novices would rely more on declarative and, to a lesser extent, on general or weak heuristics based on procedural knowledge, experts rely more on judgement knowledge [25]. In the context of interaction design this is the process of learning to recognise situations where the previously learnt technique or design element should be applied.

- *Wisdom* (*why*) knowledge refers to meta-cognitive monitoring which may lead to a new course of action. It is related to judgement knowledge referring to the ability to reflect, question, and come up with new courses of action. It involves an element of moral reasoning [25]. Wisdom is the most vague and intimate level of understanding [4]. It is much more abstract and philosophical than the other levels and less is known about how to create or affect it. Wisdom is a kind of 'meta-knowledge' of processes and relationships gained through experiences. We cannot create wisdom as we can with declarative and procedural knowledge and we cannot share it with others as we can these levels of knowledge. In the context of interaction design this is the process of understanding the rationale of the technique or design element, and understanding why it comprises a good and effective design, why when applied creatively it would enhance the user experiences, etc.

In terms of design skills these four *levels of learning* can be defined as [4]:

- *Knows*: Factual knowledge about interaction design elements or simple skills. It is the product of research or creation (such as writing), data gathering and discovery.
- *Knows how*: Methods (ability) enabling the application of the knowledge or skills. It is about presentation organisation.
- *Shows how*: Appropriate use, i.e. the ability to identify situations where skills or knowledge, or particular design elements can be applied. It is about conversation, storytelling and integration.
- *Knows why*: Understanding stuff, i.e. the ability to argue about why a specific skill or method or design element will be appropriate or not. It is about contemplation, evaluation, interpretation and retrospection.

Interestingly, although we have to keep these four levels of knowledge in mind when teaching interaction design, the same four *levels* should also be kept in mind when *designing interactive experiences* [4]:

- The *what* knowledge is just data: It is the raw material we find or create and then use to build our communications. Most of what we experience is merely data. It is often boring, incomplete, or inconsequential. Data isn't valuable as communication medium on its own, because it isn't a complete message.

- The *how* knowledge makes data meaningful for audiences because it requires the creation of relationships and patterns between data. Transforming data into information is accomplished by organizing it into a meaningful form, presenting it in meaningful and appropriate ways, and communicating the context around it.
- The *when* knowledge is communicated by building persuasive interactions with others, or with tools, so that the patterns and meanings in the contained information can be learned by others.
- The *why* knowledge cannot be created, as we can with what, how, and when, and we cannot share it with others as we can these other levels of knowledge. We can only create experiences that offer opportunities and describe processes. Ultimately, wisdom is an understanding that must be gained by oneself.

4.2   A Framework for Design Exercises

The proposed framework for design exercises for interaction design and HCI is based on the theoretical frameworks discussed above.

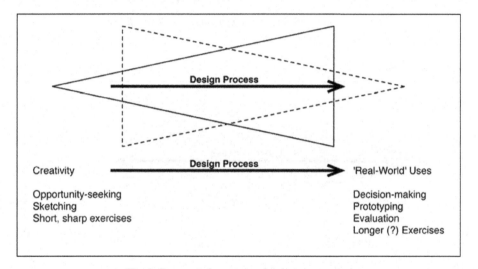

Fig. 3. *Framework structure for design exercises*

Fig. 3 illustrates the idea that design is in some ways a continuum ranging from purely creative work to real-world implementations, i.e. sketches to prototype to use the terminology from section 4.1.1. Design exercises can be aimed at any point of this continuum, either starting at a specific point, or ending at a specific point. There is no wrong or right way of 'designing' design exercises entrenched in this model. When aiming at the creative side, exercises should be short, sharp and varied, requiring students to work with a variety of interaction design elements (see section 3).

If we superimpose the Kotzé et al. [13] pyramid of competence on the reduction funnel of the framework illustrated in Fig. 3, we found that it has a natural fit, as illustrated in Fig. 4. It follows the traditional way we teach in the fields of engineering and computing and the way in which HCI courses has been taught in the past. It also follows the arguments of learning theory, on which the Kotzé et al. pyramid of competence is based.

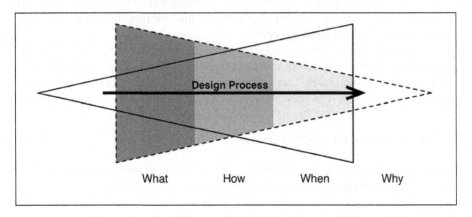

Fig. 4. *Pyramid of competence mapping to reduction funnel*

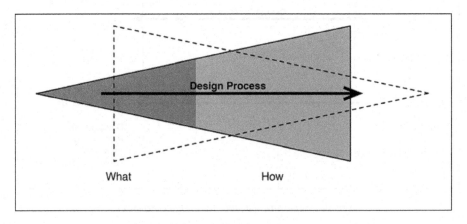

Fig. 5. *Pyramid of competence mapping to elaboration funnel*

When we are creative we take particular thoughts, ideas and elements and connect them together in a fresh way so as to produce an experience which is novel, interesting and possibly of value. The elaboration funnel is therefore different from the reduction funnel in the way it links to the pyramid of competence, as illustrated in Fig. 5. As it is focused on opportunity seeking, it does not necessarily reach the 'why' or even the 'when' stages, although they are not completely excluded (in fact the reduction funnel will take over to reach these stages). The primary focus of the elaboration funnel is using skills and methods to manipulate the skills ('what') in a new way ('how') to create something that is not pre-specified (and not necessarily usable or useful).

Creativity is therefore a judgement of a different kind, and involves a product, process, and a situation, the same aspects that are often present in the reduction funnel, although often used in opposite ways of a range.

Table 2. *Sim and Duffy's knowledge transformers*

Knowledge Transformers	How is knowledge transformed
Abstraction / detailing	Abstraction generates a new, less detailed version through the use of abstract concepts and operators. Detailing generates new knowledge with more detail.
Association / disassociation	Association determines a dependency between entities based on some logical, causal or statistical relationships. Disassociation asserts lack of dependency.
Derivations / randomization	Derivations derive some knowledge from another piece of knowledge (based on some dependency between them), Randomizations transforms one knowledge segment into another by making random changes.
Explanation / discovery	Explanation derives additional knowledge based on existing domain knowledge. Discovery derives new knowledge without existing underlying domain knowledge.
Clustering/ decomposition	Clustering involves the grouping of past designs according to their similarities when considering certain perspective and criteria. Decomposition removes the groupings.
Generalization / specialization	Generalization creates a description that characterises the entire concept based on a conjunction of all the specialisations of that concept. Specialisation increases the specificity of the description.
Similarity comparison / dissimilarity comparison	Similarity comparison derives new knowledge about a design on the basis of similarity the design and similar past designs. Dissimilarity comparison derives new knowledge on the basis of lack of similarity between two or more designs.

Sim and Duffy [27] propose a set of knowledge transformers that could assist in making the link between learning and creativity on the design continuum. They distinguish between seven opposite knowledge transformers:

- Abstraction vs. detailing.
- Association vs. disassociation.
- Derivations (reformulation) vs. randomization.
- Explanation vs. discovery.
- Group rationalisation (clustering) vs. decomposition.
- Generalisation vs. specialisation.
- Similarity comparison vs. dissimilarity comparison.

The reduction funnel aims at the knowledge transformer mentioned first, while the elaboration funnel aims at the knowledge transformer mentioned second. Table 2 elaborates the meaning of each of these knowledge transformers.

As already mentioned in section 4.1.1, Laseau [12] describes three approaches to creative exploration:

- Open-ended images that suggest a number of different perceptions or interpretations.
- Transformation of images.
- Structuring or ordering of images.

These approaches can also be seen as knowledge transformers, as Laseau [12: p.115] explicitly states: 'These approaches are aimed at re-centrering visual thinking'. According to Laseau, re-centrering visual thinking means 'unlearning' a certain viewpoint and thus enabling the ability to find new, unexpected viewpoints. Table 3 defines these three knowledge transformers (and provide our own definition for the opposites for each transformer).

Table 3. *Laseau's knowledge transformers*

Knowledge Transformers	How is knowledge transformed
Open-ended images (vs. constrained images)	Open-ended images allow for ambiguity, collage and multi-valency of sketches and invite new interpretations and ideas. Constrained images remove this ambiguity by limiting interpretations.
Transformation of images (vs. preservation of images)	Transformation is invoked by open-ended images, and changes perspective or perception, making familiar seem strange. Preservation maintains the meaning and structure of images.
Structuring or ordering of images for non-specified context (vs. real-world context)	Create artificial context within which new responses can be made vs. specifying a real-world context.

Comparing the two sets of knowledge transformers, we immediately notice some similarities (though not complete overlap), for example, between Sim and Duffy's derivations vs. randomization and Laseau's transformation, and between clustering vs. decomposition and structuring.

Integrating Laseau's model, Kotzé et al. framework for teaching and learning, and both Sim and Duffy and Laseau's sets of knowledge transformers, we propose CTUDE (Creativity to Real-world Use Design Exercises), our framework for design exercises, as illustrated in Fig. 6.

To use CTUDE, the lecturer has to decide where to position the exercises on the continuum and on which funnel, and then plan the experiences to fit this purpose using/suggesting appropriate knowledge transformers. If the purpose of the design exercise is experiencing creativity, one will aim for the left hand side of the continuum and equip one's students with the tools and techniques matching the knowledge transformers suitable for this side of the continuum. If the aim is for students to design a small-scale real-world application, one would design the experience around tools, techniques and knowledge transformers at the opposite side of the continuum.

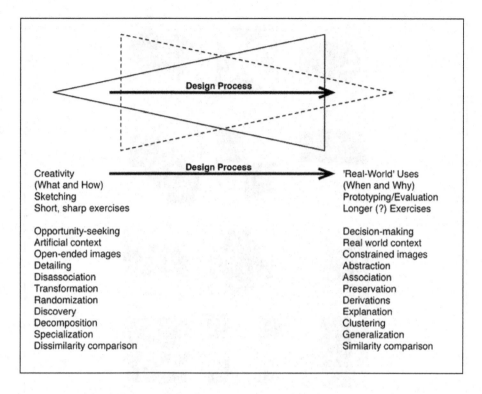

Fig. 6. *Framework for design exercises and knowledge transformers*

5 CONVIVIO Faculty Forum Design Examples

We analysed the various design exercises presented at the CONVIVIO Faculty Forum [3] for their fit onto this framework for design exercises. The exercises varied from purely creative, at the start of the elaboration funnel (for example the Varey, Petrie, Ozcan, and Baumann cultural probe examples), to examples with deliverables at the other side of the spectrum of the reduction funnel with mock-ups or working prototypes (for example the Garay-Vitoria examples). Several of the exercises started off in the elaboration funnel but concluded in the reduction funnel (for example the Oestreicher, Baumann circular handover, Van der Veer, Silva, and Kotzé examples), or were positioned mid-way along the design continuum, requiring students to design or analyse something, but not requiring any kind of implementation (for example the Van Greunen, Jounila, Mavorommati examples). A variety of knowledge transformers were used, with discovery and transformation of images the most popular for the creativity exercises, and clustering, association and similarity comparison the most popular for 'real-world exercises'. We provide detail on two of these examples to illustrate the differences.

Fig. 7. *Examples of Graphic Design problem undertaken by students as part of tutorial programme.*

The first is an example provided by Varey [3], using short visual thinking exercises solving communication problems through experimentation and exploration to allow her students to think creatively, and therefore aims at the opportunity seeking funnel. Possible solutions must be generated and concepts represented in a visual form. The exercises are designed not to rely on draughtsmanship skills, but rather to encourage the generation of solutions that have impact and are memorable, visually interesting and communicate the appropriate message. For example, students have to create graphic images, using four black papers squares of the same dimensions, to express the meaning of words such as order, tension, playful and bold. These blocks are their sketching tools. The task intentionally limits the variables to encourage students to be creative and to develop design skills based on the principles of illusory space, framal reference, contrast and the dynamics of relationships. The exercises involve opportunity-seeking, discovery, transformation and structuring of images, all creative knowledge transformers. After completion of the design exercise, it also requires students to select the most effective solution, developing their critical and reflective skills, i.e. moving into the reduction funnel. Fig. 7 illustrates some of the examples produced by students.

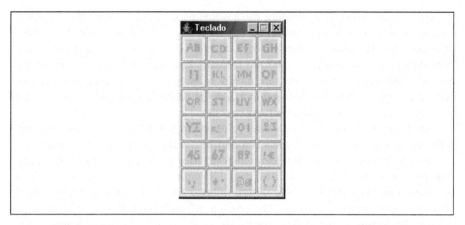

Fig. 8. *Visual interface of the reduced keyboard application to be developed.*

Garay-Vittoria [3] describes an exercise for the design of reduced keyboards (the number of keys are less than the number of standard characters that can be produced), aimed at the reduction funnel. Although it starts off with some creative elements, the final aim is to develop a working prototype within a relatively constrained specification. The exercise involves decision making, constrained images, association, preservation and similarity comparison, all aimed at the right hand side of the design continuum. Reduced keyboards usually work on the principle of pressing a key repeatedly to obtain a particular character (e.g. the keypads of mobile phones). For example to type the word 'KEY' you have to press 44229. However, this method has a problem with ambiguities. For instance, if you want to write 'MOON', you have to write 555555555, but this combination can be interpreted as 'NOMO', 'MONO', 'ONMO', 'OMNO', 'NOOM', 'OOOO', etc. Some of the possible interpretations may have no sense in natural language. The exercise requires the students to develop an interface that work with scanning input with a single-button, using a reduced keyboard with 24 keys that are distributed in 6 rows and 4 columns (as illustrated in Fig. 8). This distribution is due to the fact that they use a remote control from Creative (Creative CIMR 100) to compose messages. The interface must be designed so that interface options are selected after a period of time when a key is pressed or when pressing another different key. The selected character is the last one shown in the display. Although pre-specified design instructions for the prototype were given, some students did try to enhance interaction strategy, searching for other operational ways, i.e. moving into the elaboration funnel.

6 Conclusion

The main contribution of this paper is a CTUDE, a novel framework for design exercises with it foundations in graphical thinking, learning theory and knowledge transformers.

Apart from providing a structure for positioning design exercises, the proposed framework also exposes a number of bare spots in interaction design and HCI design education. While some of the aspects covered by the model (especially the 'prototyping' or engineering facets) are typically represented quite well, sketching and especially the creative 'how', are mostly missing from these programmes. Our study also suggests that there is need to extent the problem space, or the knowledge set, over which some of the transformers operate.

One more direction to follow would be to research whether the isolated training of the use of knowledge transformers could make a difference in design education. It would be interesting to see if students that practice the application of knowledge transformers with suitable exercises would benefit in their design skills. Such exercises would be quite simple to design following CTUDE, and, as an additional advantage, quite easy to evaluate. The problem of evaluating designs is often cited because the lecturers find it difficult to assess the methods used in reaching the design: CTUDE will provide a framework to position the designs and the methods used and thus a template for assessing them.

Acknowledgments

Our sincere thanks go to all the participants of the CONVIVIO Faculty Forum, who sparked the idea for the framework during the brainstorming session, and to the CONVIVIO European Network for Human-Centred Design of Interactive Technologies (www.convivionetwork.net) for sponsoring the Faculty Forum financially.

References

1. R. Reimann, So you want to be an interaction designer, *Cooper Interaction Design Newsletter*, **June 2001** (2001).
2. K. Baumann, P. Kotzé, L. Oestreicher, L. Bannon, A. Varey, D. Van Greunen, G. Van der Veer, H. Petrie, I. Jounila, I. Mavrommati, N. Garay-Vitoria, O. Ozcan, P. Purgathofer, and P.A. Silva, EISH - Exercises in Studying HCI, in: *Creativity3: Expereincing to Educate and Design - Proceedings of HCI Educators 2007*, edited by P. Alexandra Silva, A. Dix, and J. Jorge, (Designeed, Aveiro, 2007), pp. 134 – 137.
3. CONVIVIO, Design for HCI, Proceedings CONVIVIO Faculty Forum: Teaching Design for HCI, (cited 2007-01-05); http://www.hcieducation.com/pmwiki.php?n=WorkShops.CONVIVIO2006 (CONVIVIO, Graz, Austria, 2006).
4. N. Shedroff, Information interaction design: A unified field theory of design, in: *Information Design*, edited by R. Jacobson, (MIT Press, 1999), pp. 267 - 292.
5. J. Preece, Y. Rogers, and H. Sharp, *Interaction Design: Beyond Human-computer Interaction* (John Wiley & Sons, Inc., New York, 2002).
6. D. Hill, Architecture and Interaction Design, via Adaptation and Hackability, (cited 2006-12-22); Http://www.cityofsound.com/blog/2006/05/architecture_an.html, 2006).

7. D. Saffer, *Designing for Interaction: Creating Smart Applications and Clever Devices* (New Riders, 2006).
8. D.H. Malouf, Elements of Interaction Design, (cited 2006-12-22); http://synapticburn.com/comments.php?id=143_0_1_0_C (Synaptic Burn, 2006).
9. J. Gibson, The Ecological Approach to Visual Perception, (1979).
10. D. Norman, *The Design of Everyday Things* (MIT Press, London, 1998).
11. P. Dourish, *Where the Action Is: The Foundations of Embodied Interaction* (MIT Press, 2001).
12. P. Laseau, *Graphic Thinking for Architects & Designers* (Wiley, 2000).
13. P. Kotzé, K. Renaud, and J. Van Biljon, Don't do this - Pitfalls in using anti-patterns in teaching human-computer interaction principles, *Computers & Education*, DOI: doi:10.1016/j.compedu.2006.10.003, (2006).
14. B. Buxton, What sketches (and prototypes) are and are not, in CHI'06 Workshop, City, 2006), pp.
15. D. Schön, *The Reflective Practitioner* (MITPress, Cambridge, MA, 1983).
16. J.E. Holt, Practising Practice by Design, *International Journal of Engineering Education*, **18**(3), 256 - 263 (2002).
17. R.H. McKim, *Experiences in Visual Thinking* (Brookes/Cole, Monterey, CA, 1972).
18. M. Polanyi, *Personal Knowledge - Towards a Post-Critical Philosophy* (Routledge and Kegan Paul, London, 1958).
19. A. Reber, *Implicit learning and tacit knowledge* (Oxford University Press, Oxford, 1993).
20. M.W. Kirkhart, The nature of declarative and nondeclarative knowledge for implicit and explicit learning, *The Journal of General Psychology*, **128**(4), 447 - 461 (2001).
21. N.A. Taatgen, Learning without limits: from problem solving towards a unified theory of learning, (cited 2005-06-05); www.ub.rug.nl/eldoc/dis/ppsw/n.a.taatgen/ (Universal Press, 1999).
22. D.C. Berry, *How Implicit is Implicit Learning?* (Oxford University Press, Oxford, 1997).
23. M.E. Gorman, Types of knowledge and their roles in technology transfer, *Journal of Technology Transfer*, **27**(3), 219 - 231 (2002).
24. G.E. Miller, The assessment of clinical skills/competence/performance, *Acad Med*, **65**, 563 -567 (1990).
25. C. Lebiere, D. Wallach, and N.A. Taatgen, Implicit and explicit learning in ACT-R, in: *Proceedings of the Second Conference on Cognitive Modelling (ECCM 98)*, edited by F. Ritter and R. Young, 1998), pp. 183 - 189.
26. J.R. Anderson, *Rules of the Mind* (Lawrence Erlbaum Associates, Hillsdale, NJ, 1993).
27. K.S. Sim and H.B. Duffy, Knowledge transformers - a link between learning and creativity, Learning and Creativity Workshop - 2002, (cited 2006-12-22); http://www.cad.strath.ac.uk/AID02_workshop/Workshop_webpage.html, Cambridge, UK, 2002).

Teaching Human-Computer Interaction from Real World Examples – Furnishing Creativity?

Lars Oestreicher
Computer Science Unit, Department of Information Science
Uppsala University, Uppsala, Sweden
larsoe@dis.uu.se
WWW home page: http://www.anst.uu.se/larsoest/

Abstract. This paper argues that it can give good results to use bad and good design examples when teaching Human-Computer Interaction provided that the examples are elaborated by the teacher in a manner that enables a changed (shaken) mind-set in the students. In the paper examples from lectures, exercises and larger assignments using concrete material as a base, are discussed from the perspective of general theories of education. The key issue in the teaching process in order to reach this level is the proper elaboration of the used examples and exercises, leaving the reflection on the problem to the students to a large extent. One conclusion is that it is possible to use elaboration to support the students' learning so that he or she is enabled to understand the general problem and create new solutions to given problems. Elaboration of concrete examples can in this way support even a creative level of learning.

1 Introduction

It is often said that creative thinking should be encouraged in students of Human-Computer Interaction. But how should this be done in practice? This paper takes a standpoint in this issue of teaching Human-Computer Interaction (HCI) to Computer Science Students. One way to stimulate creative thinking is in my experience to support the students' thought processes to break away from traditional ways of thinking about design and problem solving.

I have been an academic teacher since 1991, when I received a lecturing position in Computing Science, with an orientation towards Human-Computer Interaction.

Please use the following format when citing this chapter:

Oestreicher, L., 2009, in IFIP International Federation for Information Processing, Volume 289; *Creativity and HCI: From Experience to Design in Education*; Paula Kotzé, William Wong, Joaquim Jorge, Alan Dix, Paula Alexandra Silva; (Boston: Springer), pp. 60–77.

The courses I have taught cover various topics in the area, ranging from Introduction to Human-Computer Interaction, Usability engineering, User-oriented software design and Task and Work analysis. In my teaching I use many examples of bad (and occasionally good) design cases to try to create a new mindset in the students mind. In this paper I will argue that the proper use of practical examples or illustrations (good or bad) can act as a catalyst for creative thinking in HCI design.

Over the years, I have collected many pictures, error dialogues, cartoons and other educational material, which to some extent have been published on the Internet as a free, public resource for teachers, e.g., in Human-Computer Interaction. The material is available on my personal home page [1] and the figures in this article are all displayed on the site. One example of the material that I use is shown in Fig. 1.

Fig. 1. *An example image that is used to illustrate the problem of complex technology in a different way than in an ordinary interface. (photo by the author)*

In this figure I have heaped all the remote controls that are used to (mis-)handle my home video system. These are the controls that I have to manage before I can turn on the TV-combo to see the popular Christmas show (hence the four surrounding candles) if I manage to do this in time. The example appears to be a much more telling way to talk about technological complexity than just showing a complex interface, e.g., to a power plant, or in a cockpit. The students remember this picture, because turning on a family show or the children's channel should not require an engineering degree, whereas most people do not imagine running a power plant or fly an aeroplane. The ridiculous situation has even provoked discussions on power distribution in family life, starting from the question about who has the knowledge needed to turn on the TV. I will get back to how this type of pictures is used in later parts of this paper. (By the way, I actually happened to get the remote for the car GPS added to heap in Fig. 1 by mistake, which one is that?)

From teaching HCI at the Åland Polytechnic (Åland is a small Swedish speaking island, belonging to Finland) I have also had some experience from teaching in areas with (at least on the surface) minor cultural variations. This has provided an opportunity to see how minor cultural differences may influence the design process. Åland is a society with strong marine connections, inheriting a fishing and seafaring culture, which can also be seen in buildings and smaller design items. The use of cultural issues in teaching is mentioned further in section .

Most of the experiences, and the informal studies described in this paper are from students of Computer Science at Uppsala University, and at the Åland Polytechnic. None of the examples in this article are results from a controlled study, but they are examples that have been selected to reflect observations that have been collected over a long period of teaching in real classroom settings.

In section 2 a theoretical background is given to the approaches I use for teaching. In sections 3, 4 and 5, I will discuss how the theory affects lectures, exercises and assignments through a series of examples. I will also report on the experiences from the exercises when these have been used with groups of students with different backgrounds. Finally in section 6 I will draw some conclusions from the examples, and try to see how teaching can be supported through the ideas in this article.

2   Teaching Human-Computer Interaction

During my employment as a teacher, the focus has often been on making the students grasp the *problems* with software design. I have also tried to extend the area of interest during the courses to the problem of designing machines in a more general sense, but still with computers as the main area of interest. By widening the scope of the topic, the students are more or less forced to see human-machine interaction as an applied science. It also makes them aware of the fact that computers are intruding everywhere in society, and not only as visibly computer-shaped. However, I still use a fair amount of computer-based examples in my teaching, to attach to the students' final profession (for some samples see my home page [1]).

2.1   Theoretical Foundation

In my teaching I have gradually included ideas that are based on more firm didactic principles. Even if the theoretical approaches to teaching are difficult to apply in the practical teaching situation, the theoretic framework is a good starting point to understand the process of creating exercises and examples for the students to use. The basic ideas in my teaching are still founded on associative learning, such as described by Anderson [2]. In this simple model association is supported by elaboration of concepts into associative networks. Elaboration can be simple, such as just adding related ideas to the concept to be memorized, or it can be extensive by creating more elaborate 'stories' around the concepts. However, only employing associativity is a too simple teaching strategy, since it mostly addresses simple memorizing, but does not promote such phenomena as understanding. Also more complicated things such as creativity are difficult to address in associative theories of learning.

A second model or framework for learning that has been used extensively is Bloom's taxonomy [3]. The taxonomy does not in itself provide direct models for teaching but can be used as a reference when teaching material is designed. In the revised model, there are several differences from the original [3]. The revised taxonomy is especially interesting in that it considers learning processes rather than the goals of the learning. The following learning processes are mentioned:

1. REMEMBERING: Can the student RECALL information?
2. UNDERSTANDING: Can the student EXPLAIN ideas or concepts?
3. APPLYING: Can the student USE the new knowledge in another familiar situation?
4. ANALYZING: Can the student DIFFERENTIATE between constituent parts?
5. EVALUATING: Can the student JUSTIFY a decision or course of action?
6. CREATING: Can the student GENERATE new products, ideas or ways of viewing things?

Thus the taxonomy in some respect defines knowledge on different levels as how the student uses the knowledge, from the simplest level, where the student just recalls the knowledge (e.g., as when learning the decimals of the irrational number π), to the most complex level where new knowledge can be synthesized from the old, which is closest to what we would like to achieve when we teach how to design. This taxonomy can also be compared to the idea about competences, separating different kinds of knowledge, dependent on what a person can do with it. This is also referred to as the pyramid of competence model [4]:

- Declarative knowledge – What?
- Procedural knowledge – How?
- Judgement knowledge – When?
- Wisdom knowledge – Why?

In order to be skilled designer the 'why'-aspect needs to be a more or less constant awareness. Much of textbook information is giving declarative and procedural knowledge, whereas judgment knowledge and wisdom knowledge is often left as something that grows as a skill. One question is whether the upper levels in Bloom's taxonomy can be achieved through the teaching process, and thus also provide the knowledge displayed in the top of the pyramid of competence.

A fourth model that can be applicable in this context is the scaffolded instruction [4] that stems back to the work by Vygotsky [6]. In this model the tutor prepares the learning process by a scaffolding instruction incorporating the following features [4]:

1. *Intentionality*: The task has a clear overall purpose driving any separate activity that may contribute to the whole.
2. *Appropriateness*: Instructional tasks pose problems that can be solved with help but which students could not successfully complete on their own.

3. *Structure*: Modelling and questioning activities are structured around a model of appropriate approaches to the task and lead to a natural sequence of thought and language.
4. *Collaboration*: The teacher's response to student work recasts and expands upon the students' efforts without rejecting what they have accomplished on their own. The teacher's primary role is collaborative rather than evaluative.
5. *Internalization*: External scaffolding for the activity is gradually withdrawn as the patterns are internalized by the students.

There are many other perspectives on the scaffolding instruction process, but from this perspective it can be used as laying a foundation for learning on the various levels. This means that a teaching process can use the basic features of this model in different ways, depending on the knowledge level that is aimed at. By laying the proper foundation, the students have an easier task to incorporate the new knowledge.

In most cases it is better the closer to the evaluation/creation and judgement/wisdom levels of knowledge we can take students through our teaching. The question is whether it is possible to teach Human-Computer Interaction in such a way that these levels are stimulated?

2.2   Mind-Shaking Teaching

A large part of the education has to be based on a mixture of practical and theoretical materials for the student as was discussed at the INTERACT'99 workshop on Teaching HCI (cf. [7]). During the workshop the need for mind-shaking experiences for the student was explicitly stated [8–9]. The conclusion was the introduction of an approximate general procedure for teaching Human-Computer Interaction based on six 'golden rules' for shaking the students mind when teaching Human-Computer Interaction [8] that were listed as one result from the workshop:
1. Provide thought-provoking literature that illustrates the problem.
2. Let the students observe real users, using real artefacts, anchoring the observations in the literature.
3. Let the students analyze the results of the observations, and stimulate the understanding by making them write reports!
4. Mix the results from the analysis with theory, e.g., cognitive psychology, perception psychology, computer science.
5. Apply the experiences in a redesign of the artefact.
6. Iterate the observation phase with the new artefact.

The foundation of this approach is to encourage an experiential knowledge acquisition in the student. The basic assumption is that it is only by actual practical experience that the student can understand the nature of the knowledge and also understand how the knowledge can be applied. This is in my experience especially true when we teach the topic to students who are not specifically Human-Computer Interaction specialists, but software engineers, or web-programmers etc. These students may be less motivated in learning good design, since they are more intent on the technical problems in software design. In this context good practical examples are crucial to awakening the necessary understanding of the problem.

In all these models there is also a need for a separation between implicit and explicit learning, where the former is learning that 'just occurs', without the learner consciously trying to learn, and the second is based on an intention to learn something specific. In some cases implicit learning gives a more immediate acceptance of the knowledge, whereas explicit learning requires more learning efforts. Used in the proper way the scaffolding instruction process can be applied to the teaching in a way that seems to make implicit learning much more immediate and effective.

In the following sections I will describe a series of activities used in lectures, exercises and assignments, and which I suggest do address not only the lower levels of the models referred in this section, but also have the potential of addressing the upper levels, thus giving the student a more applied knowledge that can boost creativity in the HCI area.

3   Mind Shakers in Lectures

Many of the courses I have taught have been short courses that can be classified as crash introductory courses, where a course goal has been 'to make the students aware of the problems with human-machine interaction'. One problem with the short courses is that it has been difficult to include the whole design process from scratch in the teaching. One way to work around this has been to work from concrete design examples. However, in order to explain essential concepts and to urge the students to take the ideas further it is not sufficient to provide illustrative examples of good or bad designs. It is also necessary to provide examples that make the students reflect, and even make the students reflect on the further consequences emanating from the more general problems illustrated through the examples. To do this, it is not sufficient just to present the examples, but it is also necessary to complement the examples by prodded real-time reflection and the addition of follow-up material, such as exercises or questions to ponder.

Teaching good design is in itself a big challenge. Teaching good design without delimiting the creativity in the students mind is an even greater challenge. One of the best appreciations I have had as a teacher in HCI was a former student who came back, five or six years after his graduation, telling me that 'You have destroyed my life! I can't open a door or turn on a water faucet, without thinking about you!'. By the concrete examples used in the lectures, the student had been forced to start reflecting on the things around him. His statement left me with a feeling of being successful in the first part of my mission as a teacher, in shaking the students' minds. This reflects my ideas on the effects of successful teaching of Human-Computer Interaction — the making aware and inspiring of a constructive curiosity.

The problem is not to teach the students to make the best design, but to teach the students in daring to use alternative designs, while still being aware of the advantages and disadvantages of their own designs. During both lectures and practical exercises I try to encourage the students to try on new designs that go outside of the normal thoughts and furthermore to have them challenged in critical examinations. In this process I also encourage the students to observe cultural phenomena, such as shapes and colour schemes that they can observe in their surroundings. By picking up and also stressing cultural design features in the teaching process, it is easier to make the students reflect on the designs that they produce in the end. Often the cultural specialties in the environments are not considered by the students until they are pointed out specifically, as for example, during the lectures.

3.1   Hot or Cold Showers

The first example of such material for use in lecturing is displayed in Fig. 2 below. This particular example has been used to discuss the concept of accessibility, but it contains several other possibilities (see the full example with comments on the web page [10]).

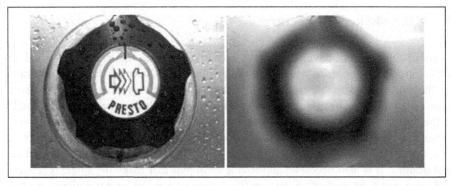

Fig. 2. *Two different pictures of the same faucet displaying a typical problem of accessibility (photo and post processing by the author)*

During a typical lecture, at first the left picture is shown, displaying a faucet that is used to change the temperature of water in a shower at a public bathhouse. The students are asked about what they can see in the picture. Then the picture is changed to the right picture in Fig. 2, showing the situation when someone with bad eyesight removes their glasses. The question is, which way to turn the tap in order to get colder water when you get scalded? The students quickly realize that the normal condition of usage does indeed mean an accessibility problem for some parts of the bathhouse population. Remarkably enough, even the students ordinarily wearing glasses often find themselves a little surprised by this example.

Now, this example by itself does not contribute much unless we use it by adding some complementary exercises, where the students are asked to hand in their own examples of something that might be difficult to use for someone with special needs. In the assignment they also have to explain why the problem occurs, and a possible way around it. The exercise is constrained by using specified disabilities.

The extra elaboration around this example serves several purposes:

- It gives the student a better retention of the example itself.
- It forces the student to adapt the problem to other, similar problems, thus making the problem a more general observation.
- By suggesting a solution it is necessary for the student to engage in a more creative process than the simple viewing of the example.

In the exercises that follow the example it often turns out that the students find a motivating challenge in finding alternative solutions, and they seem to get a better understanding and appreciation of the problems with accessibility, which in many cases does not make any impression on the students during the short courses (between four or five weeks) that we have at our University.

3.2   Less Extra Sugar?

The second example shown in Fig. 3 is also a picture that is used during a lecture to illuminate a problem, namely the problem of achieving clarity in interface messages. The lecture example is in this case immediately followed by a larger design exercise (performed in the same way as he exercises described in section 0), where the students are encouraged to focus their design ideas around clarity of the concepts. Unfortunately the example is from a Swedish coffee vending machine, but the idea should be easy to get from the labels anyway (the figure caption gives the proper translation).

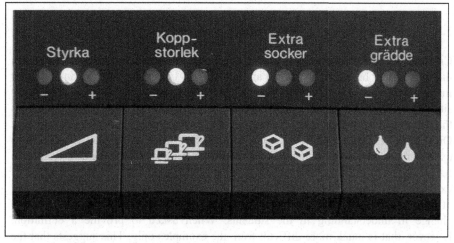

Fig. 3. *The adjustment buttons on a common coffee vending machine in Sweden. The labels on top read 'Strength', 'Cup Size', 'Extra Sugar' and 'Extra Cream' from the left to the right. The question is what the minus signs signify in combination with the expression 'Extra...' (photo by the author)*

The example in Fig. 3 is from a very capable coffee vending machine, which provides the customers with an assortment of hot drinks including chocolate and mixtures of coffee and chocolate. The machine also offers the user to adjust some parameters in the ordered drink. You can, for example, have a stronger or weaker drink than normal (first button from the left) and you can have a larger or a smaller cup than normal (second button from the left). It also allows you to adjust the amount of cream and sugar added to the coffee (this will not work for chocolate drinks, although this is not visible in the interface). However, here is also where the problem starts. The two remaining buttons are labelled 'Extra Sugar' and 'Extra Cream'. But the labels beneath marked '+' and '–', indicate that you can also have 'Less Extra Sugar' and 'Less Extra Cream' added to your cup. If we would compare the function of these two buttons to those for cup size and for strength, 'Less' should denote, less than normal, but now it is modified by the word 'Extra'. So we end up with having 'Less Extra Sugar than Normal' in our cup. The problem is therefore to explain how much sugar is actually added to a normal sized cup.

Often the students at first don't even discover that this is a problem, since they are already used to the machine. When they start seeing the problem they often remark, 'Well, it is no really big thing'. But then of course, if it is not a big thing, then why is the button there at all? Once here, the students sometimes find themselves engaged in a discussion on what the expression 'Less Extra Sugar' means in practice, which normally also means it is time for a real-time coffee break in the lecture (possibly for some exploratory experimentation on the coffee machine).

As a follow-up to the lecture, the students are presented with an exercise where they are challenged to first pinpoint the more general problem with this interface, i.e., the lack of visibility of status and function availability, and then to suggest an alternative design that avoids the problems that they have found.

3.3   Changing Mindsets – Stimulating Creativity

Creativity is in this context not something that can be taught, but rather an ability in the student that has to be awakened and stimulated. Understanding human-computer interaction is in my opinion very much an issue about managing to put oneself in the situation of the computer users [8]. This is a difficult thing to teach, and sometimes the theoretical explanations do not support this change of perspective in the student. One typical example is how to explain *affordance*, since the notion is difficult to explain in simple terms. When provided with definitions, students are often able to repeat and even in some cases explain the idea behind it. However, when, instead of explanations, they are provided with a few, to them well-known, cases of bad affordance, and the following discussion of the problem, there is a remarkable change in understanding in the students. When asked to provide a definition, however, that is much more difficult from the examples only. This suggests that the examples have to be accompanied by the explanation during the afterwork after the examples. The examples then serve as a platform on which to build the more general framework through elaboration and discussion.

By providing good design examples and by discussing bad design examples, it is quite possible to induce a change in the mindset of the forthcoming software engineers. In this context I believe more in the bad examples, as long as they are not just shown, but also elaborated in an appropriate way. The examples shown in this section are typical for the type of examples that I have collected over the years. A general property of these examples is that the problem with the design is easy to understand in each case, but the solution more difficult to find. The students also recall these examples and use them as starting points when discussing the more theoretical issues around the design exercises, and during the exams. Therefore, the examples are published on the website with ample explanations and elaboration suggestions for the teachers.

One of my first sources of inspiration for this kind is the first book by Donald Norman: The Psychology of Everyday Things [11]. In this book, everyday users' experiences of the world are brought up from the subconscious to the conscious level of thinking. However, in some way the process stops at the point of observation the phenomenon. In my teaching I often try to go further with the observations, and try to make the students reflect further on the problem and its consequences. Challenging them to redesign things that don't work with clear constraints on the new design often causes them to start thinking in a more lateral way.

One (informal) observation I have made over the years is that software engineers tend to be caught in traditional ways of thinking around software. In their opinion, graphic user interfaces cannot be too different from what they look like today. In this perspective I see it as an important task to encourage non-traditional thinking about the interface. In these contexts, therefore, examples like the ones shown in this section are the more important, since they challenge the traditional ways of thinking on interfaces. In the next section it will also be shown how restraining can force the students into lateral thinking, when the traditional solutions are constrained away.

4   Creativity Stimulating Exercises

Creative exercises do not exist in themselves; rather it is the context and the setup that does make an exercise inspire creativity. I have over the years used a number of exercises that were designed to talk to the creative sides in the students. There are several aspects that are important for triggering free thinking in the student:

- *Inspiring curiosity*: Curiosity is one basic incitement for creativity. By inspiring the students to use curiosity, it is easier to open their minds to understanding problems and solutions. The 'what if'-type of questions are very important catalysts for new designs.
- *Group dynamics*: I value the use of group dynamics both for design and for evaluation. Using parallel design (or snow-ball group dynamics) the students are forced to rethink their design suggestions several times over time. By constructive evaluation they are also forced to not only criticize the design but also suggest improvements, i.e. rethink the problem situation.
- *Grounded exercises*: The exercises have to be based on real problems. They should be relevant to the student and based on their reality if possible. By considering well-known areas, the 'why haven't I thought about this before' part of the brain is often activated, possibly inspiring further curiosity.
- *A constrained design space*: By added constraints in the design space (not the actual design or the creative process) the students are forced to move away from the traditional solutions. This removes the uncertainty from the students about

what is and is not allowed in the exercises. Furthermore, it allows the teacher to remove conventional solutions from the design space.

I will start by presenting the exercise process and then the exercises in more detail. I will get back to the importance of the process also in the evaluation of my design examples and the assignment.

4.1   Process

In this section two design exercises are presented. They are each performed in four separate stages:
1.   Individual design.
2.   Small group redesign (2 – 3 students per group).
3.   Large group redesign (15 – 20 students per group).
4.   Final examination/evaluation of exercise.

Stage two and three also involve a critical assessment of the previous design, if possible with written comments and motivations. If time permits, the critique is also discussed in the groups, in order to train the critical thinking. After the large group redesign, I have also tried a method of 'The critical eye', where all students have been asked to take down three essential advantages and three essential disadvantages with the 'final' design. Each exercise normally takes about four hours to complete, with a longer mid-exercise break in the middle.

During the first two stages of the design exercises the students are left more or less to themselves, with the teacher/session leader moderating the discussion in order to avoid inactivity. During the presentation of the final stage the teacher enters a different role as a constructive critic. In this role the students are challenged to defend their choices and also defend their non-choices, i.e. the solutions that they have discarded. Informally they describe a partial design rationale (cf. [12]). All the design work is made only on paper, preferably large display sheets. Computer tools are not allowed for the design. This makes the students focus on the design, rather than the technology.

One point of caution is worth mentioning here. In the group design stages (2 and 3) there is a large risk that there is someone (or a couple of persons) who drives the design process, ruling out other suggestions. This is especially difficult in interdisciplinary groups, if one of the participants has a deeper knowledge in the application area. Avoiding this could be a matter of the teacher monitoring the group work. In general, it is better the more active all the participants are in the larger sessions.

4.2   Design Exercise Examples

The two design exercises I present in this paper were also included in the position paper for the CONVIVIO 2006 workshop (see [13]) but the descriptions have been extended in order to make the examples more clear. The two examples are to some extent similar to each other. Normally I let the students alternate between computer-oriented design examples and design examples that are more anchored in the 'real' world. The sample results presented in section 4.3 come from courses held with Swedish speaking students at the Åland Polytechnic.

4.2.1 Example Exercise 1

The first example exercise is to redesign a printing dialog that allows a user to print a document on a printer and really (!) get the *desired* printout. The functionality is specified in advance, and corresponds to a standard ink jet printer dialog, including the 'Page Setup'-function. The dialog should allow the user to achieve the result in a minimum number of steps with respect to the intended task. There are a few general restrictions placed on the final design:

- It should be task-driven and not consider technical difficulties (such as that round windows may be more difficult and inefficient to draw).
- It should use a minimum number of buttons and traditional controls such as dropdown menus, tabs, etc.
- It should adhere to minimalist design
- It should provide immediate feedback on actions

Prior to the exercise, the students are also told that one important aim is to achieve a design that has to be as non-standard as possible, while still offering a good and usable interface to the printer.

4.2.2 Example Exercise 2

The second example exercise is to design an interactive display that allows a car buyer to select from a vast number of cars on a site for used and new cars. The selection dialogue is to be primarily directed towards a non-technical user, while still being interesting to use for more knowledgeable car buyers. Prospective buyers have to be provided with sufficient support in order to make the appropriate choices for a new or used car.

In this exercise more stress is also placed on that they find good solutions for the designs than on that they cover all possible options for selecting a car. The functionality is therefore not completely specified, but the students may instead add their own functionality.

In the task setting there are also a few general restrictions on the design:

- It should not be primarily text based,
- It should be a minimalist design,
- It should allow fuzzy requirements, or multi-valued choices in an easy way

Like in exercise 1, the students are told that non-traditional solutions are preferred to standard interface alternatives. This is stressed during all the three design stages of the exercise. It also turns out to be a major difficulty throughout for the more computer science oriented students.

4.3   Exercise Results

The following presentation of the experiences from the exercises is divided into a set of general observations on the procedure and type of exercises, as well as the actual outcome on the teacher side from the respective design exercises. Since the final designs from the student groups were presented on drawing boards or black boards, there are unfortunately no figures available showing the resulting design suggestions from the students.

4.3.1 Exercise 1 – Results

The solutions to the exercise with the printing dialogue that were presented evolved gradually over the design stages, and in the evaluation processes, the restrictions were among the first things that were discussed and often the properties that were not conforming to the restrictions were changed or removed in the designs after the first evaluation – redesign cycle.

In this exercise the gradual extension of the design group from individual design to smaller groups to a single large group proved constructive, when the design solutions were presented. In general the students found that it was interesting to try to provide the given functionality in the new design, without complicating it by using standard widgets, such as tabs. Most of the specified functionality was also incorporated in the design solution that was presented after stage 3 or 4, i.e. as soon as they 'got the gist of the design problem'.

Example of a final design: The final solution used a preview type of display with direct manipulation switches that directed choices, such as orientation, size, number of copies, etc. A number of visual switches displayed on-off type of attributes, such as binding edges and similar properties in the printed material.

4.3.2 Exercise 2 – Results

The search form for used cars appears to have been more difficult from the start, and it was clear that the students were less experienced car buyers. There were initial problems specifying the relevant criteria for selecting a used car, and due to time constraints there was no time to arrange for the students to interview real car buyers. Also there were initial problems with the constraints on the design, such as how to avoid using text for selecting various criteria. In one or two cases it was even necessary to intervene and discuss the problem with the group, before they could start. Interestingly enough this also seemed to make them more restricted in the thought to traditional (i.e., the results were more similar to the existing web search sites for used cars).

Also the change between the stages was subtler, changing more in details than conceptual design, compared to in exercise 1. The final solution was also using more features of the individual suggestions, and did not evolve quite so much over the stages as the printing dialogue.

Example of a final design: The design presented was based on a picture of a car body that changed visually as the user was selecting important features. The visual presentation of the body changed when the user selected properties such as seating, loading capacity and similar. In case of multiple selections, the picture was duplicated. Additional features such as engine type, type of gear box, etc. was indicated graphically on the pictures.

4.4   General Observations on the Exercises

The exercises were generally well liked by the students. For the more constrained examples it was considerably easier to get students started on the exercise. The process used for the exercises seems to gradually allow students to proceed from an applied type of knowledge, to knowledge that uses justification of the design decisions. There are also indications (especially in the first exercise) that the students shift from a traditional design perspective to a more inventive view, when they consider the constraints of the exercise. Thus, they are approaching the upper learning or competence levels in the models presented earlier.

The first exercise seems to induce a more direct connection to the students' imagination, probably (according to some comments from the students during the design discussions) since the students have been using the print dialogue extensively and also seen the problems with the dialogue. The second exercise was more difficult for the students to get started with. Common comments were such as 'How can you display information without using text?' and 'It is difficult not to make something that looks like those sites that already exist!'. Some mental 'prodding' seems necessary in order to get the students into non-conform thinking.

The outcome of these exercises has also been interesting from a methodological standpoint. Many students tended to fall back to designing a conventional type of display. Utilizing direct manipulation was often not considered an option, and a more or less standard 'Apply' or 'OK' button (although often 'disguised' in order to comply with the given restrictions on the interface) was not an uncommon feature in the dialogue.

In a 'Pilot' exercise I gave the students free hands on the first exercise, which actually rendered it much more difficult for the students to begin working on the exercise. This does not mean that it has to be specified in details, but rather that the overall constraints have to be well specified, giving the students a solid framework for the exercise.

5 Example Assignment

Even the major assignments on a Human-Computer Interaction course need to be aimed at the upper levels of Bloom's taxonomy and the pyramid of competence (cf. section 2.1). Most assignments on the courses I teach have been designed to promote a synthetic or at least an analytic aspect of the design problem.

The assignment described here is a slightly older assignment, but one that has been very successful over the years. Even though technology has speeded ahead, the design challenge is still the same, although for an updated version I would probably rather use displays of mobile phones, PDAs or why not, remote controls for home video systems as example applications. However, the essential design problem remains the same, i.e. achieving good functionality in a limited space.

5.1 Process

The larger assignments on my courses have often included a separate phase of task analysis including interviews with potential users of the artefact, prior to the following design task. This means that the assignments have been run over longer periods of time, to give the students ample time for reflection over the problems involved.

Assignments of the type described in this chapter normally run over a period of two to three weeks, with smaller groups (< 20 students) of computer science students. The assignments are initially run in the same manner as the exercises in the previous section (see section 4.1). They are in most cases started as snowball group exercises, i.e., where the work is initially done in small groups (or individually) and the groups are gradually merged into larger groups by a sequence of constructive group critique/redesign cycles, composing larger and larger design groups. In this way the students are forced to rationalize their designs from the beginning. In the assignments, the students are required to hand in a larger part of a design rationale, which is now formal, rather than informal as in the exercises (cf. section 4.1). In contrast to the exercises the assignments are run in smaller end groups, consisting of at most six students (but often less). This means that the overall positive effect of snowballing becomes smaller.

5.2   Designing a Telephone Switch

The assignment that the students have been working with is to design an innovative telephone interface (to a standard telephone) using a colour touch-screen display. The display was intended to allow a user to handle all the necessary switchboard functions on the normal home telephone, such as wakeup calls, moving calls from the home phone to another number, etc. These are the functions in a standard telephone that are (or were) handled via combinations of two-digit numbers and '#' and '*' buttons. These combinations are of course difficult, if not impossible, for a user to remember unless he or she is an expert on handling the telephone switchboard.

The following restrictions were given for the final design:
- The maximum size of the display was set to eight by eight centimetres.
- The display should allow for also users who are blue-collared workers, i.e., the controls should be easy to handle also with big hands.
- The display should be readable by people with normal or slightly reduced eyesight.
- All the functionality (approximately 10 different functions) that was described in the official manual had to be represented in the final system.

There is also an informal requirement stating that the resulting product should not primarily look like a computer display. This requirement was initially slightly difficult to carry through, primarily due to the lack of good prototyping tools. Today, this prerequisite would be much easier to fulfil with the drawing tools that are available. On the other hand, the best prototypes were often the ones that were 'hand made' and where no toolkit was available, since then the students were able to focus on the design, rather than the implementation (cf. the use of paper designs in section 4.1).

The first designs are sketched individually and then disseminated in a first common seminar. Then the students are regrouped into pairs, and a new design process initiated. This continues throughout the whole assignment, where in the end the whole group sets out to create a final design for presentation.

5.3   Results

The assignment described in this section has been used over a period of totally 6 years, and interestingly enough, there has been a large variation in the suggested design solutions over time. In the beginning the assignment was less specified in the instructions, but it turned out that when the restrictions on the assignment were more specified, the students made much better initial designs.

The students often commented on that they were encouraged to change their ideas when they saw the other group members' solutions, and many also agreed on that the group discussions added to their understanding of both the problem and the requirements on the solutions. Over the 6 years there were only five or six 'similar' design suggestions, from the smaller groups (four students) before the final common design phase.

On the negative side it is possible to note that there is a tendency to use good examples from lectures and literature in a quite literal manner, in that the students ended up using many of the design suggestions given during lectures in their designs. This implicates that in order to increase the amount of creative thinking, the teacher has to be carefully considering *how* solutions to given problems are discussed, e.g., in lectures.

6   Conclusive Summary

Over the doors of the main lecture hall in the old university building at Uppsala University there is an old motto from around 1850, which states: "To think freely is good, to think correctly is better".[2] The original intention of the motto is that it is preferable to follow the logic of thought rather than free elaboration. However, it has often been misinterpreted, taking 'right' to be standing for proper thinking or being politically correct. Now, I still think that in some cases there is a firm belief from the students in a single 'right' thinking, which does prohibit 'free' thinking. A frequent problem is that the students expect to find 'the single right solution'. They more or less expect that there is a 'solutions page' also for such free and open ended exercises, as the ones described in this article. In fact, they sometimes initially get disappointed to find that there are many possible solutions to a problem.

From the experiences of using lecture illustrations, exercises and assignments such as the ones in this paper, it can be seen that it is possible to use good and bad design examples to start the students off towards creative thinking in human-computer interaction design. But it also turns out that it is almost mandatory to give the students a constraining framework to work within. So how do we handle the balance between using free exploration in the exercises (to encourage creativity) and constraining the exercises and assignments (to support the knowledge forming in

---

[2] The quotation is a great source of smiles to most visitors of the university.

'good' directions)? The issue is of course whether we should encourage 'free' thinking and look away from 'right' or 'wrong', or look more decisively at right or wrong designs with the risk of reducing the creativity in the students?

From my experiences with the assignments, there are good reasons to expect that exercises will produce better and for all, more creative results if there are well-defined restrictions on the design space, and on the methods that are allowed to achieve the goal (this was discussed at the second CONVIVIO 2006 workshop [13]). This will give the students a stricter framework to work within, thus reducing their problems to understand the task. Thus by using examples and exercises that stimulate the upper levels of the educational models, while at the same time restraining the framework within which the students can work, we may even increase the students' abilities to use lateral thinking in the design exercises and assignments.

Furthermore, it is also suggested in this paper that neither lecture examples, exercises or assignments (regardless of their quality) will on their own bring the students to the wisdom level of competence (according to the pyramid of competence [4]), or the creative level of learning (according to Bloom's extended taxonomy [3]). The teacher must prepare this development in the students by a proper combination of examples, exercises and assignments, in combination with a good (and preferably guided) discussion on the problem area. The use of real world examples requires a large amount of preparation on the part of the teacher. Also, it is essential that the students are given ample time to consider and reflect on the teaching elements described in this article, something which might be difficult in short courses.

A good example is still only an example, and it does not become knowledge without additional effort, from both the student and the teacher.

Note

Those interested in the material discussed in this article are welcome to check out my home page [1] with some of the material I use in my lectures, with supportive annotations and comments on how to use it. Also, the remote control for the GPS in Fig. 1 is the small black one, closest to the leftmost candlestick.

Acknowledgements

I want to thank all the colleagues that have been a source of inspiration during the workshops on Human-Computer Interaction Education that I have organized and participated in during the years. I also want to thank all the students that have acted as guinea pigs over the years of development of teaching materials.

References

1. L. Oestreicher, The author's home page with educational resources http://www.anst.uu.se/larsoest/pmwiki.php?n=Education.EducationalResources (cited June 26, 2007).
2. J.R. Anderson, *Cognitive Psychology and its Implications.* (Freeman, New York, 1990).
3. M. Forehand, Bloom's taxonomy: Original and revised, in: *Emerging Perspectives on learning, teaching and technology*, edited by M. Orey (cited on January 2, 2007): http://www.coe.uga.edu/epltt/bloom.htm (2005).
4. P. Kotzé, K. Renaud, and J. Van Biljon, *Don't do this - Pitfalls in using anti-patterns in teaching human-computer interaction principles*, Computers & Education, DOI: doi:10.1016/j.compedu.2006.10.003, (2006).
5. L. Lipscomb, J. Swanson and A. West, Scaffolding. In: M. Orey (Ed.), *Emerging perspectives on learning, teaching, and technology.* (cited on January 2, 2007): http://www.coe.uga.edu/epltt/scaffolding.htm (2004).
6. L.S. Vygotsky, *Mind in Society.* (Harvard University Press, Cambridge, MA, 1978).
7. M. Cox, L. Oestreicher, M. Quinn, M. Rauterberg and M. Stolze, HCI in Education: Theory or Practice. *Proceedings of INTERACT'99,* (Kluwer, Edinburgh, UK, 1999).
8. L. Oestreicher (ed.), The Six Golden Rules to shake the Students Mind — Report from a workshop on HCI education in Edinburgh. (cited on June 26, 2007): http://www.anst.uu.se/larsoest/uploads/Research/SixRules.pdf (IFIP Working Group 13.1:8, 1999).
9. L. Oestreicher and P. Kotzé, Teaching Human-Computer Interaction: Qualitative Support for an Alternative Approach, In: *Usability: Gaining a Competitive Edge, Proceedings of IFIP World Computer Congress,* Montreal, Canada, p. 267 - 281. (2002).
10. L. Oestreicher, The 'Hot or Cold Shower?' example with colour pictures (cited on June 26, 2007) http://www.anst.uu.se/larsoest/pmwiki.php?n=Education.-HotOrColdShowers (2007).
11. D.A. Norman, *The Psychology of Everyday Things* (Basic Books, New York, 1988).
12. S. Buckingham Shum, Design Argumentation as Design Rationale. In: *The Encyclopedia of Computer Science and Technology* (Marcel Dekker Inc: NY), Vol. 35, Supp. 20, 95-128. (1996).
13. K. Baumann, P. Kotzé, L. Oestreicher, L. Bannon, A. Varey, D. Van Greunen, G. Van der Veer, H. Petrie, I. Jounila, I. Mavrommati, N. Garay-Vitoria, O. Ozcan, P. Purgathofer, and P.A. Silva, EISH - Exercises in Studying HCI, in: *Creativity3: Experiencing to Educate and Design - Proceedings of HCI Educators 2007*, edited by P. Alexandra Silva, A. Dix, and J. Jorge, (DesignEd, Aveiro, 2007), pp. 134 – 137

Teaching Creative Interface Design: Possibilities and Pitfalls

Janet Wesson
Nelson Mandela Metropolitan University
PO Box 77000
Port Elizabeth 6031, SOUTH AFRICA
+27 41 5042323
janet.wesson@nmmu.ac.za
WWW home page: http://www.nmmu.ac.za

Abstract. Interface design is an essential aspect of any interactive system and thus a core component of most Human-Computer Interaction (HCI) curricula. Teaching creative interface design is, however, a challenging task, as it involves both an understanding of HCI theory and practice. A trade-off exists between enforcing the use of standard design aids such as guidelines and patterns, or encouraging the development of creative design solutions. This paper discusses the tensions that exist between these two approaches and explores the possibilities for developing a combined approach to teaching creative interface design. This approach, called 'Usable Creativity' aims to produce usable and creative design solutions.

1 Introduction

Creating good interfaces requires designers to think really hard about how they want to visually represent the interface. In essence, interface design comprises designing the external (visual) representation; determining how data is visualised (information visualisation and visual properties); choosing an appropriate design metaphor; and providing effective interaction techniques.

This paper firstly discusses how design guidelines and patterns can be used to support the design process and how design metaphors can be used to assist users with the learning process. Several different approaches to teaching creative design are then reviewed. Finally, a combined approach for teaching creative interface design is presented together with some student examples developed using this approach.

Please use the following format when citing this chapter:

Wesson, J., 2009, in IFIP International Federation for Information Processing, Volume 289; *Creativity and HCI: From Experience to Design in Education*; Paula Kotzé, William Wong, Joaquim Jorge, Alan Dix, Paula Alexandra Silva; (Boston: Springer), pp. 78–89.

2 Design Guidelines and Patterns

Design guidelines are a commonly used and generally accepted aid for interface design [1]. Guidelines specify what to provide and what not to provide in the interface and are intended to help designers explain and improve the interface design [2]. Design guidelines are typically derived from a mix of theory-based knowledge, experience and common-sense. Examples of such guidelines include Shneiderman's eight golden rules for interface design [3]:

1. Strive for consistency.
2. Enable frequent users to use shortcuts.
3. Offer informative feedback.
4. Design dialogues to yield closure.
5. Provide error prevention and simple error handling.
6. Permit easy reversal of actions.
7. Support internal locus of control.

Usability principles (heuristics) are similar to design guidelines, except more prescriptive, and are used mainly as a basis for the heuristic evaluation of interactive systems. These include Nielsen's ten heuristics [4] as well as others for designing specific types of systems, such as IBM's web design guidelines [5] and Gong and Taresewich's guidelines for mobile interface design [6] .

Interaction design patterns have been proposed as alternatives to design guidelines [7]. Some evidence exists that interfaces designed using patterns are better than the equivalent interfaces designed using guidelines [8]. More research is needed, however, to determine if there is a significant difference in quality between the designs produced using patterns and the designs produced using guidelines [9].

3 Design Metaphors

Choosing an appropriate design metaphor implies designing the visual representation of the interface to be similar to a physical entity but with its own behaviour and properties, for example the desktop metaphor and the search engine. A design metaphor can be based on an activity, an object or a combination of both.

The use of an appropriate metaphor can exploit the users' familiar knowledge, helping them to understand 'the unfamiliar' [1]. Metaphors conjure up the essence of an unfamiliar activity, thereby enabling users to leverage familiar knowledge to understand other aspects of the unfamiliar functionality.

Using design metaphors can have several benefits as they can:

- make learning new systems easier;
- help users understand the underlying conceptual model; and
- be very innovative.

Several problems, however, also exist with metaphors, since they can:

- break conventional and cultural rules;
- constrain designers in the way that they conceptualize a problem space;
- conflict with design principles;

- limit the users to only understanding the system in terms of the metaphor;
- cause designers to inadvertently use existing bad designs; and
- limit the designer's imagination in creating new paradigms and models.

It is clear that several pitfalls exist with using design metaphors for interface design. However, this does not have to be the case. Provided designers are aware of these pitfalls and endeavour to develop metaphors that effectively combine familiar knowledge with new functionality, many of the above problems can be avoided [1]. The use of analogy as a basis for interface design can also be very innovative and successful, expanding the use of computers to a greater diversity of people.

4 Prototyping

Generating alternative designs is an essential aspect of the interaction design process [1]. Considering alternatives and thinking about different perspectives can provide the designer with considerable insight into the problem space. These alternative designs are normally represented in terms of low-fidelity (paper-based) or high-fidelity (software) prototypes.

Prototyping requires converting the user requirements and needs into a visual representation (conceptual model) of the system. The basis for designing this model is the set of user tasks that the system will support. Three different aspects need to be determined:

- Which *interaction mode(s)* should be used? This will depend on the nature of the users' activities, for example exploring and browsing.
- If an appropriate *design metaphor* exists (Section 3). This requires an understanding of what the system will do and which are the critical tasks.
- Which is the most suitable *interaction paradigm*? This requires an understanding of the user and the proposed context of use.

Developing a prototype therefore involves addressing these aspects and using appropriate design guidelines (Section 2) and metaphors (Section 3) to produce a design solution which meets the users' requirements.

The process of generating alternative designs is, however, not as straightforward as one might expect, for several reasons [1]:

- Humans generally stick to what they know works.
- Considering alternatives is important to 'break out of the box'.
- Designers are trained to consider alternatives; software developers generally are not.

This raises the question of how do you generate alternative design solutions? Several ideas have been proposed including:

- *Flair and creativity:* This requires research and synthesis.
- *Seek inspiration:* The designer can look at similar systems or look at very different systems.

The problem of generating alternative and innovative designs has resulted in research into teaching creative design, which is discussed in the next section.

5   Teaching Creative Design

Several approaches have been developed to encourage and foster design creativity. These include the following:

- *BadIdeas*, a technique that uses bad or silly ideas to inspire creativity [10]. This approach generates silly or bad ideas to solve a problem rather than aiming directly for good ideas, thus allowing the student designer to derive metrics with which to evaluate and extend these ideas. It is not clear, however, if the suggestions made to remedy these bad ideas would include the use of design guidelines and result in a usable system.
- *Worksheets*, which are used to capture aspects of a scene or situation [11]. Worksheets can be used to record stories and anecdotes as well as people. The use of Worksheets allows designers to gather and structure information about the problem space, thus enabling them to easily identify if important information is missing. This technique obviously assists in the requirements analysis phase, but does appear to support creative design.
- *Rapid Contextual Design*, which includes the use of contextual interviews, affinity diagrams, personas, scenarios, visioning and paper prototypes [12]. Although some aspects of this method, especially contextual interviews, can prove very useful, it is not clear how it encourages creative thinking.
- *Metaphors*, which can be used to understand the nature of human thinking, and thereby lead to opportunities for creating better designs [13]. Using metaphors can, however, have several pitfalls as discussed earlier in Section 3.

There is no doubt that insufficient time is given in HCI curricula to encourage and foster creativity [14]. To address this issue, Beckhaus proposed seven factors which are needed to support teaching creative design [15]. These factors are:

- Formation of a group and a supportive environment.
- Building confidence in creativity.
- Balance of a clear goal with space to evolve.
- Preparation of a task document.
- Motivation.
- Assessment.
- Assistance versus interference.

In general, successful interface design requires balancing constraints and requirements and teaching creative design requires a similar approach. The issue of assessing creativity is, however, not straight forward, as discussed in the next section.

6   Assessing Creativity

The issue of assessing creativity is one of the greatest challenges currently facing teachers. While many teachers believe that it is possible to help students be creative, few believe that it is possible to assess creativity effectively [16]. Yet evaluation is considered critical to the idea of creativity. In addition, the issue of evaluating design quality is still largely unresolved, which can lead to inaccurate results [17]. Usability is fairly easy to evaluate using standard techniques like heuristic evaluation (Section 2), but evaluating design creativity has not been adequately addressed. There is almost universal agreement, however, that understanding a student's creativity depends on his/her ability to understand and explain it. Reflection would thus seem to be a necessary partner to creativity.

Evaluation of creativity can focus on several aspects including the products produced, the process followed or a combination of these [16]. Several characteristics of a creative product (or system) are included in the definition of *'Functional Creativity'*, which is well known in the domain of Engineering. These characteristics are as follows:

- *Novelty* (is it original and surprising?).
- *Relevance and effectiveness* (does it do what it is supposed to do?).
- *Elegance* (it is a simple and easy to understand solution?).
- *Germinal* (does it lead to new ideas and/or products?).

Although this definition is typically used to evaluate the creativity of products produced by engineering students, it can also be used to assess the creativity of interface designs produced by HCI students. Three characteristics of this definition are particularly relevant for assessing design creativity, namely Novelty (is it original or innovative), Relevance and effectiveness (does it do what it is supposed to do) and Germinal (does it lead to new metaphors and/or designs). The other characteristic, namely Elegance, is included in the ten usability heuristics as proposed by Nielsen (as Aesthetic and minimalist design) [10].

The next section proposes a combined approach to teaching creative interface design which encourages creativity whilst still ensuring that the design solutions produced comply with standard design principles

7   The Usable Creativity Approach

As discussed previously, design guidelines and patterns can be used to assist with interface design. If combined with a user-centred design approach, these design aids can be used to produce usable design solutions. These design aids do not, however, encourage and foster creativity or the generation of new metaphors or alternative designs.

Some of the current approaches to teaching creative design actively promote innovation and creativity. These approaches do not, however, include the use of the design aids discussed in Section 2 and thus do not address the issue of usability.

An approach is needed, therefore, which provides structure whilst encouraging innovation in order to produce usable and creative design solutions. This approach is expressed in the formula for *'Usable Creativity'*:

$$Structure + Innovation \rightarrow Usable\ Creativity$$

where:

- *Structure* is provided by design aids such as guidelines and patterns (Section 2); and
- *Innovation* is provided by metaphors and prototyping (Sections 3 and 4).

This approach to teaching creative design requires exposing students to HCI theory in terms of guidelines and patterns, and HCI practice in terms of generating alternative, creative designs taking due cognisance of these design aids.

This approach also requires most of the seven factors identified by Beckhaus (Section 5) in order to provide a favourable environment for inventivity and creativity. In particular, the students need to work in small groups to encourage collaboration; the requirements and goals of the project must be clearly defined; a task document should be established; the students should be motivated by allowing them to choose an area in which they are interested; and the choice of prototyping tools should be left to the students.

The approach towards 'Usable Creativity' discussed in this section was used to teach a postgraduate course in HCI to 15 students at the Nelson Mandela Metropolitan University in the first semester of 2006. Two examples of the student designs produced are presented and discussed in the next section.

8   Examples

The students were asked to select any interactive system and design prototypes for this system, working in groups of 2 or 3 students. The design documentation required to be submitted comprised the following:
- a description of the users' goals;
- the envisaged context of use;
- the functional and non-functional requirements for the system;
- a low-fidelity (paper-based) prototype for the system;
- feedback from informal user testing; and
- a high-fidelity prototype.

The students were required to include sufficient screenshots to show how the key user tasks and goals would be satisfied. The following sections present a description of the development methodology, two example designs submitted by the students and a discussion of how these designs were evaluated.

8.1   Development Methodology

The students were required to use the Interaction Design (ID) Model, as proposed by Preece *et al.* to develop these prototypes [1]. This methodology comprises four main steps, namely:
- identify requirements;
- develop alternative designs;
- build interactive prototypes; and
- evaluate the prototypes.

The key aspects of this methodology are a user-centred approach, identifying usability and user experience goals, and iterative design and evaluation. This methodology does not, however, prescribe any specific interface design method(s). The students were therefore given lectures on the use of design aids such as guidelines and patterns, and the use of interface metaphors to support design. The students were also informed that the evaluation of the design of their prototypes would comprise two main aspects, namely usability and creativity. The approach to teaching interface design thus followed the steps outlined in the 'Usable Creativity' approach as discussed in Section 7.

8.2   Medical Mobile

Medical Mobile is a PDA/Pocket PC based system designed to replace the currently inadequate practice of doctors relying on pagers or cell phone messages. Currently, pagers or text messages are still often used to notify doctors of medical emergencies or patients that require urgent attention when they are out of the office or hospital. Such devices do little to indicate the exact nature of the situation that requires their attention. *Medical Mobile* attempts to remedy this situation by providing an interactive system which alerts doctors to situations that require their urgent attention. The system will provide doctors with exact details regarding the priority of the situation and allow them instant access to patient files and medical histories (see Figures 1 and 2). They will also be able to respond to the messages they receive, and thus provide better care for their patients.

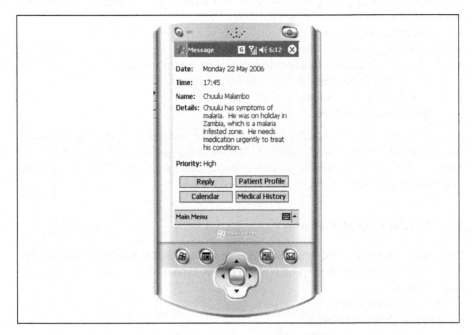

Fig. 1. *Message screen in Medical Mobile*

Fig. 2. *Patient Profile in Medical Mobile*

8.3   TravelSA

TravelSA is a PDA based system which allows tourists to obtain information about cities within South Africa and book accommodation in a particular city (Figure 3). Locating areas of interest within a particular city is done using a city map (Figure 4). Users can then view information about a city and the different areas within that city, with the aid of pictures and textual descriptions. Users can also search for accommodation in a selected city based on certain criteria such as price range, accommodation rating and/or distance from the airport (Figure 5).   A facility also exists for users to book accommodation and receive confirmation of reservation with a reservation number.

Fig. 3. *Selection of a city in TravelSA*

Fig. 4. *City information in TravelSA*

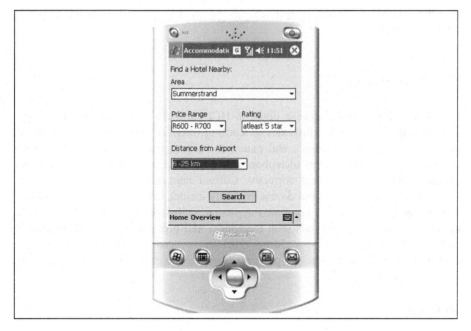

Fig. 5. *Searching for accommodation in TravelSA*

8.4   Evaluation

The students' prototypes were assessed in terms of usability and creativity, as outlined in Section 8.1. The usability of the prototypes was assessed by the author using a heuristic evaluation method together with Nielsen's ten heuristics [4]. Usability was determined in terms of the number of usability problems identified and the severity of these problems. The creativity of the designs was assessed according to the three creativity characteristics identified in Section 6, namely Novelty, Relevance (and effectiveness) and Germinal. The Novelty was assessed in terms of the degree of innovation shown; the Relevance in terms of the effectiveness of the solution in the specific context of use; and the Germinal in terms of the extension of existing interface metaphors and the development of new metaphors.

Both of the student examples presented in Sections 8.2 and 8.3 were evaluated as having a high degree of usability and creativity. Standard design aids, such as guidelines for mobile interface design were used, resulting in a high degree of usability (Section 2). Interface metaphors and iterative prototyping were used to develop the prototypes, resulting in a high degree of creativity (Sections 3 and 4). Existing metaphors were extended and adapted to a mobile context, exploiting the users' prior knowledge. *Medical Mobile* uses an Outlook metaphor to provide a mobile system for doctors; whilst *TravelSA* uses a map metaphor for selection of cities and areas of interest within a given city, and a search engine metaphor for finding accommodation within a city. These examples therefore provide evidence that the 'Usable Creativity' approach can be used to effectively teach creative interface design.

9   Conclusions

Insufficient time and attention is given in HCI curricula to encouraging creativity and innovation. Standard approaches to teaching interface design include the use of design aids such as guidelines and patterns. These approaches do not, however, encourage creativity. Design metaphors can offer several benefits for innovation provided that these are used correctly. Current approaches to teaching creative design encourage creativity but do not explicitly include the use of these design aids. This paper has proposed a combined approach, called 'Usable Creativity', which combines standard design aids with metaphors and prototyping to produce usable and creative design solutions. More research is needed, however, to develop evaluation methods and criteria to properly assess design creativity.

References

1. J. Preece, Y. Rogers, and H. Sharp, *Interaction Design: Beyond Human-Computer Interaction* (John Wiley & Sons, Inc., 2002).
2. *Microsoft Windows User Experience: Official Guidelines for User Interface Developers and Designers*, Microsoft Professional Editions (Microsoft Press, 1999).
3. B. Shneiderman, *Designing the User Interface: Strategies for Effective Human-Computer Interaction*, Third Edition (Addison-Wesley, Reading, MA, 1997).
4. J. Nielsen, *Ten Usability Heuristics*, http://www.useit.com/papers/heuristic/heuristic_list.-html, 1994.
5. IBM, *Web design guidelines*, (cited 12 June 2000); http://www-3.ibm/ibm/easy, 1999.
6. J. Gong and P. Tarasewich, Guidelines for Handheld Mobile Device Interface Design, in: *Proceedings of DSI (Decision Sciences Institute) 2004 Annual Meeting*, (Boston, Massechusetts, 2004), pp. 3751 - 3756.
7. M. van Welie and H. Traetteberg, Interaction Patterns in User Interfaces in: *KoalaPLoP 2000* (Melbourne, Australia, 2000).
8. J.L. Wesson and N.L.O. Cowley, Designing with Patterns: Possibilities and Pitfalls, in: *IFIP INTERACT'03 Workshop on Software & Usability Cross-Pollination: The Role of Usability Patterns* (Zurich, Switzerland, 2003).
9. N.L.O. Cowley and J.L. Wesson, An Experiment to Measure the Usefulness of Patterns in the Interaction Design Process, in: *Human-Computer Interaction - INTERACT 2005, Lecture Notes in Computer Science 3585*, (Springer, Berlin/Heidelberg, 2005), pp. 1142 - 1145.
10. A. Dix, T. Ormerod, M. Twidale, C. Sas, P.A.G. da Silva, and L. McKnight, Why bad ideas are a good idea, in: *Inventivity: Teaching theory, design and innovation in HCI (HCIEd 2006)* (Limerick, Ireland, 2006), pp. 9 - 14.
11. M. Lennon and L.J. Bannon, Worksheets in Practice: Gathering Artefacts for Reflection in Interaction Design Education, in: *Inventivity: Teaching theory, design and innovation in HCI (HCIEd 2006)* (Limerick, Ireland, 2006), pp. 29 - 34.

12. M.K. Larusdottir, Using Rapid Contextual Design at Reykjavik University, in: *Inventivity: Teaching theory, design and innovation in HCI (HCIEd 2006)* (Limerick, Ireland, 2006), pp. 35 -39.
13. E. Frakjaer and K. Hornbaek, Metaphors of human thinking, in HCI: Habit, stream of thought, awareness, utterance and knowing, in: *Human Factors and Ergonomics Society of Australia and the Australian Computer-Human Conference (HF2002/OzCHI2002)* (Melbourne, Australia, 2002).
14. B.L.W. Wong, Inventivity in HCI Education, in: *Inventivity: Teaching theory, design and innovation in HCI (HCIEd 2006)* (Limerick, Ireland, 2006), pp. 67 - 72..
15. S. Beckhaus, Seven Factors to Foster Creativity in University HCI Projects, in: *Inventivity: Teaching theory, design and innovation in HCI (HCIEd 2006)* (Limerick, Ireland, 2006), pp. 91 - 95.
16. N. Jackson, *Assessing Students' Creativity: Synthesis of Higher Education Teacher Views*, http://www.heacademy.ac.uk/assets/York/documents/resources/resourcedatabase/id560_as sessing_creativity_synthesis_of_teachers_views.doc (The Higher Education Academy, 2005).
17. A. Sutcliffe, J. Karat, S. Bodker, and B. Gaver, Can We Measure Quality in Design or Do We Need To?, in: *Proceedings of the 6th Conference on Designing Interactive Systems* (University Park, Pennsylvania, USA, ACM Press, 2006), pp. 119 - 121.

HCI and Design Research Education
A Creative Approach

Bert Bongers and Gerrit van der Veer
[1] University of Technology, Sydney
702-730 Harris Street, Ultimo NSW 2007, Australia
+61 2 95148932
bertbon@xs4all.nl
[2] School of Computer Science,
Open University Netherlands, Valkenburgerweg 177,
6419 AT Heerlen, The Netherlands
gerrit@acm.org
WWW home page: http://www.cs.vu.nl/~gerrit

Abstract. This paper describes the latest insights in HCI education inspired and informed by the creative disciplines, how education is implemented, and how it could be fed back into the artistic fields. It contains examples, contrasts different methods, and discusses and concludes the findings for HCI education in general. A course on HCI is described which is supported by a creative approach, related to art, architecture and music. Experiences are described in of HCI tools and insights such as structured design methods, interaction frameworks and interface design heuristics relevant to the arts fields.

1. HCI and Education

The domain of Human-Computer Interaction (HCI) is a multidisciplinary area involved in research, development and design, which should all be reflected in the education of HCI. HCI is a relatively new field combining human sciences, engineering and design. In addition to developing its own knowledge and practices, it draws knowledge from a number of more established disciplines, as shown in Fig. 1 below. On the left hand side of Fig. 1 a number of relevant human science disciplines are shown, on the right hand side relevant engineering disciplines are listed while the list on the top gives an overview of the design disciplines. In the middle it is stated what it is about in this broad approach: the interaction between people and technology. The outer circle gives what can be called the meta-disciplines: philosophy, art, mathematics, and science [4].

Please use the following format when citing this chapter:

Bongers, B. and van der Veer, G., 2009, in IFIP International Federation for Information Processing, Volume 289; *Creativity and HCI: From Experience to Design in Education*; Paula Kotzé, William Wong, Joaquim Jorge, Alan Dix, Paula Alexandra Silva; (Boston: Springer), pp. 90–105.

The three main approaches to HCI historically are from (cognitive) psychology, computer science, and design. Although many research centres and HCI courses still reflect one of these biases, in the last years particularly we have seen the field mature to a new discipline combining the different approaches. Some of the major text books in this field are written by multiple authors from a variety of backgrounds reflecting the main approaches mentioned above [8, 25]. Even though the course described in this paper is based in a Computer Science department (at the Vrije Universiteit in Amsterdam), it is set up and taught by people with various backgrounds and expertise in psychology, technology, design, and the arts.

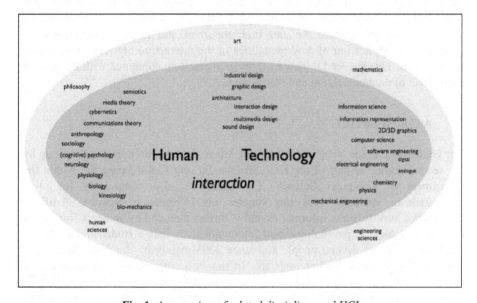

Fig. 1. *An overview of related disciplines and HCI*

As it is increasingly understood that the design of interaction is about creating experiences, the HCI field can often borrow from the knowledge that creative disciplines have developed, such as theatre, music and video art. Methods, processes and approaches from these field inform the HCI field, while at the same time HCI teaching can help the artistic and design disciplines to develop interactions in a more user / audience centred, structured and formal way. The way the courses that are discussed in this paper are set up, reflects this interrelation between HCI and creativity.

2. Teaching HCI

In order to develop better interfaces between people and technology, knowledge is required about all partners involved in the interaction: humans and technology, or in a broader sense, the natural and the artificial. From the human mind(s) it is not possible to directly influence the environment. We use our bodies to express ourselves in speech, movement, etc. The physical world comes in through our senses; light, sound, smells, movement etc. New technologies develop fast, and have the ability to profoundly change the way we live, work and play. Mankind has always developed technologies, created artefacts, reshaping the environment. Computer technology is intertwined with other technologies, our whole environment, real and virtual.

The discipline of HCI research looks at ways to further improve the interaction between people and computers. In order to do this, it is necessary to have a good understanding of the human mind, body, and social interactions. At the same time the technology must be understood, how things function, what is possible and what is not (yet), and how to develop interfaces. Artistic disciplines are studied: in music, visual art and architecture we can find important and inspiring developments, including the application of new modalities in the interaction between humans and environment. This has lead to new insights in interaction, combined with knowledge of the field of communication and media studies.

2.1   A Course on HCI

The HCI course at the Vrije Universiteit in Amsterdam has been originally set up by the second author as part of the *HCI, Multimedia and Culture* program within the department of Computer Science. The course is also compulsory for other undergraduate students from the courses on Information Science, Artificial Intelligence and Business Informatics and is further attended by students from other departments such as psychology, and international exchange students. The course has been taught by several people and since 2003 mainly by the first author, with guest lecturers and a student assistant. In the last years about 100 students are involved in the course per year. This is a rather theoretical course followed by a practical course "User Interface Design", in which teams work on a specified project developing an interface in a structured design approach.

The teaching method aims at developing understanding, insights and the ability to reason about the HCI topic rather than purely learning facts and fixed methods. While the main part of the teaching is about structured design approaches, the emphasis on the creative elements is supported by many examples and case studies from artistic and design disciplines such as electronic musical instrument design, video performances, installation art, art history, interactive architecture, etc. Many image materials are used, gathered particularly over the last few years. For instance, to illustrate interactions between people and technologies the use of little video clips can be very illustrative.

The course consists of 14 lectures of two times 45 minutes. Practical experiences are gathered through assignments. The course is assessed by a written exam and writing an academic paper. An overview can be found on the course web site. This serves increasingly as an e-learning environment. Section 2.1.3 provides details and the URL.

2.2.1 Thematic Structure

To cover the broad field of HCI the course consists of four themes. These themes reflect the three approaches as mentioned above (human sciences, engineering and design) as well as the independent knowledge of the HCI discipline. The themes are:

- Technology for interaction.
- Human factors in interaction.
- Design of interaction.
- Structured design methods.

The first two themes provide background information about the two entities involved in the interaction: humans and computers. The physical aspects of the interaction are emphasised, and technology in general is discussed. While these themes are to a large extend informed by the traditional disciplines (as shown in the right and left hand sides of the diagram in Fig. 1), the other two themes are mainly covering the knowledge and insights in the independent field of HCI. The course starts with two lectures to introduce the field of HCI, its relevance (illustrated with many examples of human-computer struggles), and an ecological design approach for UbiComp and pervasive computing paradigms in the course. Throughout the course, many examples from the field of art and design are used (music, video, installations, architecture). Many images, movie- and video-fragments are used. All lectures are supported by examples from the authors' own recent research practice. Furthermore, a number of 'advanced interaction' topics are covered within the themes.

In the sections below the themes and the lecture content is described in more detail.

Technology for Interaction

In two lectures the history of technology is briefly described, starting from the first pre-historic human artefacts. It is argued that, in a way, the first designers were the early hominids who designed their tools such as the stone axe both functionally and ergonomically. Technological categories are introduced, from mechanical systems (objects, passive mechanics, active mechanics), electrical (electric, analogue electronic, digital electronic) to computer technology (which is programmable). Other technologies are discussed as well, such as optical, chemical and magnetic technology. The discussion on the relation between people and technology is informed by the work of writers such as Lewis Mumford [16, 17], Marshall McLuhan [15], Neil Postman [23] and Malcolm McCullough [14].

This theme then focuses on the computer category, with the strongest need for a good interface as it is the least physical (most invisible) and at the same time functionally the most powerful technology. The interface is described in sensors and actuators, and a framework is introduced to describe and analyse the physical layer of the interaction. This framework, the Physical Interface Design Space (PIDS), describes or designs the interaction by splitting the movements up in Degrees-of-Freedom and for each DoF determine the *range*, *precision*, and *haptic feedback* [5, chapter 6]. An assignment is given in which the students practice the analysis with several devices of their choice. In this Device Parsing exercise they are encouraged to literally take devices apart, determine the technologies used (mechanical, electronic etc.) and describe the interface in the terms of PIDS. The assignments are handed in through the course web site, and marked by the lecturer. Fig. 2 shows a collage of devices in parts in the course in 2006. In the following lecture the work is presented by the students, based on selections made by the lecturer and a student assistant.

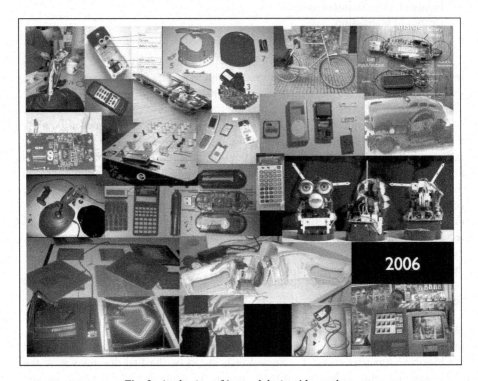

Fig. 2. *A selection of 'parsed devices' by students*

A lecture on musical instruments illustrates the technological stages, and shows how intimate and precise these instruments are. Particularly the developments in electronic instruments serve as inspiration for interface design [2], [5, Chapter 2].

Human Factors in Interaction
In the lectures about the human side of the interaction the senses, memory and cognition, and action are described. The emphasis is on the human as a multimodal being, using many senses and output modalities simultaneously. Particularly the tactual modalities are discussed, to establish a firm understanding to support physical interaction paradigms. Models of human information processing are described, with a focus on the abilities for multitasking as well as an experiment demonstrating a low-level bottleneck in this (the PRP-effect) [1], [21]. In addition to cognitive psychology, physiological factors are introduced because of their relevance for understanding physical interaction.

Particularly, visual, auditory and haptic perception is described in detail as *activities* (based on the ecological approach to perception of Gibson [10, 11]), which is more relevant for HCI than the more *passive* modes as considered in other fields of psychology). Also recent insights in the role of affect and emotion in the interaction are discussed [19], [22].

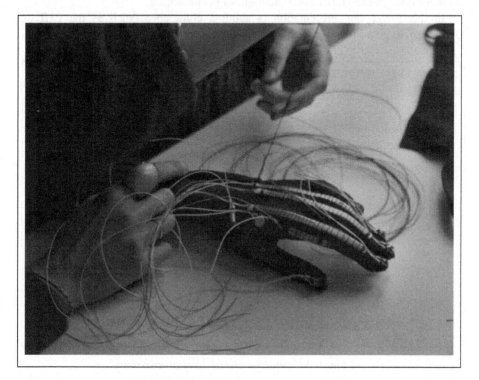

Fig. 3. *The making of an electronic musical glove*

The Design of Interaction

Several lectures on information representation [31], communication theory [26] and multimodal interaction [27] constitute the theme on the design of interaction. Some basic semiotic theory is introduced, extended with the notion of affordances from the field of ecological perception [9], [11], [18]. The aim is for the students to gain insight in reading our environment (natural and artificial) as a rich source of information, both explicit and implicit. By giving examples from everyday life, students are encouraged to translate this view to the design of interfaces. In the display of information from the system, both, the information representation, and various kinds of feedback are described. A framework for analysing and designing multimodal interaction is presented [6].

The relevance of UbiComp and Pervasive Computing paradigms is accentuated [7], following an ecological approach to HCI as an electronic ecology or *e*-cology [4], [5]. A lecture on Interactive Architecture is part of this theme, presenting historical as well as recent work on interactive buildings the first author has been in involved in [20], [30], [12]. Fig. 4 shows an interactive architectural structure as developed at the Hyperbody Research group at the Delft University of Technology.

Two assignments are part of this theme. One is about observing and describing information and signs in our everyday environment (Sign Subversion). The other is about analysing interactions using the frameworks presented.

In this theme one presentation is about a conference (such as the CHI or UbiComp), to give students insights into the experience of a conference visit.

Fig. 4. *An interactive architectural structure*

Structured Design Methods

The Structured Design Methods theme is strongly based on the DUTCH approach of the second author [32, 33], Designing for Users and Tasks from Concepts to Handles (Fig. 5). It includes introductions to Task Analysis, ethnography, usability testing methods, qualitative research methods, etc. usually taught by the second author.

Also recently developed techniques from design research such as Cultural Probes, Scenario based design, QOC method, Personas etc. are presented, and illustrated by a research project from industry that the first author was involved in [28, 29]. Guest lectures on Experience Design (by Dhaval Vyas) and Requirements Engineering (by Dr. Johan Hoorn) are part of this theme.

The knowledge from this theme is particularly relevant for the design project (see below in section 2.1.2). There is no assignment associated with this theme because of this link with the project, although in a situation where this is not the case an assignment including usability testing can be part of the course.

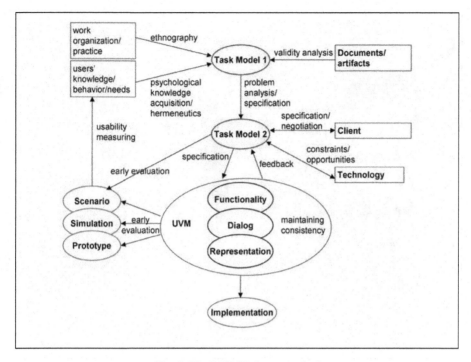

Fig. 5. *The DUTCH design method*

2.1.2 Design Exercises

After passing the HCI course, students can gain further practical experience in the User Interface Design (UID) course. In about 12 weeks students have to work in groups on the design of an interface in a structured method, usually following all the stages of the DUTCH method. The lecturer, student assistants and the students meet on a weekly basis to present and discuss the progress. In the end a final design (prototype at a proof-of-concept level) is presented, including the results of the user tests carried out. Afterwards every group hands in a report with detailed descriptions of all stages of the design process and their experiences. In the last year, the groups could make a choice of topics: a novel communication device, a computer game with physical interaction, or interfaces for a UbiComp environment. Fig. 6 shows an example proposals for an interface of a mobile device made by the students.

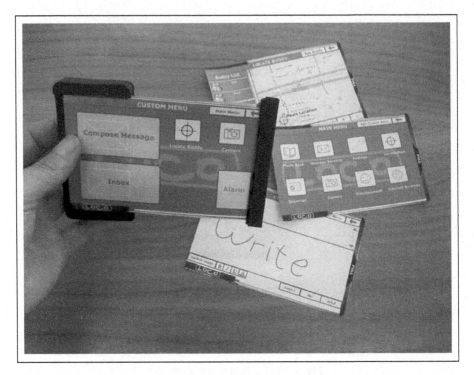

Fig. 6. *Mock up of an interface developed by students in the UID course*

2.1.3 e-Learning Environment

The course web site[3] was completely redesigned as a basis for e-learning in 2005 by Marcin Wichary, as a project for his internship for the post-masters programme of User-System Interaction at the Eindhoven University of Technology [34]. It contains not only information about the lectures and the teachers involved, but also background material about HCI, pointers to other sources, and interactive exercises such as a practical introduction to Fitt's Law. The web site is not just *about* HCI, it *is* HCI. The designer has incorporated many examples of good web site design heuristics, and added many explanations on the site itself. The content of the web site is subject to the Creative Commons License, so other parties can extend or customise the material. In 2006 the site was further developed by student assistant Elbert-Jan Hennipman, also an assistant lecturer in the course, and it is now possible for students to enrol in the course, hand in coursework and check their progress. Another interactive exercise has been added, developed by student intern Niels Rietkerk, demonstrating the psychological issue of impulsivity as originally researched by the second author in 1985.

---

[3] The URL of the site is currently http://fww.few.vu.nl/hci, and will soon be changed but linked from the www.bertbongers.com web site.

Many further extensions to the web site are currently being developed, through the involvement of the Open University in the Netherlands, with the objective to create a full HCI e-learning environment. Fig. 7 shows a screen shot of the HCI Education web site.

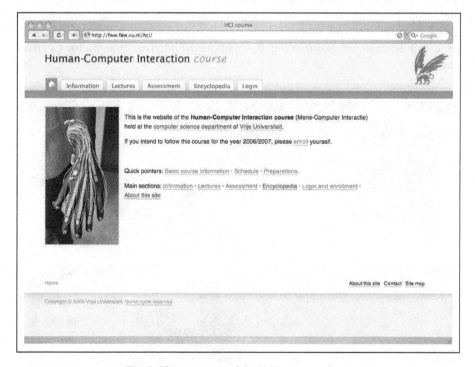

Fig. 7. *The start page of the HCI course web site*

3. HCI Teaching in Multiple Contexts

Further insight in the teaching materials has been gained by presenting (parts of) the courses to other groups of students at other places, including several outside of the general HCI audience. The format varied, but was often presented in a workshop assembled of elements as described in Section 2. Through these workshops new course elements were developed, which were then added to the main course.

3.1 HCI and Technology

The multimodal HCI approach from the human factors theme (including the assignment) was presented in a one week course for Industrial Design Master students at the Technical University in Eindhoven, and as part of a Minor in Physical User Interfaces at the department of Media Technology Bachelor programme in

Utrecht. In the latter school a preliminary structure of the HCI themes was applied. The technology theme (including the assignment) is used in a one week course for the User-System Interaction (USI) post-masters programme at the Technical University in Eindhoven[4]. Part of the workshop was for the students (in groups) to develop physical interaction styles. Functional prototypes were developed of interaction proposals for channel changers (zapping), multimodal feedback on seating posture at a work desk, an electronically enhanced hand shake, a computer game, and the example shown in Fig. 8, a multimodal interface redesign for a coffee machine.

Fig. 8. *One of the results of a physical interface proposal at the USI course*

The assignment of designing an interface for a UbiComp environment has also been carried out by 2nd year Bachelor students of Industrial Design at the Technical University in Eindhoven, coached by the first author in 2005 and in 2006 [24].

3.2   Architecture

The discipline of architecture has always been concerned with the design of spatial layout. It is an essential source of knowledge for interacting with the building environment and for developing interfaces on a larger scale. With computers

---

[4]   See the programme's web site for more information: http://usi.tm.tue.nl

becoming increasingly embedded and networked in man-made environments, it is no surprise that architects have been involved in the same issues as the UbiComp sub-discipline within HCI. Long term collaborations between the first author and architects involved in Interactive Architecture, led to the development of spatial interaction paradigms [3]. Particularly at the Hyperbody Research Group of prof. Kas Oosterhuis at the Architecture department of the Technical University in Delft[5], practical experiments have been carried out in relation to several years of teaching in workshops.

Fig. 9. *Spatial interaction with architectural models in Protospace*

3.3   Music

Considerable inspiration in HCI teaching and research comes from musical instruments, and from teaching workshops on instrument building by the first author.

The relationship between instrument design and general HCI has been addressed in the yearly conference New Interfaces for Musical Expression (NIME) since 2000[6].

---

[5]   www.protospace.bk.tudelft.nl

[6]   www.nime.org

Presenting recently developed HCI lecture materials to students of musical topics resulted in additional insight. For instance, during a two day workshop at the Institute for Musicology at the University in Cologne, students and staff members actively participated in groups to develop new electronic musical instruments after discussing the technology theme.

Currently a new workshop is being prepared to confront HCI structured design methods and instrument design.

4   Discussion and Conclusion

In this paper a creative approach to HCI has been illustrated with an interdependent relationship, of inspiration and application of knowledge from artistic and design disciplines in HCI, which has then been placed back in some of these contexts such as in Interactive Architecture and Electronic Musical Instrument design. We intent to keep developing this interdependence cycle as it yields fruitful research approaches.

As HCI is a relatively young and fast developing discipline, a lot of flexibility in teaching is required. Although a number of heuristics and structured approaches have been developed, which are a great help for the novice, rules are not cast in stone but subject to constant development. We found that young students, with their constant involvement and practical experience in the latest interactive technologies and new media, are a valuable source of information for our HCI research. Not only in direct feedback during teaching (which has to be more explicitly solicited for in larger groups such as at the VU in Amsterdam than in smaller groups such as at ID in Eindhoven), but also structured involvement during experiments (qualitative contributions such as in interviews and questionnaires) and examinations lead to new insight in HCI as a teaching domain. Essays and research papers produced by our multidisciplinary students stimulate new insight and often contribute references that inform our HCI research. Explicitly targeted exam questions yield insights in this diverse population's varied approaches to new technologies.

As always, teaching a structured course can be an excellent way of developing and validating a certain body of knowledge, as for instance Donald Norman acknowledged with the content of his book on Emotional Design [19]. We found this effect strongest at post-graduate student levels and beyond.

Over the last years, the teaching about new interaction paradigms based on physical interfaces and multimodal interaction has been greatly facilitated by the increased availability of sensor and interface hardware such as the Phidgets, the Making Things Teleo modules and other PIC chip based solutions [13]. In the electronic arts and particularly in music such interfaces were available for a long time (often based on the MIDI protocol, such as the iCube of Infusion Systems), but the current USB based interfaces are often easier to use and work with general tools such as Flash and Visual Basic, as well as with dedicated development environments such as Max/MSP for audio and Jitter for video manipulation.

The current student generation tends to be rather visually oriented. The lectures therefore were thoroughly aimed to encourage students to open up their other sensory modalities. However, a lot a visual material was used, both in pictures as in videos. Using a small digital camera, the first author has acquired a rich vocabulary of images to illustrate the topics taught, in addition to a large amount of textual media offered. A side effect may be that students are encouraged to acquire their own images in order to express themselves, rather than using stock photography. In the results of the assignments (particularly those on everyday interaction with technology, and the one on sign subversion) it was shown that students had successfully taken up this challenge.

It was also very relevant and interesting to see how the same content was interpreted and picked up by various communities. Particularly the design exercises were approached in different ways. For instance the assignment to design an interface or interaction style for a UbiComp environment was developed in an analytical and structured way by Computer Science students (creating the necessary extensive overview of functionality of such an environment), while Industrial Design students were more solution and product oriented and less structured (although in one case they developed their own wildly iterative design approach partially based on insights from the discipline of marketing! [24]). This is a challenging assignment anyway, as it is often too easy to come up with the design of yet another remote control.

In comparing the results of assignments and coaching of students, we see a difference in the teaching model at "traditional" Computer Science Departments like at the VU, based on the classical model of teaching lectures, and a competency-based teaching model as used at Industrial Design curricula. In the latter the students are more independent and more apt to search for their own resources, where in the former the students tend to be more structured.

Architecture, video art and music have been a source of inspiration for the presented HCI teaching method. And in these artistic fields it was found essential to introduce HCI methods and knowledge. Students and scholars in the fields of musical instrument development, media art and architecture are increasingly looking for design aids which HCI can provide, such as structured design methods, frameworks for interaction analysis, and interface design. It is this reciprocal influence that we intend to develop further.

References

1. Bongers, A. J., Investigating the Parallel Use of the Sense of Touch in Multimodal Human-Computer Interaction. Unpublished MSc. Thesis, UCL London, 1999.
2. Bongers, A.J., Physical Interaction in the Electronic Arts, Interaction Theory and Interfacing Techniques for Real-time Performance. In: Wanderley, M.M. and Battier, M, Trends in Gestural Control of Music. IRCAM Paris, pp. 41 – 70, 2000.
3. Bongers A. J., Interactivating Spaces, Proceedings of the Systems Research in the Arts conference, Germany, August 2002.
4. Bongers, A. J. Interaction with our Electronic Environment; an e-cological approach to physical interface design. Cahier Book series, Hogeschool van Utrecht, 2004.
5. Bongers, A. J., Interactivation - towards an e-cology of people, our technological environment, and the arts. PhD thesis, Vrije Universiteit Amsterdam, 2006.

6. Bongers, A. J. and. van der Veer, G. C. Towards a Multimodal Interaction Space, categorisation and applications. Journal of Personal and Ubiquitous Computing, special issue on Movement-Based Interaction, 2007.
7. Denning, P. J. (ed.), The Invisible Future, the seamless integration of technology into everyday life. McGraw-Hill, 2002.
8. Dix, A., Finlay, J., Abowd, G and Beale, R. Human-Computer Interaction. Prentice Hall, 3rd edition, 2004.
9. Gaver, W., Technology Affordances. In: Proceedings of the CHI conference, New Orleans, Louisiana, 1991.
10. Gibson, J. J., The Senses Considered as Perceptual Systems, Houghton Miffling, Boston, 1966.
11. Gibson, J. J., The Ecological Approach to Visual Perception. Boston, MA: Houghton Mifflin, 1979.
12. Guallart, V. (ed.), Media House Project – the house is the computer, the structure is the network. IaaC /Actar Barcelona, 2005.
13. Igoe, T. and O'Sullivan, D., Physical Computing – sensing and controlling the physical world with computers. Thomson Course Technology PTR, 2004.
14. McCullough, M. Abstracting Craft, The practised digital hand. Cambridge MA: MIT Press, 1996.
15. McLuhan, M., Understanding Media, the extensions of man. Routledge, 1964.
16. Miller, D. L., The Lewis Mumford Reader. Pantheon Books, New York, 1986.
17. Mumford, L. Art and Technics. Columbia University Press, 1952.
18. Norman, D. A., The Design of Everyday Things. MIT Press, 1989.
19. Norman, D. A., Emotional Design. Basic Books, 2004.
20. Oosterhuis, K., Hyperbodies – towards an E-motive architecture. Birkhäuser, 2003.
21. Pashler, H. E., The Psychology of Attention. Cambridge, Massachusetts: MIT Press, 1998.
22. Picard, R. W., Affective Computing. MIT Press, 1997.
23. Postman, N., Technopoly – the surrender of culture to technology. Vintage Books, 1992.
24. Reeskamp, W., Rutten, D. H. G., Vegt, N. J. H., Toering, E. B. and Bongers, A. J., Überzapper, a different kind of remote control. Proceedings of the Designing Pleasurable Product Interfaces conference, pp. 510-511, Eindhoven 2005.
25. Rogers, Y, Sharp, S. and Preece, J. Interaction Design, beyond Human-Computer Interaction. Wiley, 2nd edition, 2007.
26. Rosengren, K. E. Communication, an Introduction. Sage, London, 2000.
27. Schomaker, L., Münch, S., and Hartung, K., (eds.) A Taxonomy of Multimodal Interaction in the Human Information Processing System. Report of the ESPRIT project 8579: MIAMI, 1995.
28. Sluis, R. van de, Bongers, A. J., Kohar, H., Jansen, J., Pauws, S. C., Eggen, J. H., and Eggenhuisen, H. WWICE User Interface Concepts. Philips Report, company restricted, September 1997.
29. Sluis, R. van de, Eggen, J. H., Kohar, H., Jansen, J. User Interface for an In-Home Environment. Proceedings of the Interact conference, Tokyo 2001.
30. Spuybroek, L. Deep Surface – the unvisual image. In: Architectural Design magazine, special issue on Hypersurface Architecture II, 69/9-10, Wiley & Sons, 1999.
31. Tufte, E. R., Envisioning Information, Graphics Press, 1990.

32. Veer, G.C. van der, Welie, M., Task Based Groupware Design: putting theory into practice, In: D. Boyarski. W.A. Kellogg (eds), Proceedings of DIS - Designing Interactive Systems conference, pp. 326-337, 2000.
33. Veer, G. C. van der, Bongers, A. J. and Vyas, D., DUTCH - teaching method-based design. Proceedings of the IFIP Convivio workshop on HCI and Education, Graz, 2006.
34. Wichary, M., E-learning: the HCI example. Final report for the USI post-masters programme, published by the Stan Ackermans Institute, Eindhoven University of Technology, 2005.

Transdisciplinary Design Approach
An Experimental Model to Project-based Teaching and Creative Problem Solving

Tatjana Leblanc
University of Montreal
Faculty of Environmental Design
School of Industrial Design
C.P. 6128, succursale Centre-ville
Montreal, QC H3C 3J7, Canada
+1-514 343 – 6034
tatiana.leblanc@umontreal.ca

Abstract. In 1992, the Faculty of Environmental Design at the University of Montreal added multidisciplinary workshops to its academic program with the intention to encourage collaboration and communication between disciplines and to prepare students for the collaborative aspect in their professional life. However, experience has shown that simply joining disciplines is not sufficient. Established boundaries and hermetic discourses that academic disciplines developed over time tend to make collaboration complex and hinder the process of transcending boundaries. This paper discusses inter- and transdisciplinarity in design and describes our experimental project-based teaching model developed for the purpose of conveying methods of creative problem solving while stimulating transdisciplinary thinking.

1   Introduction

The School of Architecture, the Institute of Urban Planning, the School of Landscape Architecture, the School of Industrial Design and the School of Interior Design are all part of the Faculty of Environmental Design at the University of Montreal. They form a gathering of expertise and share a common goal of envisioning and exploring 'the new' and shaping the environment that people live in. Each of these disciplines has its specific area of interest, intrinsic epistemology, methods and language, which are the foundation for a theoretical framework, elevating it to an autonomous system and setting it apart from each other. Despite the common interest that all disciplines

Please use the following format when citing this chapter:

Leblanc, T., 2009, in IFIP International Federation for Information Processing, Volume 289; *Creativity and HCI: From Experience to Design in Education*; Paula Kotzé, William Wong, Joaquim Jorge, Alan Dix, Paula Alexandra Silva; (Boston: Springer), pp. 106–122.

share within our Faculty, they failed to provide a space for communication, collaboration and exchange of knowledge.

Recognizing the need for collaboration and knowledge sharing, the Faculty of Environmental Design in 1992 added a multidisciplinary workshop to its academic program, with the initial intention to foster collaborative and communicative practices between departments within the Faculty, and more importantly to promote exchange among students and teachers from different disciplines.

In later years the multidisciplinary workshop focused its efforts towards better preparing students for their professional careers and a multidisciplinary work environment. This pedagogic structure invited third-year students from all disciplines of the Faculty to participate and to work on a common project.

The workshop in this form (Fig. 1) did not live up to the expectations. Although meant to encourage exchange and communication, the experience exposed fundamental problems, which led to disciplinary clashes. From early on, students did not intertwine, choosing instead to follow independent solving paths, engaging in activities that were familiar to them. Cultural differences and language barriers also made integrative practices difficult. The benefits of the multidisciplinary workshop in this format were therefore not convincing, and required a different format and a revision of teaching methods.

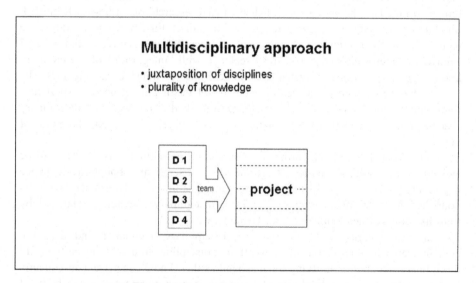

Fig. 1. *Multidisciplinary workshop structure*

The intent of this paper is to critically review the initial workshop structure and its associated teaching approach, to describe an evolved approach to teaching integrative practices, and to argue the need for transdisciplinary thinking.

The paper will discuss the need for an extended knowledgebase, describe the evolving role of design as a cross-discipline, reflect on the integration of transdisciplinarity in design education as well as illustrate these thoughts through a teaching case study. A dedicated section will address the applicability of these transdisciplinary approaches to other areas such as intelligent living environments and the design of human-computer-interfaces. The paper will conclude with some thoughts on interdisciplinary practices and evaluate the workshops outcome while commenting on the impact of transdisciplinary thinking

2   Extending Knowledgebase

'Various disciplines... over the course of the 20th century became increasingly sub-divided', as Burnett [1] rightfully observed, '... and as they grow more specialized, they cease to see or even envisage the potential connections they may have to other disciplines'. At the same time, modern scientists, such as Morin [2], stressed the need for transdisciplinary thinking, when pointing out that fragmentation of knowledge and monodisciplinarity lead to blind 'intelligence'. By compartmentalizing knowledge, disciplines can lose the ability to contextualize or to position the knowledge in its natural context. In response to the need to bridge disciplinary knowledge, multi- and interdisciplinarity practices have emerged.

Multidisciplinarity is characterized by a juxtaposition of disciplines and their knowledge base, providing multiple views on a subject matter and '...its goal remains limited to the framework of disciplinary research' according to Klein [3]. She further stressed that the characteristics of multidisciplinarity are only 'additive in nature rather than interactive' and lead to 'parallel perspectives' and limited exchange. Interdisciplinary research seeks a full integration of disciplinary knowledge, interactions between disciplines and a transfer of methods. Its 'approaches arise mainly because of a perceived misfit among needs, experience, information, and the structure of knowledge embodied in conventional disciplinary organization,' [3] and thus emphasizing the need of rejecting a singular point of view.

Nicolescu [4] goes even further by suggesting that complex issues have to be tackled from multiple angles, 'regardless of disciplinary boundaries', hence expressing the need for holistic thinking: transdisciplinarity. 'Transdisciplinarity is nourished by disciplinary research; in turn, disciplinary research is clarified by transdisciplinary knowledge in a new, fertile way'.

Transdisciplinarity seeks to transcend disciplinary boundaries and does not content itself with interaction between different disciplines. It is looking for their full disciplinary integration, unifying them as well as their knowledgebase, consequently leading towards a 'new thinking' and towards a new and 'autonomous body of knowledge' [5]. De Coninck [6], however, stressed that transdisciplinarity is not to be considered as a new discipline, but rather as an 'attitude'. 'A perspective of transdisciplinarity arises exclusively from a person's or researcher's own consequent dealing with reality' and therefore relies on an individual's own dynamic cognitive processes [7].

Burnett [1] commented on recent changes in nature and on the role of disciplines and their notable transformation from specialized approaches to integrated strategies, linking different disciplines in research and practice. According to him, the shift from disciplinarity towards inter- and transdisciplinarity occurred as a result of the alteration of social and cultural conditions for creation and communication of knowledge, driven by the scientific research itself and the proliferation of communication technologies, joining disciplines, such as arts with science.

Even if they all agree that technological innovation is essential for progress in society, many critics reproach that many 'technologically charged products' are mainly technology-driven (instead of user-driven), thus leading to a lack of acceptability by many users [8]. Technology needs to conform to the user, and not the user to technology. This is why, Veryzer [8] insisted, interdisciplinary practices involving not only engineering and marketing but especially industrial design from the onset, can lead to context-sensitive and user-friendly design, more meaningful to the user.

3 The Evolving Role of Design

The role of design is not only to conceive products, environments or services, motivated solely by economic or technological reasons, but also to take into consideration cultural, socio-political, environmental, psychosocial, and ethical issues that preoccupy modern society while exploring new possibilities. Design, should be viewed as 'a way of projective thinking, planning and communicating, not based on a set of universal values and objectives, but on criteria of appropriateness and process quality' [9]. Therefore, design cannot be confined to disciplinary boundaries while searching to 'explore the future and anticipate change' [9].

Findelli [10] stressed the need for a holistic approach in design and the extending of boundaries by emphasizing that 'a design project will more likely produce sense-making results the further one extends the limits of the system in which this project evolves.' He referred to the Bauhaus that understood the need for extending knowledge in design when introducing science such as sociology, cognitive psychology and *Gestalt* thinking [11] to its design curriculum [10]. It recognized that the quality of the physical environment affects people's behavior and psychosocial well-being; therefore, design has to understand what moves people and how they perceive their environment.

Design evolved towards a discipline that is relating and connecting other expert fields, as such; Jonas [12] characterized the role of design as being anticipative, generative, illustrative, use-oriented, context sensitive and especially integrative.

Today, several design schools acknowledge the cross-disciplinary nature of design by adapting design programs accordingly and by creating stronger ties with other disciplines.

Alberta's School of Arts and Design is one of them, having formed connections with other disciplines, such as computer science, engineering, business and marketing as well as social sciences [13]. Nonetheless, many of these collaborative practices still remain pluridisciplinary in nature, meaning that each discipline continues pursuing disciplinary goals and will therefore continue experiencing disciplinary boundaries as an obstacle.

4   Transdisciplinarity in Teaching

The previous discussion emphasized the need for looking beyond one's discipline and inciting systemic thinking. In order to incorporate a transdisciplinary approach in its teaching methods, the Faculty of Environmental Design decided to create a learning environment promoting cross-fertilization.

A broader knowledge and a common conceptual framework would enable students to develop common approaches, and experience transdisciplinary thinking. However, gaining an understanding of a new culture requires immersion. Lacking a common knowledge base and common language -- both of which are essential for communication and collaborative practices -- the initial workshop did not make such immersion possible. The new format of the workshop had to make these fundamentals available to students, and more importantly, provide an environment where divergent thinking and a variety of approaches are conceivable. Therefore, an interdisciplinary approach to creative problem solving was suggested, leading to the formation of multidisciplinary groups, which, after being exposed to each other's domain, were confronted with a real-life problem, allowing students to contribute with their expertise to a common body of knowledge while developing interdisciplinary skills (Fig. 2).

It was important to nurture exchange among students and teachers and promote critical thinking. The overall goal was to experience how 'borrowed tools and methods stimulate cross-fertilization' and how 'new concepts and theories transform the way that objects are treated' in traditional disciplines [4].

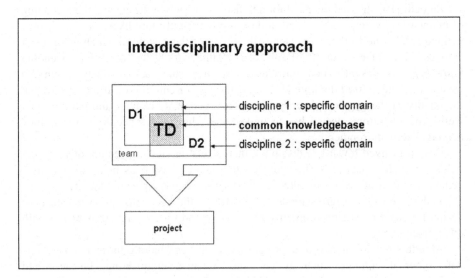

Fig. 2. *Interdisciplinary approach*

The following paragraphs describe the new objectives, the evolved scope and educational structure of the 12-week immersion workshop.

The transdisciplinary workshop was divided into four experience modules: architecture, urban planning, landscape architecture and industrial design. Each experience module lasted three weeks during which the students were immerged in a new discipline. 'Of course, a person cannot be inspired by a domain unless he or she learns its rules.' [14, pp. 89-90]. Therefore, the first effort consisted of teaching students some fundamental rules. Within each experience module, disciplinary notions were transmitted and subsequently applied to project-type exercises. To convey an entire body of knowledge within a three-week period is obviously an impossible task and it was not the objective of the workshop. And so, fundamental theoretical and methodological elements of each discipline were carefully chosen to address the transdisciplinary aspects of the workshop, and were limited to the topics at hand. After completing a module, students transferred to the next, until all four disciplines have been explored. (Fig. 3)

An overall topic, *Nature and Artifice,* tied all four modules together. This topic provided a good opportunity for gauging differences and even oppositions between the different disciplines (and their cultures). It was expected that this topic, from a philosophical point of view, would provoke discussion among all disciplines and stimulate creativity. All subtopics specific to each experience module were governed by this overall theme.

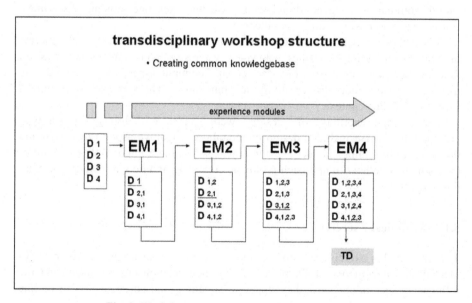

Fig. 3. *Workshop structure, transdisciplinary approach*

Since all experience modules pursue the same goal and follow a similar pedagogic structure, the following sections will describe, as an example, the content of the industrial design experience module, its approach, its exercises and some of the results.

5   Experiencing Industrial Design

The Department of Industrial Design (ID) at the University of Montreal encourages students to adopt critical thinking by teaching creative problem solving and an experience-driven design approach rather than focusing on the product itself, thus promoting a deeper understanding of the user and his interaction within the contextual environment. With this vision in mind, the discipline's theoretical basis constantly evolves to include teachings of elements from other scientific domains, such as philosophy, art history, anthropology, sociology, ergonomics, behavioral and cognitive psychology, and engineering.

The ID experience module intended to enrich students from the other disciplines, but also to bring a whole new educational experience of a transdisciplinary approach to problem solving. Its content was specifically designed, on one hand, to accommodate the short duration of the workshop, and on the other, to control the complexity of the subject matter. This was achieved by proposing a project-based learning and topics familiar to each discipline.

The overall workshop theme was *Nature and Artifice* and the subtopics, specific to the ID module, were: *to illuminate, to circulate and to communicate*. It had been anticipated that looking at a familiar subject from an industrial design point of view would stimulate divergent thinking and foster exchange among disciplines, consequently promising a different outcome.

When approaching these subtopics, students were instructed not to think in terms of objects or artifacts (lamps, signage systems...), but rather in terms of functionality. No other restrictions were given. Economic aspects were ignored. The focus was on methodology, creativity and innovation. The subtopics were only a vehicle, providing context.

Fundamental notions of design were addressed through lesson-type presentations. These included design methodology, cognitive aspects of design and the perception of things, modern design practices, but more importantly case studies that demonstrate how to approach problems creatively and how to convey meaning through artifacts.

5.1   Analytical Exercise

The goal of this exercise was to analyze a situation in an urban environment, to identify and decompose problems, to clarify their relationship, to understand the influencing factors and how they impact a situation, and subsequently, to outline design objectives addressing unmet user needs.

Csikszentmihalyi [14, p.365] explains that 'how you define a problem usually carries with it an explanation of what caused it'. Therefore it is essential to analyze a problem from as many angles as possible.

Students were instructed to adopt a phenomenological approach by focusing on people's experience of the environment (physically and emotionally), by observing user interactions and their relationship with the contextual environment. More specifically, they needed to investigate how things appear to the user, how they are being perceived and how they are being interacted with.

Specifically, this exercise consisted of analyzing one of the proposed subtopics (*to illuminate, to circulate,* or *to communicate*) by using a holistic approach. It required the collection of critical information, observation of a real-life situation and documentation of critical findings. Therefore, it was suggested to explore the city center of Montreal, and especially to envision this exploration as a first-time experience. The following guidelines were given to help structure the investigative process:

1. Identify a specific area of interest and how can or should it be defined?
2. Identify its role, impact and limits. (What does it mean to provide light, to communicate, to circulate, for example?)
3. Identify the users (primary, secondary…).
4. Observe the user experience (considering physical as well as psychological aspects).
5. Consider what may affect the experience (e.g. climate conditions, a specific situation such as rush-hour, stress, tourism).
6. What challenges do or may (some) users face?
7. What conditions need to be fulfilled to make it an efficient, pleasurable or/ and memorable experience?
8. How are those needs met today (*to illuminate, to circulate, to communicate*)?
9. Are there better ways of fulfilling those needs (comparative study, different culture…)?
10. List and prioritize design criteria based on observations and conclusions made.

Comparative studies completed the analytical part of the exercise, leading to conclusions and design recommendations. The findings were summarized and presented to the group using various communication tools: photo documentation, user scenarios, charts, diagrams and information extracted from articles or other sources. Below are a few of the topics that students have singled out and chosen to address:

- *Vertical Circulation*: Analysis of the unique infrastructure of Montreal with its underground system, connecting horizontally neuralgic points of the city: subway stations, commercial plazas, subway system and skyways, office buildings with shopping centers, museums and cinemas. Special attention was paid to the (missing) identifiers for the vertical connections between all these layers: underground, street level and high-rise buildings.
- *To Circulate with Visual Deficiencies:* Analysis of challenges that visually impaired people face everyday while living in a city environment, exploration of sensory needs and how technology integration may address those needs.
- *Street Crossings and Traffic Control*: Study of the effectiveness of the means of enforcing authority and traffic regulations in modern culture.

5.2   Ideation Exercises

Creativity is a mental operation of generating new ideas and concepts and 'refers to the act of changing some aspect of a domain' or the way a discipline is being practiced [14 p.291, 370].

Once problems were identified and design objectives established, students were ready to explore ways of solving them. The second exercise consisted of several structured brainstorming sessions, designed to stimulate students to contemplate as many ideas as possible. A panel of ten students was formed and one of them was designated as moderator. Techniques borrowed from the linguistic domain (semiotics, semantics, categorization) structured the ideation session.

5.2.1 Synonyms, antonyms, metaphors

The first part of the brainstorming consisted of generating as many synonyms, antonyms and metaphors (or free associations) as possible for each given keyword (e.g. keyword: inform, synonyms: communicate/ report/ update/ enlighten, antonyms: hide/ conceal/ veil/ deceive, metaphors: sign, message, note, pigeon). Following are some of the terms generated for the '*to circulate*' topic:

- *Synonyms*: move, travel, advance, flow, diffuse, disperse, propagate, spread, disperse, disseminate, distribute…
- *Antonyms*: stop, stagnate, bring to halt, arrest, discontinue, interrupt, hinder, immobilize, paralyze, prevent, suspend…
- *Metaphors*: grid, network, circuit, bypass, moving forward /backward /up-and-down/in circles/not at all…

5.2.2 Categorization

Categorization is a cognitive process of organizing information 'based on semantic coding'. The goal is 'to reduce the infinite differences among stimuli to behaviorally and cognitively usable portions,' [15, 16] and to structure and classify data (terms, objects, concepts…) in form of a semantic web. In our case specifically, it served as a basis for new concept generation.

Students were asked to identify and classify information gathered previously into cognitive structures. It involved grouping the suggested lexical terms into distinct categories that 'appear to substantially share features that show a clear correlation' [17].

The vertical (super-ordinate-, basic-, and sub-ordinate levels) and horizontal classifications provided an extendable information structure (mapping) to which other terms could/should be added, once a logic pattern submerged. For instance, an initial list of users (pedestrians, cars, bikes, trucks) has been later extended by adding: emergency vehicles, tramways, taxi, and isolated as categories with distinctive needs.

This following is an excerpt from the list generated for the '*to circulate*' subtopic.

- *Identification of road users:*
  a) Pedestrians: kids, adults (elderly), adolescents, animals…
  b) Vehicles:
    − Motorized: car, motorbike, emergency vehicle, taxi, van, bus, tramway, subway …
    − Non-motorized: bike, skateboard, roller, stroller, …

The vertical structure for the road user category included terms such as pedestrian, child, where as the horizontal classification for the pedestrian category included terms like child, adult, pet... The grouping of users in sub-categories suggested distinctive needs, thus requiring different solutions.

- *Identification of context:*
  a) Street, intersections, walk way, parking lots, boulevard.
  b) Commercial district, office district, residential area.
  c) School area, playground, parks, plaza/squares, bus stops.
  The classification of contextual situations helped identify stakes and specific user needs: traffic related, service related, use related.
- *Identification of experience related emotions:*
  a) Negative: to endure rush-hour-stress, to suffer from fatigue, pressure, impatience, danger, annoyance by noise, pollution,
  b) Positive: alive, vibrant, motion, colorful, sound, people music, engaging people, window-shopping, meetings, exchange...
  This category drew the attention towards contextual and perceptual differences (efficiency for motor vehicles vs. safety and conviviality for pedestrians). A hierarchical representation of categories and sub-categories helped organize and visualize relationships among them, thus inferring new concepts [17].

5.2.3 User Scenario
A user scenario is an important tool in a design process which helps visualize and better understand a user's interaction with the physical and cultural environment. By looking critically at a specific problem a designer learns to better understand the actual needs. A user scenario is usually generated once all information, gathered from qualitative and quantitative research (observations, interviews, opinion polls, focus groups...) have been analyzed. For the purpose of this exercise however, students would only be required to rely on previous observations and personal experience.

The categorization exercise served as an initial tool that helped to identify different users and pinpoint some of the possible needs or expectations in terms of infrastructure, safety measures and accessibility to services.

5.2.4 Qualifying attributes
This part of the creative exercise consisted in emphasizing the perceptual and cognitive aspects of a design project and involved the listing of functions and qualifying attributes. The use of 'manipulative verbs' [18], such as, for example, modify, magnify, minify, or substitute, allowed for extending the search. For example, the notion of safety for pedestrians triggered the following ideas: separation, isolation, segregation enclosure, hierarchization as well as tunnels, barriers, bridges, etc. Some of these terms instantly suggested concepts (Fig. 4).

There are numerous other techniques for creative exploration, such as the use of free associations or the technique of 'forced morphology' [19], consisting of listing features and qualifying attributes in semantic categories and randomly associating some of these attributes, making unique feature configurations possible. However, if applied arbitrarily or mechanically, it may lead to irrational propositions. A critical evaluation and validation of ideas are therefore essential in a design development process.

5.3   Embodiment and Communication of Ideas

Design is a process of creating meaning and of embodiment of ideas using multiple modes of communication. To convey meaning, design uses a design language, which, similar to linguistics, is composed of signs and symbols that carry meaning through its physical representation. Design uses multiple modes to communicate and to embody meaning, either material or immaterial, two-, or three-dimensional. Quoting Kazmierczak [20]:

'In design literature, content is interchangeably referred to as *information, data, message, subject,* and *meaning.* The differences in names are the result of differences between terminologies specific to the domains from which these terms were borrowed. Although the names might differ, the approach to them remains the same... The designer's role is to provide the form needed to make a predefined content/ information/ data/ meaning, and message... perceptually accessible in other words, to translate from one form to another.' [20, p.46].

By studying the cognitive processes, the users' perception and interaction with the environment, by identifying noticeable behavioral patterns and by understanding the multi-sensorial nature of a user experience, design is able to propose meaningful interfaces and environments capable of inferring significance to the user [21].

Considering the limited scope of our workshop, a complete analysis of each specific situation would have been too ambitious. Consequently, this exercise started with a brief introduction to communicative and cognitive processes and the perception of semantic qualities [22], enough to draw attention towards perceptual phenomena and to encourage students to reflect on how and in what form they should express meaning and assess the semiotic potential of their concepts as well as the chosen mode of representation [23].

The focal point of the third and final part of the ID experience module was the process of discrimination of ideas and embodiment of coherent design concepts. It involved evaluating the initial ideas, comparing them with the pre-established design objectives, selecting the most promising ideas susceptible to solve the identified problems and develop them into coherent proposals. Then, the task was to visually 'articulate' the refined design intent in a meaningful way [23].

Due to time constraints, the subsequent phases, such as concept refinement, concept validation, design development and design implementation, which would usually complete a design process, were excluded, in favor of creativity and exploration of new methods and tools. Students had to choose appropriate communication tools (sketches, schematic views, reduced scale mock-ups...) to express the main thoughts and values of their concepts. The following section will present some of the concepts generated while following the recommended process.

Fig. 4 shows a concept generated for the subtopic *'to circulate'*. The team, consisting of an urban planer and an architect, analyzed challenges that visually impaired people face on an everyday basis. Inspired by the analytical and creative exercises, students defined design criteria, specified needs, and generated ideas. By suggesting a separate infrastructure for pedestrians (upper level), they were able to address simultaneously the safety issues and propose a new conviviality through walkways with boutique entrances, plaza, café, etc... The lower level was dedicated to moving traffic, public transportation and provided access to parking and commercial distribution. Strategically located elevators connecting all levels were offering access to underground parking and subways.

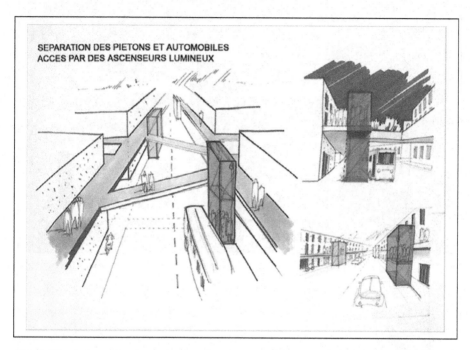

Fig. 4. *Hierarchy, safer circulation in urban environment separating pedestrians from moving traffic (image taken from student project 2006, by É. Albouy, D. Rivard, submitted to   T. Leblanc, AME 3030)*

This concept is attempting to address a problem of divergent but coexisting needs by infiltrating territories of other domains, which students - this can be safely assumed - with a purely disciplinary approach would not have attempted.

As depicted in Fig. 5, an industrial design student and an architecture student tried to solve a problem of providing natural and artificial lighting without just creating another lighting fixture, but by improving systems already in place.

Inspired by the overall theme *Nature and Artifice*, and by adopting the suggested methodology, both students detached themselves from the object and instead focused on the function of illuminating. After analyzing the topic of natural and artificial lighting, the student team came to the conclusion that windows should not only assume the role of providing natural but also artificial lighting, especially considering the fact that users at night tend to veil their windows in order to gain privacy.

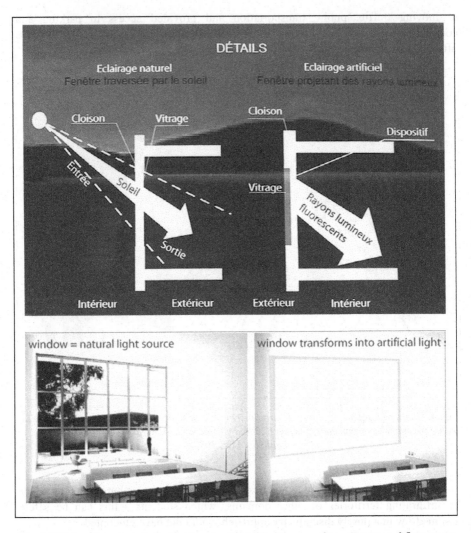

Fig. 5. *Window as a source of natural and artificial light, using photo sensors and fluorescent technologies (image taken from student project by G. Pierre and A. Khansaa, submitted to T. Leblanc, AME 3030,2006)*

The second concept proposed by the same team looked at alternatives for a traditional window structure (Fig. 6). The effects of light and shadow in nature inspired students to attempt recreating similar effects within the interior environment. During the day, the interior is animated by the play of natural lighting and shadows, while at night the building exterior appears animated by the interior artificial lighting exiting the walls.

Fig. 6. *Wall unit, window alternative (image taken from student project by A. Khansaa and G. Pierre, submitted to T. Leblanc, AME 3030, 2006)*

6   Transdisciplinarity and Design Research

Integrative approaches in the field of computer science have long been recognized as crucial, especially when designing and developing highly innovative products. Many user interfaces are too complex which represents a major challenge for certain users. Therefore, context-sensitive and user-centered design approaches are imperative in the design of digital products and services and should favor simple and intuitive solutions that are meaningful to a potential user. More and more researchers integrate design because of its cross-disciplinary nature and its ability to provide such user-oriented perspectives.

The School of Industrial Design at the University of Montreal increasingly facilitates interdisciplinary projects with other universities, which allow design students to apply the described methods. One of these interdisciplinary activities involves the School of Industrial Design and DOMUS, a research group at the University of Sherbrooke, uniting students and researchers from several disciplines: computer science, psychology, health science, ethics and design. The goal of this project is to develop intelligent living environments capable of assisting people with cognitive disabilities. This topic is of utmost importance for the Canadian public health sector that is facing numerous challenges due to its aging population, a shortage of resources and a spike in healthcare costs.

Many designers and researchers are trying to tackle such socioeconomic problems. Not only are they directing their efforts towards the prevention of a diminishing quality of care, but they also attempt to address patients' psychosocial needs, with the goal of increasing their autonomy and independence. Modern technologies and intelligent living environments are being widely considered a promising alternative.

Indeed, our information culture is a social phenomenon that has remarkably impacted social habits, engaging the younger generation but unfortunately leaving a great part of our aging population behind. In fact, those who would benefit most from being connected are our most vulnerable population, people with disabilities such as dementia, who are unable to perform simple everyday tasks due to partial memory loss, and are driven to isolation, insecurity and loss of autonomy.

The design research was looking at how technologically driven products and environments affect people's perception, interaction and experience in order to create new user interfaces that are simple to understand and easy to use.

Two subprojects [24] have been focusing on the embodiment of technology and the generation of tangible and intuitive user interfaces, specifically designed for people with dementia. One was addressing the need of assisting the user in localizing objects, and the other was looking at how to assist a user in completing a complex task.

By joining DOMUS in this interdisciplinary endeavor, design students and researchers were merging knowledgebase, learning from each other and generated new creative concepts for tangible user interfaces. The project results have been presented at the 75th congress of Acfas 2007 (Association francophone pour le savoir) in Trois-Rivières, Canada. [25]

7   Conclusion

Interdisciplinary approaches have become common practice in the last years, bringing together experts from various domains, e.g. design, engineering, marketing. Such practices have proven themselves necessary, and well-known corporate structures and design consultancies worldwide recognized the benefit of combining multiple expertise. However, what many interdisciplinary teams struggle with are the boundaries of disciplinarity, which obstruct the effectiveness of an interdisciplinary approach. It is the role of academic institutions to better prepare students for such integrative practices.

This paper intended to stress the importance of teaching transdisciplinary approaches to creative problem solving by describing a teaching model that evolved from a multidisciplinary to a transdisciplinary focus.

Judging from the outcome of the workshop and students' commentaries, one can conclude that exposing students to different cultures, new approaches and divergent perspectives, are key concerns to the success of integrative practices.

As previously explained, transdisciplinary thinking can only be the result of an individual cognitive process. Therefore, only students who were able to assimilate this process felt inspired and enriched by this workshop experience. Few of those, who were not able to break away from traditional thinking, produced rather predictable results. Most of the students, nevertheless, commented positively on the workshop experience acknowledging that the exposure to multiple design approaches made them realize that there are different ways of looking at a problem. Students also pointed out their increased respect for the other disciplines and more remarkably, some were emphasizing the confidence they gained in their newly acquired creative problem- solving skills.

The paper also made the point that the approach as described in the industrial design experience module is not a method reserved to industrial design, but a process of divergent thinking and observing, placing the human being, his experience, and his interaction with the environment of use in the center of his concern. This paper has shown that the subject matter can vary greatly. Nonetheless, in any case, whether designing a building, a lamp, a website or a software product, it means designing for a user and a socioeconomic context. To gain deeper understanding of the phenomenon surrounding a specific problem, one has to search for answers in various fields, engage in interdisciplinary activities and seek the input and expertise of other disciplines. Therefore it is necessary to point out that transdisciplinary thinking and creative problem solving is not reserved to a discipline in particular. Learning to think in broader terms, seeking to understand complex phenomenon for the purpose of envisioning and defining the future should be everybody's ambition.

Acknowledgments

I would like to thank Peter Fianu, Juliette Patterson, and Hocine Serdouk for their collaboration and passion, thereby contributing to such an enriching teaching experience. I gratefully acknowledge Élodie Albouy (ARC), Dominique Rivard (URB), Asri Khansaa, (ARC) and Giorno Pierre (DIN) for the visuals used in this paper. And finally, I would like to thank my colleague Prof. Pierre De Coninck, for his thought-provoking insights and discussions on design and transdisciplinarity, encouraging me to write this paper.

References

1. R. Burnett, Disciplines in Crisis: transdisciplinary approaches in the Arts, Humanities and Sciences, in: Critical Approaches to Culture, (Communications + Hyper-media, www.eciad.ca/~rburnett/transdisciplinary.html, 2005).
2. E. Morin, La Méthode III – La connaissance de la connaissance/1. Anthropologie de la Connaissance, (ed. Seuil, Paris, 1986).
3. J.T. Klein, Crossing Boundaries: Knowledge, Disciplinarities, and Interdisciplinarities, in: Communication au Premier Congrès Mondial de la Transdisciplinarité (Convento da Arrabida, Portugal, 2-6 Novembre 1994).
4. B. Nicolescu, Manifesto of Transdisciplinarity, (SUNY Press, New York, 2002).
5. J. Piaget, 'L'épistémologie des relations interdisciplinaires, in: L'interdisciplinarité – Problèmes d'enseignement et de recherché dans les universités', Proceedings of a workshop held in Nice 1970 (OCDE Paris, 1972).

6. P. De Coninck, De la disciplinarité à la transdisciplinarité, Info-Stopper, Vol. 4(1), pp.1-7 (1996).
7. J. Papst, Transdisciplinarity: The Unifying Paradigm of Humanities, Natural and Social Sciences, Internet-Zeitschrift fur Kulturwissenschaften, No 15, (ed. Josephine Papst, Graz, http://www.inst.at/trans/15Nr/01_6/papst_report15.htm, August 2004).
8. R. Veryzer, Design and Development of innovative high-tech products, Academic Review, Vol. 2(1), pp. 51-90 (2002).
9. W.A. Jonas, Scenario for Design, Design Issues, Vol. 17(2), pp. 64-80 (2001).
10. A. Findelli, Rethinking Design Education for the 21 Century: Theoretical, Methodological, and Ethical Discussion, Design Issues, Vol. 17(1), pp.5-17 (2001).
11. D.B. King and M.Wertheimer, Max Wertheimer & Gestalt Theory, (ed. Transaction Publishers, 2006).
12. W. Jonas, On the Foundation of a 'Science of the Artificial', in HEL99 International Conference, (UIAH Helsinki, September 1999).
13. J. Frascara, Rethinking Design, Design Issues, Vol. 17(1), pp.1-4 (2001).
14. M. Csikszentmihalyi, Creativity, Flow and the Psychology of Discovery and Invention, (HarperCollins Publishers Inc., 1997).
15. E. Rosch, Principles of categorization, Cognition and categorization (ed. E. Rosch, and B.B. Lloyd, 1978), pp. 27-48.
16. E. Rosch, On the internal structure of perceptual and semantic categories, Cognitive Development and the acquisition of language (ed. T.E. Moore, New York Academic Press, 1973).
17. U.A. Athavankar, Categorization...Natural Language and Design, Design Issues, Vol. V(2), pp.100-111 (1989).
18. A.F. Osborn, Your Creative Power, (Purdue University Press, June 1999).
19. B. Koberg and J.Bagnall, The Universal Traveler- A soft guide to creativity, problem-solving and the process of reaching goals, (Crisp Publications, 2003), pp. 4-129.
20. E.T. Kazmierczak, Design as Meaning Making: From Making Things to the Design of Thinking, Design Issues, Vol. 19(2), pp. 45-59 (2003).
21. D. Bartram, The Perception of Semantic Quality, Information design Journal, Vol.3/1, (ed. The Open University, 1982).
22. J.F. Smets, Perceptual Meaning, Design Issues, Vol V(2), pp. 86-99 (1989).
23. F.J. Doloughan, The Language of Reflective Practices in Art and Design, Design Issues, Vol. 18(2), pp.57-64 (2002).
24. S. Cayouette and V. Lapointe and T. Leblanc, L'importance du design pour l'assistance à la réalisation des tâches et à la localisation d'objets, Les nouvelles Technologies au service du maintien à domicile, in C 651, 75e congrès de l'ACFAS, (Trois Rivières, 7-11 Mai 2007).
25. T. Leblanc, Le rôle du design dans la conception de l'environnement intelligent et l'approche transdisciplinaire, in C 651, 75e congrès de l'ACFAS, (Trois Rivières, 7-11 Mai 2007).

Reflections on Teaching Human-Computer Interaction to Blind Students

Teresa Chambel, Pedro Antunes, Carlos Duarte, Luís Carriço, Nuno
Guimarães
University of Lisbon
DI, Faculdade de Ciências, Edifício C6, Piso 3
Campo Grande, 1749-016 Lisboa, Portugal
{tc,paa,cad,lmc,nmg}@di.fc.ul.pt
WWW home page: http://www.di.fc.ul.pt/~{tc,paa,cad,lmc,nmg}

Abstract. What challenges and opportunities do we face when we are to teach
HCI to blind students, especially among sighted students, and having HCI
curricula a traditional strong focus on visual aspects? How do you bring
accessibility to learning and teaching a course that itself addresses
accessibility? These are a couple of the questions we raised when faced with
this challenge. This paper presents our experience, feedback and reflection on
the subject, after two cycles of the course with blind students.

1 Introduction

Perception, interaction and accessibility are core issues in human-computer
interaction (HCI), which have been researched and taught for some years now. But
in 2006 we were faced with a new challenge that necessitated us to rethink and
expand our educational methods for HCI: we had two blind students among a
population of almost two hundred HCI students. At that stage we have already done
research on accessibility, taught many HCI students, and some of us had already
taught these, and other blind students, in other computer science courses. However
teaching HCI to blind students appeared to be different from teaching other computer
science subjects to blind students. But how were it different? In what ways? How
should we approach the teaching? These questions motivated us, leading us to face
the challenge. This paper reports on our experiences after two cycles of the course
with blind students as part of the HCI group. Our main focus is on the first cycle, but
we will also comment on the results of the second one.

Please use the following format when citing this chapter:

Chambel, T., Antunes, P., Duarte, C., Carriço, L. and Guimarães, N., 2009, in IFIP International Federation for
Information Processing, Volume 289; *Creativity and HCI: From Experience to Design in Education*; Paula Kotzé,
William Wong, Joaquim Jorge, Alan Dix, Paula Alexandra Silva; (Boston: Springer), pp. 123–142.

In the more than twenty years of computer science and informatics engineering teaching in our department, there was never a blind student until about six year ago: a girl, and around the same time, a visually impaired boy. Both of them successfully completed some courses, a couple of them in computer science, but left before the HCI course. The girl already held a diploma in education and she started working in a special school for blind people, teaching them how to use computers. The boy decided to graduate in statistics instead, which he already did successfully. The new blind students, another girl and boy, joined us three and a half and two and a half years ago, respectively. After teaching them three other courses ourselves, why would HCI be a different challenge? The first answer popping up was its traditional strong focus in visual aspects, and in particular the nature of the project students used to do. The second was that accessibility – the problem we were facing – is in fact one of the topics addressed in HCI.

So how do you bring accessibility to learning and teaching a course that itself addresses accessibility? Maybe the answer was inside, and while answering this question, we might also contribute to the course itself.

In trying to answer these questions, more specific ones appeared:

1. What challenges and opportunities do we face when we are to teach blind students, especially among sighted students?
2. How does blindness differ from other disabilities? Is it related with blind people cognitive models, their references from the outside world, their memories if they ever had the chance to see? How do they deal with space, fonts, colour, etc?

How should we approach teaching them?

1. Contents: should we teach them the same contents - in theory, practice and laboratories? If not, how should they differ? What are the easiest and more difficult topics for them to learn?
2. Access and Presentation: How to make information accessible? Should we explore different modalities and devices (e.g. Braille lines, screen readers, Digital Talking Books, 3D tactile models of diagrams and screens)? Should we present information in a different way, different analogies, explain it further?
3. Evaluation: should it be different, in what ways? In the project and or the exam? Individual or group projects? Involving blind students only or also sighted students?
4. Are these challenges analogous to those present in other computer science courses or specific to HCI? Does HCI hold a different kind of social, professional and humanitarian responsibility? Does it have the means to make a particular contribution?

Information and communication technologies provide us with key elements to facilitate social inclusion, and HCI addresses ways to approach it, sometimes with the goal of universal design [1]. In the context of HCI teaching, we believe these aspects are to be addressed at two levels:

1. Making HCI learning accessible to blind students;
2. Increase accessibility awareness in HCI, with the help of blind students.

Our search for literature in this area did not result in many hits. There is scarcely any literature focusing this specific topic of teaching HCI to blind students. This was also the experience of Prof. Tony Stockman from Queen Mary, University of London, who we came to meet recently in this process and who we will introduce later in the paper. This is probably due, in his opinion, to the small number of blind individuals that appear in these courses, every few years; so there is often no documentation of best practice or even of what does or does not appear to work. Also from our experience at the university, we do not get a special training for these cases, and even with some support from the Services for Students with Special Needs, the approaches we tend to adopt are somehow general, taking into account the means to make different types of content in books and slides accessible to the students, also providing students with general purpose access equipment like Braille lines and screen readers, and a few guidelines for type of explanations, extra time to answer exams, and lots of common sense and personal commitment in trying to reach them. Therefore, we did not have anything specific to teaching these students HCI.

So we tried to make our best. In the first year, we integrated them with the others in classes, and defined a special project that involved these two blind students and four other students, since we believed the regular project to be the less accessible aspect in the mainstream course. In the second year, we had one of these blind students again, and based on previous experience we decided to have her doing the mainstream course as a complement to what she had done the previous year. Although we received very positive feedback from the students, we wanted to explore the topic further, learn from previous experiences and guidelines that would help us to better understand the problem, and to compare them with what we were doing, helping us to reflect about our experience and conclude what went well and what could be improved in the future. In the absence of closely related literature, we broadened our search to include: learning styles and abilities, general aspects of teaching blind students, teaching HCI to students with cognitive disabilities, accessibility, also in HCI, multimodality, different types of interfaces, legislation, recommendations, and ethical issues.

In the next section, we present the most relevant related topics. Section 3 describes our experience. Feedback and our own reflections are discussed on section 4. The paper ends with main conclusions and perspectives for future work.

2   Accessibility in Human-Computer Interaction Education

Accessibility raises many challenges relevant to HCI. We present and discuss some of them, concerning ethical issues, and accessibility aspects both in learning HCI and as a topic in HCI curricula.

2.1   Ethics in HCI Practice, Research and Teaching

According to Mankoff [2], the discipline of ethics provides an important critical perspective that can positively influence the research, practice and teaching of Human Computer Interaction. The understanding of its imperatives like *beneficence*, *respect for persons*, and *justice*, must be a part of the scientific process of finding a solution to applied scientific problems. As service providers, there is a natural tendency to help the customer to know what is the best way to meet their goals (beneficence) and give them freedom of choice in the solutions we hand them (respect for persons). Standard curriculum implicitly addresses these issues. Justice is not so obvious and leads to issues of inclusion, such as fairness or equity in access to technology; being accessibility to people with disabilities an instance of this aspect.

In HCI teaching, this manifests itself in two situations: (1) making HCI learning accessible to people with various abilities; and (2) teaching accessibility aspects to every HCI student.

According to Mankoff [2], an HCI student must learn: a) to understand that as designers, they have a huge amount of control over who has access to the technology they produce – thus practitioners effectively define who is disabled with respect to their products; b) that not all forms of inclusion are just, because they may just lead to inequality at a different level. Too limited time spent on this lesson of accessibility and assistive technology can lead to misguided ideals. One bias is the usual tendency to seek out those who are like oneself as designers, something that can be attacked by an extra effort in knowing the target audience and using techniques such as contextual inquiry [3].

2.2   Making HCI Learning Accessible

The major challenge facing visually impaired students in the educational environment is the overwhelming mass of visual material to which they are continually exposed in textbooks, class outlines, class schedules, chalkboards writing, etc. [4]. In addition, the increased usage of videotapes, computers, and television adds to the volume of visual material to which they have only limited access.

Overcoming a students' visual limitation requires unique and individual strategies based on that student's particular visual impairment and his/her skill of communication (e.g., Braille, speed listening, etc.). The majority of people who are blind have some useful sight even if it is light perception. There is a great variety of sight loss, including blurred and cloudy vision; vision obscured by dark patches; restriction of the field of vision causing tunnel vision or the presence of peripheral vision only. Therefore, visually impaired people do not all 'see' in the same way, so we may have to adapt our teaching accordingly. Although 'visually impaired' is sometimes considered a more politically acceptable term, we chose to use the term 'blind' throughout the paper for clarifying purposes, since we are dealing mostly with people who have no sight at all. In the literature about differences between congenitally blind people and people who lost sight later in life, there is a tendency to assume that these cope better with blindness than those who were born blind, since they have more references and memories. However, this does not match everybody's experience. For example, Prof. Tony Stockman, who has been blind from birth and attended special schools, reports that his experience supports just the opposite; except maybe in some areas, like in understanding descriptions and perspectives of 3D buildings or structures.

Dix [5] believes we are all aware of the importance of catering for physical disability and perceptual disability, like colour blindness, both in the HCI we teach and in the way we teach it (although not always so sure about how to approach it), but not so much aware for cognitive disabilities. In this context, until a couple of years ago, dyslexia was the only cognitive disability he had ever considered. The Asperger's Syndrome, related to autism, and Williams Syndrome, an 'opposite' condition, came to draw his attention, because they are relatively common amongst university computing students. Actually, Asperger's are often high attainers. Although with a few exceptions, documents and studies about cognitive disabilities at university levels also appear to be rare. Some of the practices to accommodate students with special needs are often good practice and benefit other students as well [5, 6], but that is not always the case. For example, redundant visual cues are good general HCI advice, but a thorough description of a diagram can become dull for a sighted person, beyond a certain level of detail, while of the utmost importance for a blind person to understand it. With regards to website accessibility, Hudson et al. [7] suggest that cognitive disabilities should be accounted for in page presentation and navigation, allowing the users to control presentation and content according to their needs.

Perhaps, the term cognitive 'disability' is sometimes abusively used for a 'different' way of learning. For example, Asperger's excel in technical areas, details, and learning rules, although not in learning facts. Blind people also tend to develop other perceptual abilities. Different cognitive styles [8] are more effective in some areas than others, they require different support, but somehow determine our best ways of learning. This is something we have to keep in mind, first as learners but then especially as teachers, if we want to reach and help our students to learn better. Blind students also present different styles of learning, although in what concerns perceptual styles, they have a tendency to be more audible, and sometimes kinaesthetic in regard to touch. So, different strategies should also be tailored to the different individuals.

2.3   Teaching Accessibility in HCI Curricula

Accessibility aspects, such as the design for disabled and elderly users, are increasingly important topics in the HCI curriculum, as inclusive design and assistive technology, also due to equality legislative requirements [6].

'Know thy users' is a common motto in HCI '…for they are not you', many would add [6]. It is important that students become aware of the existence of people with different characteristics, sometimes very different and some considered disabilities, and their needs; and learn how to design and evaluate systems that meet these needs. Both goals promote awareness to design for these users.

An HCI course could be designed around these topics, or use these examples as good illustrations in most concepts: eliciting user requirements, considering alternative imaginative designs, multimodality, interaction devices, personalization, and evaluation. Topics that Petrie et al. [6] recommend should be covered include: relevant legislation and legal responsibilities; characteristics of disabilities, ageing, and also, for instance, children, speakers of different languages and from different cultures; how these people use current technologies; and inclusive design as a design methodology, although difficult to teach in practice, discussion on how to achieve this may be most valuable. As best practices, Petrie et al. [6] recommend HCI teachers to: get some training in disability awareness; bring assistive technology to life in HCI classes and if possible to get a user of assistive technology, for e.g. a blind person, to give a demonstration of their practices; include a requirement for accessibility and inclusive design in any design exercises that they set. And finally, to turn accessibility into a positive intellectual challenge: it is more difficult but also more intellectually satisfying, stretching students further.

3   Our Experience

The HCI course at the Faculty of Sciences of the University of Lisbon is part of the 4th semester in the undergraduate Informatics Engineering curriculum. In the first course cycle with blind students, the central case reported in this paper, we had 188 students attending the course, among which, 2 were blind. We intended to accommodate these students the best we could, but also had a large population of other students to consider.

3.1   Classes and Evaluation

Based on previous experience with blind students, we decided to integrate these two students in the regular classes, encompassing theoretical and practical lectures as well as a few laboratory sessions. They attended the same lectures and were taught the same materials. Slides were made available in text format, with significant limitations due to the large number of graphical contents that could not be transcribed in an automatic way. Some extra attention could be given to these students in practical and laboratory classes, and sometimes extra time was necessary to provide additional explanations, trying to match the topics covered to their mental models on these concepts.

   Regarding evaluation, we followed a different strategy. While the blind students had to answer a quite similar exam, ensuring they would acquire similar basic concepts as regular students, they developed a different project where their perceptual skills were especially accounted for, since the regular project was heavily based on visual aspects.

3.2   Project

Both the mainstream and the special project were developed by groups of three students and followed the same underlying structure: requirement elicitation, design, development, and evaluation in more than one iteration, although with different emphasis and themes, and involved tasks both as designers and usability testers.

3.2.1 Mainstream Project

Regular students had two main goals: first to design, develop and evaluate a website, exploring different design criteria and guidelines in an open and creative way; and second, to suggest incremental user-interface improvements to a commercial application (a VoIP communication tool). Students also had to develop a portfolio with the results from the different project phases. Students were faced with two types of tasks all along the project: as designers of their own projects, and as usability experts assessing the colleagues' projects. Regarding the later task, in the average, each group received and answered approximately 30 questionnaires (selected at random by the web site technology supporting the portfolio development) for usability evaluation at each design stage. Considering the website, three design stages were defined: (1) requirements analysis, concerning the identification of website target audience and functional and interface specification, taking design guidelines into account, and low-fidelity prototyping of three preliminary design alternatives; (2) high-fidelity prototyping, using HTML and JavaScript, followed by a usability evaluation using online questionnaires; and (3) prototype refinement, combining the data obtained from the questionnaires with additional user feedback from task analyses and interviews, followed by another usability evaluation. The improvements proposed for the VoIP application were also subject to a usability evaluation through online questionnaires. After accomplishing each step, each group would make a presentation about their work, before the class. This way, students could share their findings and accomplishments with the others, receive additional feedback from colleagues and teacher, and last but not least, exercise their presentation abilities and public speaking skills.

This mainstream project was considered inadequate to blind students, mostly because it had a strong visual emphasis that could hardly be experienced by them and consequently could lead to frustration and disengagement.

3.2.2 Special Project

The two blind students were integrated in two special groups, each one involving one blind and two sighted students. They also had two specific goals for the project, built around their own portfolio. First, they had to make a survey on non-visual user interfaces; and second, they worked on multimodal digital talking books (DTB), instead of the website. As with the website project, some emphasis was put on usability testing, although in the DTB case, a special focus was requested on the non-visual interactions and different types of tests [9] were explored. They also answered to other groups questionnaires (mostly with the sighted students, due to the visual nature of the prototypes) and had some colleagues interviewed in their usability tests. The project had two milestones, one after the survey and the other one after the DTB evaluation. These students also made their presentations before the class. This way, they could share their work with the colleagues, and also learn from the other projects. In addition, a paper [10] was written and presented at a national HCI conference, describing the concepts involved and the experiences of evaluating DTB with a non-visual focus conducted by the students. This challenge was announced from the beginning as an extra motivation for students to excel in their work.

In the survey, the two groups explored different aspects of non-visual interaction, covering: hardware interfaces (Braille lines, keyboards, note takers, and printers, scanners with voice output, virtual touch mice, data gloves, gesture wrists, GPS with Braille pads and voice synthesizer, and wearable computers); software interfaces and applications (screen readers, voice synthesizers, digital talking books, and audio games); and accessibility guidelines, including W3C recommendations. These topics were later complemented for the paper's related work [10].

The second project stage dealt with the usability evaluation of a DTB player. The students' work was integrated within a research project currently underway in our research group, aiming at the development of tools for ensuring access to literary content for the visually impaired community. From the early stages of the project, the students were provided with the most up to date version of the DTB player and given access to the usability laboratory facilities. The DTB player is an adaptive multimodal application, supporting visual and audio input and output. Audio input is available through speech recognition. Audio output is available through pre-recordings of the books and speech synthesis of awareness mechanisms. Given the blind students experience with audio interfaces, their contribution was valuable to the application's development.

The work started with the study of usability evaluation techniques, leading to the decision of what techniques to employ during the tests. Each group designed two controlled experiments, involving a set of visual and non-visual tasks. Preparations for capturing the experiments with video cameras and screen capturing software were made.

The experiments started with a debriefing for introducing the participant to the application and background of the tests. Participants had a ten-minute period for familiarization with the DTB player. After this period, the participants executed a set of tasks, and, in the end, answered a questionnaire about the application. Prior to the experiments, each group did a preliminary evaluation of their test settings. A first run was made with the groups' elements and a second one with one element from the other group. These pre-tests allowed the identification and correction of several errors in the experiment design, both in the tasks and questionnaires. They also provided some training for the debriefing stage. Since all the participants in the experiments were sighted, and although they had some non-visual interaction situations to experiment, these pre-tests were particularly relevant, because they rendered the opportunity to thoroughly test the application and experiment design also with blind users. During the experiments, conducted under the supervision of elements of the research team, most of the activities were performed by the sighted students of the groups. The blind students were most active in the debriefing stage. Between these experiments, each group suggested improvements to the DTB player. Due to time and resource limitations, not all the suggestions were implemented in the new version of the application used in the second experiment. This resulted in the introduction of a new evaluation technique for the second experiment - the Wizard of Oz technique – to test the unimplemented suggested features, in general related to audio interaction. Fig. 1 presents two pictures taken during these tests: a) one sighted student is conducting the test; b) blind students are following one test with the help of a sighted student in note taking.

Overall, these experiments resulted in twenty usability evaluation sessions. The participants, twelve male and eight female, were all students from the Faculty of Sciences of the University of Lisbon, from different courses and curricula. No participant was visually impaired. In order to evaluate the different features and usage possibilities, three different evaluation scenarios were considered: in the first scenario, all input and output modalities were available to the participants, which were free to choose how to interact with the application; in a second scenario, the only allowed input modality were voice commands, but the output was still done using visual and audio modalities; in the last scenario, the interaction was exclusively done through audio channels. In this way, it was possible to evaluate multiple usage scenarios and compare modalities.

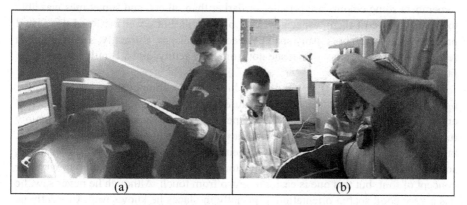

Fig. 1. *Digital talking books usability tests*

This one semester project gave the blind students the opportunity to experience the different design stages and to be involved in usability evaluation sessions, in addition to raising the awareness to the accessibility problems.

4 Feedback and Discussion

After the course and evaluation periods, the six students that participated in the special project were interviewed about their experience. In the process of reflecting upon this experience, we also discussed some topics with Prof. Tony Stockman, from the Queen Mary University London, who provided us with invaluable insights based on his own experience as an HCI blind learner and teacher. He has 18 years of experience teaching Computer Science topics, including 7 teaching HCI at a wide range of levels, although he never had any blind student. He led the HCI group at Staffordshire University for 3 years. His main area of research is the design of auditory displays, mainly for improving the accessibility of spreadsheets, providing overviews of interfaces and data, and supporting the analysis of physiological signals.

In this section, we present the main feedback we received and discuss our experience in the light of related experiences and work.

4.1   Students Profiles

The students were aged between 20 and 25, four of which where sighted males and two blind: one male and one female.

One of the blind students (A) suffers from a rare condition of the genetic Alström Syndrome, in face of which she had a severe reduced sight as a child, and completely lost her sight at the age of 15. Before completely loosing sight, she could read amplified text, and occasionally used computers, mainly for text processing. She remembers some colours are brighter or darker than others, and sometimes was able to identify some of them, especially after being told, but never mastered this visual property. She remembers many spatial objects and shapes. Currently, she uses screen readers and a Braille line, which she got from the Faculty, and a Braille printer at the faculty library.

The other student (B) is blind since birth due to complications, damaging the optical nerves, resulting from his premature birth at 6.5 months and permanence at an incubator. He has developed the shape and space concepts, perceived mainly through touch and moving around. He knows colour is a visual attribute of objects, but he is not sure how it manifests, being different from texture for example, something he can partially perceive by touch. He was also not familiar with the concept of font, but this one is easier to grasp from touch. Although he never saw, he has a very good spatial orientation, especially in places he knows well. Currently he uses screen readers, a Braille line and a printer. He already used these before coming to the Faculty, bought with social security funds. However, he got a more modern Braille line and a portable PC from the Faculty. Both of them never had contact with more sophisticated devices, like data gloves or 3D mice.

In the first year reported, all but one of the students, a sighted one, were taking the course for the first time. All students completed the project successfully, but only half were successful in the exams: blind student B and two of the others, not all from the same group. One of them never even tried due to some personal matters during the exams seasons. In this year, the second cycle of the course with blind students, student A completed the course successfully.

4.2   Contents Covered in the Course

Most of the students said it was a good idea to learn the same contents. In particular, both blind students found it useful and interesting to learn the same contents, because it is important to know what other colleagues in the area know, if they are to integrate the same professional environments. This is true even if they have an extra challenge dealing with the more visual aspects, and against some of the sighted colleagues opinion: 'I believe some of the topics are not understandable, superfluous or even useless to them.'

Most of the topics were considered understandable to the blind students. They commented they found some of the other courses more difficult, e.g. Operating

Systems. Being the biggest challenge the understanding of visual design issues, most of which they did not have to really deal with as they made a different project. This goes inline with Prof. Tony Stockman experience: 'I personally find HCI relatively straightforward [compared to other computer science courses] in terms of a typical undergraduate or postgraduate curriculum, of course advanced research papers take some reading and digesting as in any field. [...] I think colours and fonts are tricky because they are not something for which there is a clear equivalent for a blind person. [...] If someone has seen and was old enough to know the names of colours then [the concept is understandable]. To someone who has never seen, like myself, I guess I tend to think of colour a bit like being equivalent to timbre in sound, i.e. there are infinite numbers of possibilities, that it very much helps to form one's impression of the thing you are looking at and, like timbre, it is also possible to have things of very nearly the same colour or very widely differing colour. Also, because colour is so heavily used in our everyday vocabulary, blind people are very capable of understanding and using commonly used colour-based phrases, such as 'as black as night', 'green with envy', 'as pale as a ghost' etc. [...] I think layout is more tangible because some of the rules of good layout: consistency, simplicity, affordance etc. are equally applicable to Braille or auditory displays.'

In another perspective, finding some other courses more difficult also matches what Edwards et al. [11] perceive in Computer Science students, as they tend to consider HCI easy and somehow common sense, although not always being very successful at mastering it. Computer Science students tend to get satisfaction in studying a topic which is hard to understand but which becomes clear with time and effort, leading to an awareness of a level of mastery; whereas HCI requires a more open arts-like attitude, where sometimes there is no right answer. It is less deterministic, involving more subjective aspects, like human factors and design. Focus on analyzing and criticizing existing systems and using other student's designs, as well as focusing on the design process, are suggested approaches to improve effectiveness in HCI learning by Computer Science students. Our own approach matches most of these recommendations, and in particular for the blind students, more subjective issues somehow tended to be less central, since they tended to focus on usability and efficacy rather than aesthetics and liking.

Besides the visual design, another topic that was found more complex by blind students was related with the engineering aspects of interactive systems architectures, especially toolkits and window systems. Student A simply did not study these topics, while student B did not give much attention to them, because he found them unclear, in his words 'not very practical, perceivable' so he decided to focus on the other topics. This observation was confirmed by looking retrospectively into the blind students' exams. While both students were able to articulate and explain several human-computer interaction theories, most descriptive topics related to user interface components and their relationships were wrongly explained or simply unanswered. In Prof. Tony Stockman's opinion, this is understandable due to lack of diagrams, but he believes 'also, this may not be a problem for younger people, having been brought up with procedural models of programming, [but] I found descriptions of event-driven systems in some texts rather confusing, it is just an area where very clear writing makes all the difference.'

This could mean that more technical-oriented courses on user interfaces would be harder for blind students than more broad courses on human-computer interaction, with more theoretical focus, or that better supporting materials were required. More evidence is needed. For example, Prof. Tony Stockman 'has not found any aspects of HCI that with some effort, and occasional assistance from a sighted person, that he was unable to internally visualize and appreciate. [...] The text copy of Alan's book [12] was extremely helpful with this.'

4.3   Contents Accessibility and Presentation

Students had access to a text version of the course slides, and student B recorded the classes, as he usually does in every course, often also making it available to student A. So they listen to the recorded tapes and use screen readers and a Braille line to access course contents. They found the content accessibility to be similar to what they are used to. The main difficulty, as usual, is dealing with images, and they would have benefited from the textual version of the textbook as well.

Regarding our behavior in classes, whenever a blind student was present, we entered a different mode of explaining the materials, something we trained over in the different courses we taught them, and is particularly difficult the first times. We provided more descriptive information, especially related with any available sketches and diagrams, sometimes reducing related and complementary information, and avoiding some common contextual references we would provide should we have the time. It is like a cognitive breakdown [13] that gets us to a mode where we become more aware of the process of explaining, and more reflective [14]. In this mode, we tend to explain some things differently, especially when in the presence of descriptive materials, such as diagrams or pictures. We explain them in more detail – sometimes in a way that becomes too exhaustive for the rest of the audience, as many times was pointed out during lectures – tend to describe visual relationships that are obvious to the others, and make references to some things we think they are more familiar with. We try to find different examples or to explain the same examples in different ways. This however is difficult to do in very large classes, and sometimes we get distracted and get back to the more usual and somehow more experiential mode of explaining, until the next breakdown when attention is drawn back again to these students and how we are conveying the messages. In some cases, to make up for this, we tend to explain some topics further, after or outside the classes.

4.4   Examination

The exams given to the blind students were very similar to the other exams, with up to 10% different questions, addressing less visual aspects of interaction, or having additional explanations making up for the absence of figures. The blind students found the exams to be adequate, while still covering the wide range of topics. The student failing the exams blamed it mainly on the lack of study, and having to study also for other courses. One of the blind students suggested having two tests instead of a final exam, to reduce the amount of topics to study each time. However, the other student found it ok.

Blind students received their exams in digital text format on a portable PC. They wrote down their answers inline in the text file, having their screen readers and Braille lines helping in the access. They also had 50% extra time to complete their exams, according to a special regulation, which has proven to be adequate in the cases we had so far.

4.5   Project

We will discuss aspects related with the project theme: Non-visual interfaces and multimodal Digital Talking Books, and the team work involving the two groups of three students.

4.5.1 Theme

All the students found it adequate to do this type of project, different from the mainstream, exploring non-visual interfaces. They found the survey very useful to broaden their perspective and knowledge on the field, and did enjoy studying and evaluating the DTB player, in a more practical perspective and related with a research project. Main comments: 'It was a very good theme', 'the survey and the DTB project complemented each other', 'it was a fine opportunity to participate in a research project, contacting other researchers and teachers outside the classroom, and to do the evaluation tests in a usability lab', 'it was a rare opportunity to learn something different', 'I felt useful sharing my experience with others that didn't know about non-visual interfaces'

The only drawback pointed out was that they were not learning and acquiring the same skills as the other students, although they could learn some of it from the colleagues' presentations and the few usability questionnaires they answered to. The blind students did not answer these questionnaires because they felt way too far from what they could easily perceive, and it was not a central issue in their own project. However, the students believed that they could more easily catch up with the missing knowledge on their own, than with what they learned in the other project in such special conditions.

In the end, they all felt more comfortable about designing a non-visual interface. Sighted students think they would be able to approach the design of a visual interface, while blind ones are not so sure: 'Maybe with some help, I could mange to build one. I might have something to say and contribute in such a design.'

Prof. Tony Stockman's experience reinforces this belief: 'I also have not found my blindness has stopped me from being able to make suggestions about how to improve the visual layout or design of things in some cases, providing of course I have a clear understanding of the task and the interface.'

4.5.2 Team Work

All students found it important to have both sighted and blind students in the group, and sharing experiences with the other group. They recognized as most significant contributions of the blind students the explanations about their interaction experiences: their challenges in traditional interfaces, their workarounds and special tools to cope with limitations, and their experience, feedback and informed suggestions in non-visual interaction. On the other way around, sighted students, helped in understanding visual aspects of the interfaces they encountered, even on the DTB, sometimes using analogies that they could understand, and dealing with more practical matters. For instance, they were usually faster in finding information on the web, although some topics were suggested by the blind students; more at ease in conducting other people in the interviews and usability tests; managing the videos to review the recorded interviews, especially to notice what the user was doing when comments were made or how the interface responded to a particular action; and found it easier to make slide presentations and to some extent also talk before the class. However, the blind students also talked to the class, showing them a Braille line and telling them about the interfaces they used.

4.6   Research Paper and Conference

Participating in a project that lead to a research paper was perceived as a very good experience by all the students. It motivated them to do better, had their work recognized, felt they had made a contribution to something that could reach other people, and could enrich their professional experience and curricula vitae. Only one of the blind students could manage to attend the conference. The students that did not participate regret it to some extent, but they had several restrictions, including tests and projects. Student A enjoyed attending the conference because she heard about interfaces she did not know possible, and became more aware of the topics researched in the field. She felt motivated to learn more about some of the topics as a future professional and for her own use.

4.7   High and Low

For the blind students, the best aspects of the course were related with the project: its theme, the contact with a recent type of application, cooperation among the team colleagues and usability tests. Not so good, were some topics in the course that were not so accessible to them, like visual design issues. As for the others, they liked mostly the new perspective of human-computer interaction. All of them would have chosen the same project, did they have the chance to be in the same situation again.

Most of them slightly regretted not learning some of the topics in the mainstream project, like some visual design aspects and gaining more practice on HTML and JavaScript, but overall it was a very good experience. To overcome this aspect, we encouraged them to build a personal home page on their own, an idea they welcomed.

Based on this finding, this year we had student A integrated in a group with two other sighted students, doing the mainstream project. She liked the experience, especially as a complement to last year's project, and could successfully complete the project with the colleagues. She claimed that she gained more awareness of the aspects that are relevant in visual interfaces, although she recognized that she does not master the subject. In the project, they also explored some accessibility aspects, including audio feedback; and student A improved her skills in webpage construction.

As a by-product of the collaboration among the students, sighted students recognized they gained accessibility awareness, increasing their understanding of other people's needs: 'it was a very enriching experience in human terms.' One of them told us he was already creating his own webpage, where he was taking accessibility issues into account, especially those concerning blind users.

5   Conclusions and Perspectives

Facing the challenge of teaching HCI to two blind students, among almost two hundred sighted ones, and in spite of our previous experience both as HCI researchers and teachers and as teachers of blind students in other computer science courses, motivated us to re-think and expand our educational approaches in this area. Somehow, this combination seems different, holding new problems and opportunities. In one hand, HCI has a traditional strong focus in visual aspects, and in the other, the problem we were facing – accessibility – is in fact one of the topics addressed in HCI. Maybe the answer was inside, and while answering this question, we might also contribute to the course itself.

Based on our previous experience with blind students, we decided to integrate these two students in the regular classes, encompassing theoretical and practical lectures and laboratory sessions; although we tried to adjust the way we taught whenever one of them was present. In some situations, we also provided additional explanations after or outside the classes. In the first year reported, they had access to a textual version of the slides and one of them recorded the classes in audiotapes making them available to the other one. Considering evaluation, the blind students had to answer a quite similar exam, ensuring they would acquire similar basic concepts as regular students, but developed a different project where their perceptual skills were especially accounted for, since the regular project was heavily based on visual aspects. This project had the same underlying components of user requirements, design, development and evaluation, but with different emphasis and flavor. It included a survey on non-visual interfaces and some work on multimodal digital talking books (DTB) with some emphasis on usability testing and non-visual interactions. The work on DTBs was integrated on a research project and lead to the publication of a paper on a national HCI conference. In the second year, the textbook was also available in digital text format, and the blind student A, who was repeating the course, was again integrated in a group with two sighted students, but did the mainstream project this time.

In the process of reflecting on our experience, we interviewed the students involved in these special groups that integrated the blind students, and had the opportunity to share and discuss our experience with an HCI teacher who is himself blind. We also reviewed some related literature, to find there is scarcely any in this specific topic. But still, we addressed some related topics.

At this point, and in what concerns teaching blind students, we believe there are general aspects similar in every course where general purpose approaches do apply, and others specific to each course. We emphasized the ones we believe are most relevant in HCI, relating especially to visual aspects and accessibility, and raised a few question on how to approach this teaching accordingly.

Only having two blind students, and bearing in mind that there are many other factors influencing their attitudes and cognitive abilities other than their blindness, perceivable as different even in these two individuals, we tried not to jump into conclusions. However, based on our research and experience, which overall we found very positive, we believe we learned some lessons that allowed us to draw some conclusions and identify some open issues and directions for further research. These are presented next, in the context of main raised questions.

Contents: It was a good idea trying to teach them the same contents as much as possible. These students like to be treated the same way as other students and to become familiar with the same knowledge, even if they have to experience information in different ways. An open question remains on how far to go in this process, helping to expand their perceptual and cognitive limits. The answer will probably change with each individual. Visual properties and design guidelines were among the most inaccessible issues, but students still believe they would like to give it a try, should they have the adequate support.

Technical-oriented aspects of user interfaces seemed to be harder for our blind students than more broad and theoretical aspects on HCI, although not problematic for Prof. Tony Stockman, for instance. More evidence is needed to determine whether this is a structural issue, or if it only requires better supporting materials.

Access and Presentation: Blind people must have their specific perceptual abilities taken into account in order to be able to access the course materials (e.g. books, slides, classes). Some of them, and probably more if they are approaching HCI aspects, also appreciate means that help them to gain awareness or knowledge about the perception they lack.

Providing materials in text and recording classes do help them. However, although they were used to have a similar type of access to materials in other courses, and in consequence not complaining, some improvements can be made. Pictures and diagrams should be made available in an as much accessible format as possible. Prof. Tony Stockman defends that 'If blind students use either Braille or a screen reader, they will experience GUIs in a relatively serial way, and so diagrams should have value in at least conveying a two-dimensional idea of the layout [...] and screen design.'

Although some initiatives are starting this year, involving volunteer students, to describe pictures and diagrams in course material to make them accessible to blind students, this is an error prone and lengthy process, information is serialized, and some even lost. Other alternatives include tactile diagrams, drawn or printed in special sometimes expensive types of paper, and the use of 3D mice to access them online. These mice might also help them use graphical tools, which they currently do not use, sometimes adopting different descriptive approaches (e.g. a BNF based notation for Entity-Relationship modelling). Prof. Tony Stockman suggested that blind students might also find it useful to construct their own Braille-based representations of some techniques such as hierarchical task analysis, dialog design notations or user action notation.

Digital talking books [10,15] can also increase book accessibility to these students. Some recordings are also underway for a book and a couple of research papers, for this format, to make them accessible to the students. Somehow related, web lectures, in audio or in video [16], could support accessibility to classes, avoiding the students need to record the classes they attend, and improving flexibility and efficiency in storage and access methods, as well as the integration of these classes with other materials (slides, books, exercises, digital books, etc). The different materials and modalities would help to support different perceptual and learning styles. Diversity and flexibility would allow personalized tailoring of presentation and content.

This is still a problem in live classes though. How to make our presentations accessible to the diverse audience, especially when there is no balance, e.g. 1%-99%? What is adequate for sighted students can be inaccessible to the blind, and what is adequate for the blind can be redundant and dull for the others. We tried to reach a balance in class and sometimes provided extra explanations to blind students after or outside the class – but it is not always effective, although there is an interesting side effect of having them all confronted with the others point of view, increasing accessibility awareness. Another direction to exploit here is aligned with the general tendency of delivering studying materials online, where personalized access is also easier, leaving face-to-face classes the role to engage and motivate students to learn [17].

Probably due to recent advances in the field and to the small amount of blind students that enter the university, supporting services usually address general purpose approaches and do not have themselves access to most modern technology, especially in the recent years when technology is reaching more diverse audiences and accessibility became a priority in information society. Maybe this is another point where HCI people can contribute to the scenario.

Evaluation: Having comparable exams seemed a good choice, allowing to evaluate similar kinds of knowledge, although blind students usually take more time to answer, something already covered by regulations. Joining blind and sighted students in the special project seemed to be a good approach. They had a very good collaboration, complementing each others in their skills, and sharing their different experiences and perspectives. Sighted students could perceive the difficulties blind users have with common interfaces, as well as the difficulties of designing interfaces that take their needs into account. Blind users brought an important contribution with their experience and suggestions. They also had the chance to explore more diverse and sophisticated evaluation methods in a usability laboratory, and to participate in a research project. The theme of the project was perceived as adequate by all, where their perceptual skills were especially accounted for, and allowed them all to learn more about an interesting topic. To some extent, students regretted not exploring further some of the topics in the mainstream project, although they learned part of it in classes and from colleagues' presentations. This was compensated for in the case of student A this second year, having her participating in the mainstream project. The special project in the first year required a significant amount of extra support from the teacher and a couple of colleagues from the research project, especially in the usability tests. We believe this context was enriching for the students, and in the process allowed for some research contributions, but it is not mandatory in providing blind students with a different project. Anyway, some extra effort might always be required to support these students in special projects.

Although it was a positive experience, an open question still remained: to what extent could we support these students doing the mainstream project and how effective and worthwhile would it be for them to try it?

From our experience in the second year, with student A repeating the course but doing the mainstream project, we got a positive outcome. It was especially so, being a complement to previous year's project. Although some aspects related to exploring different modalities to help her gain awareness of the perception she lacks could be further explored, it was a positive experience, encouraging more work in this direction.

HCI and Accessibility: We believe that, to some extent, this experience helped making HCI more accessible to blind students and also helped to increase accessibility awareness among sighted students, and even among teachers and researchers. This was definitely true in the two groups and partially in the practical and lab section these students belonged to – one in seven. We also had a practical class on creativity where students were encouraged to invent an application, make some sketching and present their product design to the class. Some are more conservative, some are more daring and futuristic. It was interesting to notice that in the blind students section, many designs accounted for speech interaction and auditory feedback. Blind students may contribute to enrich the learning scenario, and these ones welcomed the opportunity to share their experience with the colleagues, although they did not feel much comfortable talking in public. They also had the chance to learn more about different types of interaction, and especially more about non-visual interfaces. A further step might be taken in the direction of increasing students' perception about non-dominant perceptive abilities: to help blind people grasp what it is like to see, or a sighted person what it is like to be blind. Although having contributed to this aspect, accessibility awareness and support might have been explored further and to the widest audience, stressing that it is not exclusive to people with physical impairments but also relevant to people with temporary conditions or in special conditions of use [18]. Maybe we'll take this opportunity to increase our focus on accessibility in future cycles of the HCI course, even if we do not have students with special needs attending, as suggested by Petrie et.al.[6]. Finally, it is important to increase accessibility awareness among teachers, about their diverse learners and how to go about helping them to learn better. We hope to have contributed in this direction as well.

Acknowledgments

We would like to thank Prof. Tony Stockman from Queen Mary, University of London, for his invaluable testimony, and Prof. Alan Dix from Lancaster University for introducing us. Our thanks also go to the six students participating in the special project, Ana Catarina Rua, Eduardo Santos, Guilherme Francisco, João Robalo, Sérgio Neves, and Tiago Fernandes, for their feedback. We thank our Faculty for funding the Interacção'2006 conference participation of student A and accompanying colleague, and in particular Prof. Dulce Domingos, currently the responsible person for Students with Special Needs in our Department, who dealt with this process. We also thank Prof. Ana Paula Cláudio and Prof. Isabel Nunes, previously performing these same functions, who also had an important role in the support of our blind students in the last years. The DTB research work was partially funded by Fundação para a Ciência e Tecnologia in the project POSC/EIA/61042/2004.

References

1. E. Rodríguez, M. Domingo, J. Ribera, M. Hill, and L. Jardí, Usability for all: Towards improving the e-learning experience for visually impaired users. In *Proceedings of ICCHP'2006 – Conference on Computers Helping People with Special Needs*, Univ. of Linz, Austria, July 12-14, (2006).
2. J. Mankoff, Applying ethics to the practice, research, and teaching of Human Computer Interaction. *Reflective HCI: Articulating a Research Agenda for Critical Practice Workshop at ACM CHI'2006*, Montréal, Québec, Canada, 22-27, April (2006).
3. Beyer, H. & Holtzblatt, K., *Contextual Design: Defining Customer-Centered Systems.* (San Francisco: Morgan Kaufmann Publishers, 1998).
4. Online Resources for Teaching Blind Students
   http://www.uni.edu/walsh/blindresources.html
5. A. Dix, The right mind?. *ACM SIGCHI Bulletin* HCI Education column, Jan/Feb (2001).
6. H. Petrie, and A. Edwards, Inclusive design and assistive technology as part of the HCI curriculum. In *Proceedings of HCI Educators Workshop'2006*, Limerick, Ireland, 23-24 Marh, (2006).
7. R. Hudson, R. Weakly, and P. Firminger, An Accessibility Frontier: Cognitive disabilities and learning difficulties. In *Proceedings of OZeWAI'2004*, La Trobe University, Melbourne, Australia, December 2, (2004).
8. T. Chambel, and N. Guimarães, Learning Styles and Multiple Intelligences, *Encyclopedia of Distance Learning*, (Idea Group Inc., April 2005).
9. P.W. Jordan, Methods for Usability Evaluation. In *An Introduction to Usability*, pp. 51-80 (London - Bristol: Taylor & Francis, 1998).
10. C. Duarte, T. Chambel, H. Simões, L. Carriço, E. Santos, G. Francisco, S. Neves, A.C. Rua, J. Robalo, and T. Fernandes, Avaliação de Interfaces Multimodais para Livros Falados Digitais com foco Não Visual. In *Proceedings of Interacção'2006*, Univ. do Minho, Braga, Portugal, 16-18 Outubro, (2006).
11. A. Edwards, P. Wright, and H. Petrie, HCI education: We are failing – why?. In *Proceedings of HCI Educators Workshop'2006*, Limerick, Ireland, 23-24 March, (2006).
12. A. Dix, J. Finlay, G. D. Abowd, and R. Beale, *Human Computer Interaction*. 3rd Edition, (Prentice Hall, 2003).
13. T. Winograd, F. Flores, *Understanding Computers and Cognition: A New Foundation for Design* (Addison-Wesley, 1986).
14. D. Norman, *Things That Make Us Smart* (Addison Wesley Publishing Company, 1993).
15. C. Duarte, T. Chambel, L. Carriço, N. Guimarães, and H. Simões, A Multimodal Interface for Digital Talking Books. In *Proceedings of WWW/Internet'2003*, iadis, Algarve, Portugal, 5-8 November (2003).
16. T. Chambel, C. Zahn, and M. Finke, Hypervideo and Cognition: Designing Video-Based Hypermedia for Individual Learning and Collaborative Knowledge Building, Chapter II, in

Eshaa Alkalifa (ed), *Cognitively Informed Systems: Utilizing Practical Approaches to Enrich Information Presentation and Transfer*, (Idea Group Publishing, January 2006).

17. A. Dix, *Deconstructing the experience of (e)learning for delivery ecologies*. Talk given at The e-learning Experience, Birmigham Institute of Art and Design, 15th October (2003). www.comp.lancs.ac.uk/computing/users/dixa/talks/elearning2003

18. M.S. Gazzaniga, R.B. Ivry, and G.R. Mangun, *Cognitive Neuroscience – the Biology of the Mind*. (W. W. Norton & Company, 1998).

Between the Ivory Tower and Babylon – Teaching Interaction Design in the 21st Century

Gerrit C. van der Veer

School of Computer Science,
Open University Netherlands, Valkenburgerweg 177,
6419 AT Heerlen, The Netherlands
gerrit@acm.org
WWW home page: http://www.cs.vu.nl/~gerrit

Abstract. A brief history of interaction design shows that there is an ongoing cultural change in the relation between people and computers. This results in a structural need to include new disciplines in interaction design approaches. The concept of experience is analysed, and the need for new curricula is shown. One example of a curriculum is illustrated, with its successes and failures.

1 Introduction

Interaction design is now a common concept in those modern Information and Communication Technology (ICT) curricula that include a focus on users. However, beyond the concept there seems to be a wide variety of content and meaning. The main *aim* might be the design of technology, or, alternatively, the design of people's environment and opportunities. The *format* of the product of design can vary from formal specifications, requirements, or running prototypes to sketches and scenarios. The actual *meaning* of the end-product of design may be a specification of functionality, or an intention towards the prospective users' experience.

It makes sense to briefly consider the history of technology design. Early technology tended to be designed and produced by the users themselves. Early hunters build their bow and arrows, European musicians, at least till the 13th century, cut their own flutes or harps, and in most 'primitive' cultures people make their own clothes and dwellings. Even in the early 20th century technology users tended to control their own tools: The first photographers were chemical experts; the first car

Please use the following format when citing this chapter:

van der Veer, G.C., 2009, in IFIP International Federation for Information Processing, Volume 289; *Creativity and HCI: From Experience to Design in Education*; Paula Kotzé, William Wong, Joaquim Jorge, Alan Dix, Paula Alexandra Silva; (Boston: Springer), pp. 143–158.

drivers fine-tuned their own engines; the first sewing machines came with a tool kit, and the first computer users loved to program. But as technology develops, the situation always changes. Users are no longer by default designers and builders, and separate roles develop: the professional designers, as well as the technical producers of the tools, are different from the user who acquires a tool and applies it.

The following sections deal with: a brief history of interaction design (section 2); a change in culture (3); the need for new disciplines (4); the concept of experience (5); how to integrate this in an academic curriculum (6); and the development of one such curriculum in interaction design (7). Finally, in section 8 the conclusions are summarized.

2 Brief History of Interaction Design

With ICT this historical development took a short period. Till about 1980 computers were used by professionals (mathematicians who needed to calculate complex functions, psychologists who validated formal learning theories and models of human problem solving [1]). The main issue in getting technology optimally used was to make the users accept it, for which 'user participation' turned out to be a major design focus [2]. Once the technology was accepted, the users happily learned to fine tune their system to their job. In some cases this developed into the professional pride to program, and these users enjoyed the possibility to formally specify, test, and iteratively improve their attempts to solve their professional problems, or to mathematically prove the correctness of their solutions.

The 80s saw the development of general systems for office work (starting with word processors and spreadsheets), as well as the availability of the PC and microprocessors. The main design issues now concerned how to deliver the system ready for the job of the user. The user interface was the main focus with systematic approaches towards its architecture [3], its functionality (Tauber's concept of the user virtual machine [4]), early approaches to analyse the (command) dialogue [5], and successful implementations of representation like the desktop. Users were considered in all these approaches, and even the concept of 'user participation' continued to be advocated but with a changing meaning. In most cases users were not considered to co-design but to be involved in all stages, from early envisioning to field-testing the delivered product. And, consequently, knowledge of psychological concepts and models was compulsory for design curricula [6]. Still, some professional users needed, and were provided with, tools they could and would adapt to their individual way of use [7].

The 90s saw the explosive expansion of ICT availability and use. ICT use for *professionals* still expanded. Hypertext and the World Wide Web supported quick collaboration and availability of remote sources and facilities. At the same time, ICT started to play a vastly growing role in the *consumer* context: as a time and place independent entry to public administration, private banking, and health care, as a tool for participation in society (news, entertainment) and politics (blogs, voting), for private buying (Amazon.com) and selling (eBay). New theories entered the library of user centred design, like Distributed Cognition [8] and Contextual Design [9].

The 21st century came with even more challenging developments. Apart from the still growing professional and consumer market, *leisure* applications became a major business. The total sales number of Apple's wearable juke-box iPod (first sold in 2001) passed 100 million in the 2nd fiscal quarter of 2007 [10]. At the same time, ICT is increasingly embedded in our *environment*; in vehicles for transport and in traffic technology, and in buildings [11].

3   Computers and People, a Changing Culture

For the early users of ICT the computer was a work bench that allowed them to develop their own tools. Command languages and operating systems like UNIX were a preferred environment since these gave them control. The professional wanted to know what was going on behind the console, paper tape or punch cards. A user interface would have been considered an unnecessary layer in between the user and the tool.

Our world changed, and ICT became available and used by a broad range of non-expert people, workers as well as consumers, for serious tasks as well as leisure. It became part of living in our society, and a core element of our culture, sometimes visible but increasingly embedded in the environment. Apart from the ICT experts, most users do not care 'what is inside'.

Using technology should serve the user's purpose, whether this concerns functionality and user control, or excitement and surprise. Requirements, from the user's point of view, always will include:

- Usefulness – it should support reaching the user's goal or the goal of the 'community' (employer, culture, government) the user intends to comply with. In this respect a further distinction can be made between effective and efficient [12];
- Usability – it should fit the user's possibilities [13] (which often are different for different users or users in different roles), i.e., provide universal access [14];
- Safety – use should involve an acceptable risk for the individual and the community [15];
- Motivating – using the technology should be convincing the user this is the right thing to do (providing satisfaction, in terms of [12]), should provide the intended and expected emotions (e.g., fun for leisure applications) and motives (warning for certain political or ethical communications) [16], or be to a certain extend unpredictable in this respect (games, the iPod shuffle, cultural performances).

All of this still may include aspects of control, as the traditional example of the 'programmable' video recorder and the currently newest 'high –end' mobile phone show us:

- Usefulness is limited to the individual user's ability to access the intended functionality, which, for many people, turns out to be no more than a rumour on availability;
- Usability is limited by people's ability to read small screens, understand the proper language and icons, press small buttons, remember sequences of actions and identification codes;

- Safety is a function of the chance to loose data objects or stored information, accidentally or through misinterpretation of storage and retrieval functions;
- Motivation is influenced by both physical appearance of the gadget, by its cultural image ('all my neighbours have one'), as well as by the obvious success or failure to use the thing.

4   New Solutions Require New Disciplines

In the early days of computer use, user centred design mainly developed from three disciplines: Computer Science (this discipline originally was referred to with labels like 'the art of computer Programming' [17]), Cognitive Psychology [6], and Ergonomics [13]. Cognitive Psychology originally focused strongly on usability of program languages [18] and on planning and problem solving in the case of time related monitoring processes of process control [19]. Ergonomics came into view as soon as large quantities of input and output had to be processed *by the user*. Consequently, the first contributions of this discipline concerned hardware, posture, and workplace design including lightning [20].

Since computers became small and cheap, microprocessors turned up in offices, and PCs appeared at people's desks. Design had to focus, in addition, to software design. Software industry developed applications for a large variety of jobs, e.g., text processing for secretarial work, spreadsheet for financial and planning tasks, and profile programming for lath turners. These users were professionals in their own domains. Cognitive Psychology supported design with knowledge on perception, motor skills, and learning. Human-Computer Interaction (HCI) specialists provided models like GOMS and the Key-Stroke Model (see [6]), developed design guidelines [20], and supported to standards [12]. Classical Ergonomics was considered basic knowledge, HCI is sometimes (especially in Europe) labelled 'Cognitive Ergonomics' [22].

Once universal usability and access becomes a design issue, attention is required to Culture [23, 24]. And when ICT is being used to support people working in groups (Computer Supported Collaborative Work, CSCW), Ethnography is a new source for design knowledge and techniques [25]. These new disciplines have contributed considerably towards the scientific basis for web-based applications and for software for organisations and public administration.

The newest developments, however, have again new characteristics. Current technology allows for rich and intuitive interaction with representations in many modalities and many media: very small or vary large screens, camera, speech recognition, input with gestures and tactile output, etc. Again new disciplines and expertise is needed. Knowledge can be found with industrial design (since ICT gets embedded in 'things' like furniture, consumer products, gadgets and household appliances), and architecture (for technology in 'smart' buildings, vehicles, and our physical environment like roads and parking lots). Theories and techniques have to be borrowed from Cinematography (how to induce understanding of causality and time interruption and flow), graphic arts and crafts, and semiotics (how to represent meaning).

Users (if one can still call people with this label) often are no longer explicitly, knowingly, or intentionally controlling the technology. Sometimes mastery of control is a challenge: the game industry is booming. Sometimes users explicitly refrain from control: the popular iPod shuffle slogan reads 'enjoy uncertainty' [26]. Experience is a new concept that certainly covers more than understanding.

5   An Old Story: Experience as Design Focus

'Experience' has all characteristics of a buzzword. The concept will be illustrated first of all from domains that are not connected to modern ICT, to show it is not new at all to aim a design at an audience. In both examples, the artist (the designer) aims at a representation that challenges the audience to perceive something that is a combination of what is physically presented to the human senses and what is interpreted. In both cases the audience is (correctly) expected to enjoy the sensation of the perceiver contributing to the physical stimuli in developing the total experience.

Fig. 1. *Visitors at Panorama Mesdag*

5.1   Panorama Mesdag, 1881

Our first example is about visual art. The panorama illustrated in Fig. 1 is a cylindrical painting, oil on canvas, over 14 meters high with a circumference of 120 meters. It shows a view on the North Sea, sea dunes and the village of Scheveningen.

It has been painted by one of the most famous artists from the 'The Hague School', Hendrik Willem Mesdag, assisted by his wife Sientje, by Théophile de Bock, George Hendrik Breitner, and Bernard Blommers. The graphics may look like a color photograph taken from a dune in 1881, but that was not the intention of the designer. The picture is still on display in its original setting, in a large hall, where one enters through a tunnel and a narrow staircase that climbs to a covered arbor on a sand hill (see picture). The visitors in 1881 needed to walk only 10 minutes to view the real scene. Visiting the panorama allowed them to experience and to enjoy the *virtual* environment. Visitors today imagine being on a sand dune and see what Scheveningen looked like 130 years ago, and many are tempted to even smell the salty see air. Only a very small fraction of the 1000s of visitors during the years ever will ever have taken the scenery for real. Most were happy to pay the entrance fee for the pleasure to dwell in a 'look-a-like' environment and to imagine the real scene, knowing it was their own imagination, not reality as such.

Fig. 2. *Start of the fugue from J.S. Bach, transcription G.C. van der Veer*

5.2   Bach's Fugue for Violin Solo

Johann Sebastian Bach wrote many fugues, compositions for multiple voices that, one after the other, each start with the same theme (beginning at different tones).

Bach wrote for many instruments, and he had many pupils and most of his many children were excellent musicians. The Fugue from Sonata BWV 1003, of which the start is transcribed in Fig.2, is a nice example of the complexity Bach confronted his musicians with.

One after the other the voices start, after which a single one remains to embark in exuberant embellishments till the other 2 voices join again. There is, however, something special with this composition. The title page says, in Bach's own handwriting, 'Sei Sonata a Violino solo senzo Basso accompagnato' which means: 'for solo violin only'. Even a professional violin player who studied the performance practice of Bach's time is not able to hit 3 strings at the same time. But it is well possible to *suggest* the simultaneous sounding of the voices. Apparently, Bach intended the experience for the player to make the suggestion succeed, and for the audience (as long as they have some background in the culture of Baroque Music) to enjoy being able to 'hear' what they well know cannot be sounding. In that case, the performer is a designer her/him self, and the choice of the music hall with its acoustics certainly should be part of the design of the performance. Experienced readers of western music even enjoy reading the score and imagining what could be sounding and what could be 'heard': many copies of the score are bought by music lovers who do not pretend they are able to play it. In fact, a famous violin player that should be unnamed recorded the Fugue in the '70s with multi-track recording in order to sound exactly what was written. Many music lovers abhorred the 'mutilation' of the design.

5.3   Designing for Experience

An experience is something that, in the end, is created by the audience, based on information that reaches ones senses and on knowledge about this information ('this painting is 130 years old', 'the score indicates 3 voices, but the player can only play one or two at the time'), and on actual needs ('I want to "feel" being on a sand dune 130 years ago. I do not want to use this view to predict tomorrow's weather'). Each member of the audience 'lives' the interaction with the artefact.

The designers (painter, composer, or performer) need to apply expertise from their arts and crafts to seduce the audience (maybe 130 or 280 years in the future!) to have the intended experience. The designers / artists need to understand the effects of their techniques including the cultural meaning of the signals that represent the information. They also need to understand the possibilities and restrictions of human perception, attention, knowledge, memory, and thinking.

6   Interaction Design as (Part of) an Academic Curriculum

A scientific base for ICT supported experience design (which cannot be the design of experience, but the design *for* experience) requires input from a multitude of disciplines:

- Computer Science, Industrial Design, and Multimedia technology – for applying the engineering techniques and making sure the resulting product complies to the intentions of the design;
- Human sciences, from Psychology (both Cognitive and Emotional Psychological knowledge), Sociology, and Ethnography, for understanding theories, approaches, techniques and tools for analysing and understanding single and multiple people in relation to the use of technology, and Ergonomics for matching the design to human size;
- Design disciplines ('Arts and Crafts') for professionally creating representations that aim at the intended experience.

Industrial practice was there long before Academia. Multidisciplinary teams, and projects that systematically covered multiple sciences, were common practice decades ago, e.g. at Xerox PARC (since 1970), IBM Science Centres (first research in Speech recognition in 1971), Apple Advanced Technologies (1986-1997), and Philips Design (since 1991). Leading visionaries in those settings felt responsible for interaction design that was at the same time useful, usable, and focused on experience.

6.1   Conditions and Ingredients for an Academic Level

Educating designers at an academic level requires multidisciplinary knowledge to be integrated in a single curriculum, with some strong conditions:
1. A systematic approach, i.e., design based on a solid academic theory with scientific quality that supports methods, techniques, and professional use of tools. This could mean providing enough insight and a conceptual framework in alien disciplines to request expert assistance;
2. Each multidiscipline needs a solid base in a mono discipline that acts as ground for developing theory and methods;
3. Designers educated in this way need to be willing and able to apply knowledge and techniques borrowed from other disciplines in an arguable way.
4. In the end each design discipline will need to aim at three goals:
   - design for human size possibilities and restrictions;
   - specify the system completely as far as relevant for all (types of) users and stakeholders, i.e., specify the Users' Virtual Machine [4]; and
   - aim at experience, (users' understanding, activity, sensations, and emotions, in their context and culture) [27].

Interaction design education requires a combination of the discipline groups as mentioned in section 5.3. Until the '90s the basic discipline mentioned in condition 2 was most frequently either Computer Science or Cognitive Psychology. This last discipline still plays a role in rather traditional Cognitive Ergonomic approaches where mainly single user interaction for professional tasks is concerned. Generally speaking, however, Cognitive Psychology is no longer a default home for a curriculum in Interaction Design. The main current options appear to be Communication Science, Industrial Design, Computer Science (especially Software Engineering), and Interaction Design (or Multimedia Design) as a specialisation of Artistic Design.

6.2   A Case: Interaction Design in Computer Science

The case illustrated here is based on experience in a Software Engineering section of a Computer Science department. Requirements engineering is a major design activity in good industrial practice. Moreover, in industrial design processes there is a considerable amount of user interface building involved. Consequently, there is a need for Interaction Design of a type strongly related to Software Engineering and formal modelling [28]. In that line, courses in Human-Computer Interaction as well as in User Interface Design were implemented [29]. An iterative design process was developed labelled DUTCH (Design for Users and Tasks, from Concepts to Handles [30]) and a task analysis method GTA (Groupware Task Analysis [31]) to support analysis of complex multi-user task domains as well as envisioning of changes in the task domain prior to implementation of new ICT.

The phases in the DUTCH process are:
- a client's original requirements and intentions;
- (task) analysis: knowledge elicitation, ethnography, task modelling
- task envisioning: negotiations with client and technology, modelling again, confronting stakeholders (with scenarios);
- specification: envisioning technology (functionality, dialogue, representation), formal specifications;
- confronting stakeholders: mock-ups, simulations, rapid prototyping;
- evaluation of resulting requirements for engineering: claims analysis, usability studies, experiments;

where each phase may trigger going back to any of the others, in an iterative way.

The total design process starts with requirements (from the client of design), as well as ends with them (for engineering and implementation).

Starting from this situation, the challenge was to develop a complete academic curriculum in Interaction Design. Section 7 will provide the story, and show some illustrations.

7   Development of a curriculum

The department of Computer Science of the Vrije Universiteit of Amsterdam, the Netherlands, decided for a complete and separate curriculum in Interaction Design, within Computer Science. The New curriculum should pair with an existing specialisation labelled Business Informatics, and both would be divisions of 'Information Sciences'. Graduated Information scientists of both types should be experts in their specialisation and, at the same time, should understand enough of the whole field of Computer Science to be able to collaborate at a professional level.

7.1   The mission

The curriculum should consist of a 4 year education that included a Bachelor as well as a Master degree. The department aimed at attracting a 'new' type of students, interested in people as well as ICT, that could be prepared for a practical design job in industry (moreover, the Masters degree should be of an academic level that allowed a PhD follow up trajectory).

Market research focused on two populations: highest level high school students (interview and focus group data were collected from 750 students and 25 student supervisors from 50 schools,), and relevant industries (20 multi media design companies, broadcasting companies, museums, etc).

A list of requirements for the curriculum was specified:
- contain enough Computer Science to allow students to actually engineer (and 'build') the products they designed;
- provide extensive multimedia and web design hands on experience;
- integrate artistic and cultural aspects of design, as well as knowledge of history of modern cultural developments;
- integrate human sciences and theory of interaction design; and
- provide experience in team design for real clients and real users / customers.

Based on the market study the curriculum was labelled 'Multimedia and Culture'.

7.2   The Curriculum

A core set of Computer Science courses were identified for inclusion, e.g., full programming education, data base classes, and software engineering, all of which were standard part of the other curricula in the department. Enough Business Informatics was included to prepare students for insight in their future markets and apply analysis techniques.

A total of four courses in Multimedia were included, from introduction of state of the art tools to the design of complex productions. The existing courses in human-computer interaction and user interface design were kept as core courses and a new course in groupware task analysis was added, as well as a practical group project on web design for a real client.

Relevant classes in history of modern culture could be 'borrowed' from the Faculty of Literature and Arts.

New courses were developed in Human Information Processing, in Information Representation, in Visual Design, and in the Design of Music and Sound. All courses developed complied with a general course structure:
- introduction to a systematic design approach, and theory behind this from the relevant disciplines;
- guest lectures from practitioners;

- design for a real client, where students are collaborating in several competing teams for the same client; and
- whatever the topic (visual design, music, website, user interface) the design process takes the whole way from original requirements till presentation and documentation of the design product.

The Bachelor education finishes with two projects where the student participates both in ongoing (PhD student's) research, and in a practical design project in industry. The Masters finishes with a thesis based on 6 months of work, either in industry or with an academic researcher where the student completes a well defined task and writes up the process as well as a scientific analysis or a related piece of research, in the format of an academic publication.

Fig. 3. *Sample of 'winning' design products for CHI 2005*

7.3   Example Student Project for the Course Visual Design

In 2004 three different student groups (each composed of 3 students) chose to work for the conference CHI 2005 to develop and implement a house style.

After studying visuals from previous CHI conferences, extensive communications with the management of the 2005 team, and analysing the theme of the conference, each group developed a logo with several variants as well as example applications for the various conference products: publicity (flyers, postcards, advertisements in magazines), website, printed material (program book, proceedings, tutorial notes), merchandise (mugs, t-shirts), on site decorations, and animated video clip to announce the conference one year out, including a hip-hop beat and a rap. All groups had to develop the full set of decorations and products, one design was chosen based on the presentation to the conference team and the reactions on this. Fig. 3 shows some of the products of the winning design. In fact, all three groups passed the exam of the course based on their products and presentation.

7.4   Example Student Project for the Course User Interface Design

Based on a collaboration of five students that intended to develop a start-up company, on a market research among the domains of dance education and of physical rehabilitation, and on support from the Faculty of Human Movement Science, two students choose to bring their own project to the course. Their aim was to develop a take-home device with interface for unsupervised training (e.g., at home of movements that had been introduced by teachers or physiotherapists to dance students or impaired patients. The users were supposed to practice between supervised sessions, the market of training institutes did not appreciate stand alone solutions.

To this end, the students developed a business model (as part of another course), analysed many existing types of representations of movements, iteratively worked through several design cycles according to the DUTCH approach, and developed a full formal specification as well as an interactive mock-up (running on a PC) for a single example, the basic Salsa step. In addition they developed a mood board for the dance to guide them in their graphics, and they developed moving figures based on photographs of themselves and a system of stick figure movement decomposition (see Fig. 4).

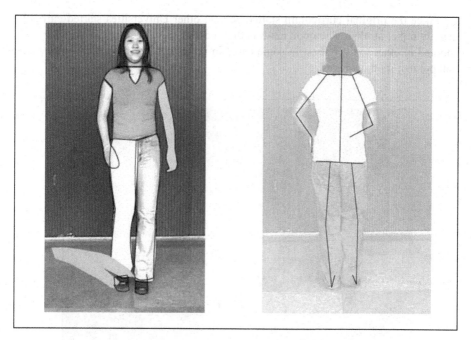

Fig. 4. *Development of a moving dancer for the 'Virtual Dance Tutor'*

The full prototype (see Fig. 5 for the main screen) as delivered allowed a choice of dancer (male, female, pair) or feet to be represented in the movements, a possibility to choose sound (simple or complex melody, with or without counting), the adjustment (slowing down) of the speed, and the optional labelling of the individual steps.

7.5   Successes and Failures

The curriculum attracted a considerable number of students (after the first two years, the number was over the yearly number of new students for either the departments of Physics, Chemistry, or Mathematics!). Students earned their degrees in time and either found jobs in industry or embarked in a PhD study.

On purpose the concept of 'creativity' was never mentioned, not even by the visiting 'artist' lecturers. In every course the methodology of systematic design approaches and explicit design decisions was stressed. Still, creativity was never banned, though a design rationale of some sort was asked for all decisions.

Students liked it, clients for the design courses liked it, and employers liked it. The Faculty of Sciences, however, that is the new higher authority of this curriculum, and with them the department of Computer Science, did not like the multidisciplinary character of the new team of lecturers and the curriculum. A financial crisis in the department led to the decision to cut back on the number of curricula, and 'Multimedia and Culture' was decided to die. One of the Professors of Computer Science stated 'My students do not need to talk to people'.

Since the original curriculum started several other Universities started curricula that are rather similar. The good news is that most of the courses developed are now adopted in other Universities, in some cases in rather concise format, in other cases without major adjustments.

Fig. 5. *Main interface screen for the 'Virtual Dance Tutor'*

8   Summary and Conclusions

Interaction design is a label with a multitude of meanings, depending on the time in the history of ICT, and on, both, the contributing disciplines, and the adopting academic discipline. 'Experience' has been identified as a leading concept in current approaches to Interaction Design. In order to illustrate the possibilities, the history and structure of one example curriculum, positioned in Computer Science, has been discussed in detail. This shows how such a curriculum can be developed, what possible successes are, and how an academic context may also lead to the destruction of it.

References

[1] A. Newell, and H.A. Simon, *Human Problem Solving*, (Prentice-Hall, Englewood Cliffs, NJ, 1972).

[2] E. Mumford, *Designing human systems for new technology: The ETHICS method.* (Manchester Business School, Manchester, UK, 1983) .

[3] G.E. Pfaff, and P.J.W. ten Hagen, (editors) *User Interface Management Systems*, (Springer Verlag, Berlin, 1985).

[4] M. Tauber, On mental models and the user interface, in: *Working with computers: theory versus outcome*, edited by G.C. van der Veer, T.R.G. Green, J.-M. Hoc and D. Murray (Academic Press, London, 1988).

[5] T.P. Moran, The command language grammar: a representation for the user interface of interactive computer systems, *International journal of man-machine studies*, **15**, 3 - 50 (1981).

[6] S.K. Card S.K., T.P. Moran T.P. and A. Newell, *The psychology of human-computer interaction*, (Erlbaum, Hillsdale, NJ, 1983).

[7] B.A. Nardi and J.R. Miller, The Spreadsheet Interface: A basis for end user programming. Human-Computer Interaction, in: *INTERACT'90* (Elsevier, Amsterdam, 1990) pp. 977 - 983.

[8] E. Hutchins, *Cognition in the Wild*, (MIT Press, Cambridge, MA, 1995).

[9] H. Beyer, and K. Holzblatt, *Contextual Design: A customer-centered approach to systems design*, (Morgan kaufman, San Francisco, CA, 1997).

[10] Apple Inc., Apple Reports Second Quarter Results, (2007) http://www.apple.com/pr/library/2007/04/25results

[11] P.J. Denning (editor), *The invisible future, the seamless integration of technology into everyday life*, (McGraw-Hill, New York, NY, 2002).

[12] ISO 9214-11, *Ergonomics requirements for office work with visual display terminals, Part 11: Guidance on usability*, (International Standards Organization, 1991).

[13] B. Shackel, Usability- Context, framework, definition, design and evaluation, in: *Human factors in informatics usability*, edited by. B. Shackel and S. Richardson, (Cambridge University Press, Cambridge, UK, 1991).

[14] B. Shneiderman, Web science: a provocative invitation to computer science, *Communications of the ACM*, **50**(6), 25 – 27 (2007).

[15] J. Reason, *Human error*, (Cambridge University Press, Cambridge, UK, 1990).

[16] D.A. Norman, *Emotional design. Why we love (Or hate) everyday things*, (Basic books, New York, NY, 2004).

[17] D.E. Knuth, *The Art of Computer Programming, Volume 1: Fundamental Algorithms* (3rd edition), (Addison-Wesley Professional, Reading, Massachusetts, 1997).

[18] T.R.G. Green, Sime, M.E. and M.J. Fitter, The art of notation, in: *Computing skills and the user interface*, edited by M.J. Coombs and J.L. Alty, (Academic Press, London, UK, 1981), pp 221 – 251.

[19] J.M. Hoc, Strategies in controlling a continuous process with long response latencies: needs for computer support to diagnosis, *International Journal of Man-Machine Studies*, **30**, 47 - 67 (1989).

[20] B. Shackel, *Man-computer interaction: human factors aspects of computers and people.* Nato Advance Study Institutes, Series E: Applied Sciences, 44, (Sijthof & Noordhoff, Alphen aan de Rijn, NL, 1981).

[21] S. Smith, and J. Mosier, *Guidelines for designing user interface software*, Technical Report MTR-010090, EDS-TR-86-278, (The Mitre Corporation, Bedford, MA, 1986).

[22] P. Falzon, P. (editor), *Cognitive Ergonomics: Understanding, learning and designing 1986) human-computer interaction*, (Academic Press, London, UK, 1990)

[23] G. Hofstede, *Cultures and organizations: Software of the mind.* (McGraw-Hill, London, UK, 1991).

[24] G. Hofstede, *Masculinity and Femininity – The taboo dimension of national cultures*, (SAGE Publications, London, UK, 1998).

[25] S. Knaster, iPod shuffle Tips and Tricks, (O'Reilly, 02/15/2005) http://www.oreillynet.com/pub/a/mac/2005/02/15/shuffle.html

[26] B. Jordan, and A. Henderson, Interaction Analysis: Foundations and Practice, *The Journal of the Learning Sciences*, **4**(1), 39 - 103 (1995).

[27] D. Vyas and G.C. van der Veer, Experience as Meaning: Some Underlying Concepts and Implications for Design, in: *Proceedings of ECCE-13*, (ACM Press: NY, 2006) pp. 81 – 91.

[28] G.C. Van der Veer and J.C. Van Vliet, A Plea for a Poor Man's HCI Component in Software Engineering and Computer Science Curricula, *Computer Science Educational Journal*, **13**(3), 207 – 225 (2003).

[29] G.C. van der Veer, B. Bongers and D. Vyas, DUTCH - Teaching method-based design (*EU CONVIVO Faculty Forum*, Graz, Austria, 2006), http://www.hcieducation.com/pmwiki.php?n=WorkShops.CONVIVO2006

[30] G.C. Van der Veer and M. van Welie, Chapter 7 - DUTCH – Designing for Users and Tasks from Concepts to Handles, In: *The Handbook of Task Analysis for Human-Computer Interaction*, edited by Dan Diaper and Neville Stanton (Lawrence Erlbaum, Inc., Hillsdale, NJ, 2003) pp. 155 - 173.

[31] M. van Welie and G.C. van der Veer, Chapter 19 - Groupware Task Analysis, In: *Handbook of Cognitive Task Design*, edited by Erik Hollnagel (Erlbaum, Inc, Hillsdale, NJ, 2003). pp. 447 - 476.

Teaching Usability Principles with Patterns and Guidelines

Kostas Koukouletsos, Babak Khazaei, Andy Dearden, Mehmet Ozcan
Communications and Computing Research Centre
Sheffield Hallam University,
Sheffield, UK
+44 114 225 4951
ccostas@teipir.gr
{B.Khazaei, A.M.Dearden, M.B.Ozcan}@shu.ac.uk

Abstract. We present a comparative study of the effectiveness of patterns and guidelines as aids to teaching web interaction design. We recruited two groups of novice designers and taught them web design from scratch using a popular authoring tool. We used two balanced sets of guidelines and patterns that in essence present the same advice in two different formats. After the initial training, subjects learned about usability and usability principles with the help of one of these sets. The groups then engaged in two common activities that professional designers must perform, that is designing and evaluating web sites. The final design artefact that was delivered in all tests was a working web site. Here we present the quantitative results for the design phase of this experiment. Evaluation of the designs was conducted by three independent evaluators, using defined metrics. We conclude that both patterns and guidelines help with the design of usable sites, however the advice presented using our patterns format had a greater impact on the novice designers' performance than the same advice in our guidelines format.

1. Introduction

Guidelines are a traditional format for capturing knowledge and experience and presenting advice about interaction design. Recently researchers in Human Computer Interaction (HCI) have started comparing guidelines with patterns, another emerging tool for capturing knowledge and experience. For example, van Welie et al. [1] argue that the main problem of guidelines is that they do not state the context in which they are applied. Mahemoff & Johnston [2] suggest that guidelines can be conflicting,

Please use the following format when citing this chapter:

Koukouletsos, K., Khazaei, B., Dearden, A. and Ozcan, M., 2009, in IFIP International Federation for Information Processing, Volume 289; *Creativity and HCI: From Experience to Design in Education*; Paula Kotzé, William Wong, Joaquim Jorge, Alan Dix, Paula Alexandra Silva; (Boston: Springer), pp. 159–174.

whereas a pattern presents a solution by demonstrating how conflicting forces in a design can be resolved. Pemberton and Griffiths [3] also argue for advantages of design patterns in comparison to guidelines, suggesting that design patterns are presented in a canonical form and provide much richer information than guidelines.

Despite their claimed shortcomings, guidelines remain the most widely accepted form of presenting experience and knowledge. Their durability and endurance are remarkable. Nielsen [4] reports that general guidelines built 20 years ago are still up to 70% valid and applicable, while 78% of guidelines from the early days of the web continue to be valid and relevant.

It may be argued that patterns and guidelines are simply two different formats serving as practical tools to present guidance to designers and practitioners about how to build better artefacts [5]. Borchers [6] states that '... patterns are, above all, a didactic medium for human readers'. This work attempts to compare patterns and guidelines as two alternative formats of providing knowledge and experience to students acting as novice designers.

Previous empirical work on patterns explores the use of patterns in assisting designers to create applications in new domains and how patterns can benefit the design process by generating and communicating ideas between the members of a design team [5, 7]. Other research compares patterns and guidelines based on the perceived usefulness of the designers that used them [8, 9].

Our approach is to develop a balanced set of patterns and guidelines; experiment with them; and finally test their effectiveness by evaluating and rating the design artefacts produced. This approach gives us a better assessment of the strengths and weaknesses of these competing formats, and their value in HCI education.

Section 2 reviews other empirical work on the evaluation of patterns and guidelines for HCI and their use in teaching usability principles, while Section 3 presents the main hypothesis. Section 4 describes the steps taken in defining and formulating a balanced set of patterns and guidelines for our experimental purposes. Section 5 describes the experimental procedure and the teaching approach. Section 6 discusses the results of the experiment and the greater impact of patterns on our subject group, and finally Section 7 gives our concluding comments.

2. Empirical Work on Patterns and Guidelines in HCI

Several researchers used and propose patterns as an aid to teaching HCI principles and design concepts. Borchers [10], having used patterns to teach two HCI design courses, suggests that patterns can lead to above average retention of design values, and concludes that patterns have great potential since there are not just interesting as a topic, but also useful as a tool and format to teach basic design principles. Seffah [11] considers patterns useful not only as a design tool, but also as a learning resource part of an educational framework for effective training and improving developers' skills in Human Centred Design. In particular, user interface design patterns are considered useful for teaching students to master visual information design, including screen layout and interaction design. Griffiths and Pemberton [12] used patterns as a means to teach the interaction design of software systems. Three different approaches were used: teaching about patterns, teaching through patterns and discovering patterns. Although students had difficulties to discover and suggest new patterns, the authors report that existing patterns improved the level of discussion within the design teams and that patterns helped students to produce an improved final artefact; however they also express the need to verify this impression more formally. Laakso et al. [13] used their teaching experience of interface design courses to develop a collection of 25 user interface patterns and pattern candidates. The authors report that initial designs have consistently improved and in some cases the students were producing high quality interface designs in very short time. Dearden, Finlay & colleagues, investigated the use of a pattern language as a tool to support participatory design of web-based systems [14-16], demonstrating that a pattern language can benefit a participatory design approach and can help users generate artefacts in a prototype form.

Although quantitative empirical evidence about the usefulness of patterns in the domain of HCI is not extensive [17], recently there have been a few studies examining the use of patterns in real design activities and investigating the problems of applying patterns in practical settings.

Chung et al. [5] evaluated the effectiveness of using patterns with designers in developing applications in the emerging field of ubiquitous computing. The designers were asked to design a location-enhanced application. One group had access to a set of patterns while the other did not. They concluded that experienced designers without patterns performed better than novice designers with patterns, i.e. patterns can not substitute experience, but that experienced designers (although not familiar with this particular domain) performed better when they had patterns available. Saponas et al. [7] investigated the use of patterns in early design activities with designers building a digital home application. The participants were split randomly into two groups and were asked to perform the same design task. Only one group was given access to the set of patterns with the help of a tool within a web browser. The study suggests that team members were able to use the patterns productively to generate new ideas and to exchange design ideas with each other. Furthermore, the designs of the patterns group had a lower mean number of heuristic violations than the control group, implying that the use of patterns promoted higher quality design products. Cowley and Wesson [9] compared patterns and guidelines based on the opinions of two groups of students, one using guidelines and the other patterns, to investigate the usefulness of patterns as a design aid. Based on initial analysis of the students' ratings of their opinion about patterns and guidelines, the authors concluded that designers consider patterns useful for design and an effective and efficient design aid. However, both patterns and guidelines groups felt equally positive in their intention for using them in future projects. Kotze et al. [18] examined the use of patterns and anti-patterns to teach HCI principles to two groups of students. The authors provide statistical results, from assessing the students, indicating that anti-patterns can be counter productive.

Our work can be regarded as a complementary approach to the ones described above. There are however, noticeable differences:

1. We are assessing completed web pages and sites instead of a prototyping task, working with a widely accepted web design tool.

2. We use a balanced set of patterns and guidelines providing a balanced body of knowledge to the two groups, thus allowing us to compare the effectiveness of the different formats.
3. We engage the subjects into a realistic course spread over a full semester of teaching.

3. Hypothesis

The main purpose of our study is to assess the effectiveness of patterns and guidelines on the design habits of novice designers. We follow a matched subjects design, studying web usability principles by means of either a set of patterns or an equivalent set of guidelines. The dependent variable is the scores of the students in a practical design test. Thus our hypothesis is:

H1: There is a difference between the performances of students taught usability principles using patterns, and students taught using guidelines.

The null hypothesis is then that:

H0: There is no significant difference between the performance of the students in the patterns and the guidelines groups.

4. Balancing Patterns and Guidelines for the Experiment

4.1   Patterns and Guidelines for the Study

Identifying a set of patterns and guidelines that could be implemented as an instructional tool for teaching design principles was critical to the success of our experiment. The following criteria were used for the selection:

1. Patterns and guidelines should be meaningful for the students, close to their technical level and experience, and appropriate to their particular level of knowledge;
2. Patterns and guidelines should be easy to apply in a web site design using existing basic technical web design skills.

Our patterns and guidelines are primarily derived from existing sources: Koyani et al.'s collection [19] for guidelines (hereafter Koyani's guidelines) and two widely known pattern languages [20, 21]. A quick review of the patterns that we considered for our experiment revealed that many of the patterns in these sources did not meet our criteria. Current patterns and pattern languages [20-22] contain many patterns that are complicated and address complex and high level design issues (e.g. e-commerce, site genres, trust and credibility, etc.). Novice designers do not possess the necessary technical knowledge and experience to apply these patterns in their design work, and such patterns deal with advanced issues that may only be clearly explored in large scale design tasks. Similar observations can be made about the available guidelines: although their complexity is somewhat lower than patterns, many are not suitable for a time limited experiment designed for a novice designer.

Another problem with existing sets of patterns and guidelines is the lack of consistency between them. This can be attributed to an existing gap between patterns and guidelines in their approach to design: patterns are used mostly as components to build web sites while guidelines as small pieces of prescriptive advice. Comparing, for example, the Koyani guidelines [19] with the currently developed pattern languages [20-22], we observed that only a small number of guidelines could be directly mapped to the existing patterns. A pattern sometimes contains advice that is spread across several guidelines.

Because of these difficulties, and in order to avoid complicated procedures of transforming patterns into guidelines or developing new patterns, with all the drawbacks that such a procedure would imply, we decided to form a body of usable guidelines complying with our criteria and then transform them into patterns, since it was easier to find guidelines that were addressing low level problems.

An additional complication in this experiment was the fact that the work was conducted in a Greek University, hence, since few HCI patterns are available in Greek, patterns and guidelines written in English required translation into Greek to make them accessible for the students.

4.2   Forming the Sets

We followed a stepwise approach of defining the set of patterns and guidelines for our experiment.

- *Step 1*: We initially collected all the patterns from the two pattern languages that met our criteria. There were not many. However we made sure that every pattern that could be used was included in the set. This set included only, what we name as, 'simple patterns' that could be directly mapped to a single guideline each. These patterns were then translated into Greek.
- *Step 2*: We selected a set of guidelines from the Koyani collection that was appropriate for our study. These were translated into Greek. The chosen set of Koyani's guidelines was transformed into a set of patterns using the format that we employed for this study. Some of the guidelines, relevant to a common design issue, were consolidated and formed a single pattern. We name patterns that correspond to more than one guideline as 'compound patterns'.
- *Step 3*: Once the set of patterns was finalised, patterns were transformed into guidelines. The patterns that were collected in step 1 were transformed into guidelines. For the rest of the patterns, since there were originated from guidelines the work involved for the transformation was minimal.

We examined all the information and advice included in each pattern and the corresponding guideline (or guidelines) to verify that equivalent information was being given.

4.3   Pattern Format

We chose to present our patterns in a format that would make balancing guidelines and patterns easy since we transformed guidelines to patterns. Also, the pattern format should be simple for the students to familiarize themselves with the pattern terminology, being introduced for the first time to the idea of patterns. The format is consistent with published formats for web design. We used mainly the formats from van Welie [21] and van Duyne et al. [20] pattern languages to structure our patterns. Patterns were presented in the following format: the name of the pattern; a picture as an example of its application; a section describing when the pattern is used; a short problem statement followed by a detailed description of the problem and the solution to the problem and the forces involved; the solution for the problem in a condensed statement; other patterns that may be taken into account; and finally more examples of the pattern.

Each pattern was formed by taking, to a great extent, the advice and examples given in each guideline and presented them in a pattern format. The advantage of this approach, in connection with the format adopted for patterns and guidelines, is that the basic content, narrative and examples, of the patterns and guidelines are equivalent. The only exception to this rule is the examples section where, in some cases in the 'more examples' section, more examples were included. This is a very distinctive feature of the pattern format and we followed this tradition of presenting patterns. Also, since patterns suggest the use of a pattern language, in each pattern, wherever applicable, in the relative section, links to other related patterns were given.

The patterns that were used for the study were simple. However, developing and implementing simple patterns, draw a parallel with the use of simple programming patterns, inspired by the success of Object Oriented Design (OOD) patterns [23]. OOD patterns focus on advanced software design problems with a target audience mostly designers and are used only in advanced design courses. More recently, related research [24-26] has been carried out into simple programming patterns that are being developed with intention to teach simple programming principles to computer science students. In a similar way, we introduce simple design patterns to teach usability principles and web design issues to novice designers.

4.4   Guideline Format

The format that guidelines were presented was adapted from Koyani's guideline format [19]. Essentially, all the information presented in the Koyani guidelines was included. The format consists of a heading-title for the guideline, the guideline itself followed by comments explaining why the guideline should be used and in some cases how it should be applied, and finally examples of the guidelines. The illustrations in the original guideline depicting bad or good examples of web designs were used. However, these examples were placed after the full set of guidelines, at the end of the booklet, as a set of examples about good design, each with the guideline title that the example refers to.

4.5   Refining the Sets

The patterns and guidelines evolved through two pilot studies [27-29] and several reviews with evaluators and experienced designers.

Some of the examples initially used for teaching were not successful in that they did not communicate the indented message to the students. After an extensive search through the Internet, focusing mainly on Greek sites, we were able to find successful and illustrative examples. Subsequently, we either included them in our collection or replaced the inappropriate ones.

Some of the patterns names and guidelines titles were changed to improve the students' understanding. We also added some patterns/guidelines, and modified the focus of others in ways that we believed would help students improve their design habits. These patterns/guidelines dealt with some of the most common mistakes that students made for example with text alignment, fonts and font sizes, links and underlined text.

4.6   The Final Set of Patterns and Guidelines for the Study

The final set formulated for the experiment was 35 guidelines and 25 patterns. Some patterns/guidelines that could not be directly implemented in the experimental design tests were included in the sets since they were considered essential for the overall training of student subjects as novice designers.

Table 1 depicts only the guidelines and the corresponding patterns that could be directly implemented and used by the students in the final design tasks (19 patterns and 29 guidelines). Column one identifies 7 broad categories of advice, these being: Home page; Page layout and Design; Navigation; Headings, Titles and Labels; Links; Text and Typography; and Lists. The second column gives the title for each pattern, and column three gives the title to the corresponding guideline or guidelines.

There were 15 'simple' patterns that could be mapped onto their equivalent 15 guidelines, 1 'compound' pattern that corresponded to 2 guidelines and finally 3 'compound' patterns that corresponded to sets of 4 guidelines each.

5.   The Experimental Study

5.1   Overview of the Experiment

We recruited a group of students and taught them web design from scratch using a widely used authoring tool. Once the tutorials about web design finished, a pre-treatment assignment was used to split the subjects into two balanced groups. Each group learned about usability and usability principles using either the set of patterns or the set of guidelines.

After this teaching, subjects engaged in two common activities professional designers are involved, that is designing and evaluating tasks. More qualitative data was also collected through interviews after completion of the task. This data will be reported elsewhere.

Table 1. *Categories, patterns and corresponding guidelines*

Category	Pattern Name	Guideline Title
Home Page	1. Home Page Link	1. Enable Access to the Homepage
	2. Home Page Length	2. Limit homepage length
Page Layout & Design	3. Consistent Important Items	3. Place important items consistently
	4. White Space	4. Use moderate white space
	5. Item Alignment	5. Align Items on a Page
Navigation	6. Users' Location	6. Provide Feedback on Users' Location
	7. Descriptive Tab Labels	7. Use descriptive tab labels
	8. Repeated Menu	8. Repeat Navigation at the Bottom of the Page
Headings, Titles & Labels	9. Nice Headings	9. Use Unique, Descriptive and Emphasized Headings
	10. Page Titles	10. Provide descriptive page titles
Links	11. Consistent and Descriptive Links	11. Provide links where users may need them 12. Match link names with destination pages 13. Ensure embedded links are descriptive 14. Designate used links
	12. Obvious Links - Consistent Links	15. Provide consistent clickability cues 16. Avoid misleading cues to click
	13. Clickable Images	17. Use Text for Links and Clickable Images
	14. To-the-Top Link	18. Allow Users to Go Back to the Top of the Page
Text & Typography	15. Consistency in Text	19. Ensure visual consistency 20. Format common items consistently 21. Use at least 12-point font 22. Use familiar fonts
	16. Visible Text	23. Use Black Text on Plain, High-Contrast Backgrounds
	17. Emphasized Text	24. Emphasize Importance in Text
	18. Aligned Text	25. Use Proper Alignment for Text
Lists	19. Lists	26. Display Related Items in Lists 27. Introduce Each List 28. Format Lists to Ease Scanning 29. Capitalize First Letter of First Word in Lists

5.2   Subject Groups

The participants for the study were students from the final year of Automation Department, TEI Piraeus, Greece. All of them had already completed three years of study, and they were quite skilful with the use of computers and familiar with internet related activities, but had not previously studied web design.

For the purposes of the experiment, a special course was scheduled for the first half of the Spring Semester 2006. The course included twenty-five plus hours of lectures and seminars about Web Design including the use of FrontPage, usability design principles and evaluation techniques. The course was set apart from any regular formal academic courses that the students were following, and had no affect on their marks.

Forty five volunteer students enrolled for the course. Three groups, with fifteen students in each group, were formed and tutorial sessions about web design techniques of two hours duration twice in a week were conducted. Throughout the course, several small assignments enabled the students to practice the techniques presented by the lessons taught. Every student was assigned to one computer, working on his/her own. We ensured that all students received sufficient training through practice by completing, to a great extent, all assignments during the tutorials.

5.3   Teaching Approach

Tutorials were conducted by the first author, while a technical assistant was present at all times to help with technical problems and the use of equipment (network, projector screen, etc.).

The tutorials introduced the use of tools and technical issues about web design. One of the tutorials was about general usability principles and evaluation of web sites. This tutorial was delivered before the pre-treatment assignment.

During the tutorials, we intentionally presented and practiced a certain number of design principles and design issues, using traditional teaching techniques without employing patterns or guidelines. That was deemed to be appropriate because we wanted students to advance with web design and to avoid making elementary usability mistakes. We made sure that students had time to practice and adopt these basic design practices found on all contemporary sites.

Apart from these design principles that were delivered to all students, the tutor would not directly suggest any quality or usability issues or how to make improvements to the appearance of a web page since that would directly interfere with quality and usability issues of web design with the individual student. Avoiding presenting advice and good practices about web design was a rule that was strictly followed during the tutorials, since advice and good practices were supposed to be delivered only during the patterns/guidelines lectures.

5.4   Pre - Treatment Assignment

Once the initial tutorials finished, a pre-treatment assignment was given to the students that required the design of a small but complete site. For simplicity, and in order to allow students to focus on major design issues rather than complex navigational schemes, the site was one level deep requiring only one main navigation menu. Each page of the web site was based on a fixed width template. This assignment was used as a criterion to split the students into two balanced groups with regards to their design ability and skills.

Based on their performance of the pre-treatment assignment, we categorized the students into 4 groups: adequate, good, very good and excellent. After that, using a stratified sampling, we divided the students into 2 balanced groups. In this way, one group was equivalent to the other with regards to their ability and knowledge about web design. For the final experiment one group would be exposed to usability issues using patterns and the other one using guidelines.

5.5   Teaching Patterns and Guidelines

The set of 35 guidelines and the equivalent set of 25 patterns, as discussed in Section 4, were presented to the two groups. Patterns were presented to one group and guidelines to the other. The students were given a booklet of 33 pages of either patterns or guidelines to use during the lecture and to study afterwards. The time needed to cover the set of guidelines and the equivalent set of patterns was 3 hours. The guidelines/patterns tutorial was given by an independent lecturer while the first author of this paper was acting as an observer. The duties of the observer were to make sure the lecturer did not favour patterns or guidelines and to make sure that every pre-planned aspect of the teaching process was covered.

Finally, a revision test was given to the students, in order to elicit at least a minimum degree of study and comprehension from the students. A two-page form, with a full list of the pattern names or guidelines titles that were presented in the class, was given to each student at the end of the tutorials. Students were asked to study patterns/guidelines and then describe, in their own words, the most essential and critical idea that was incorporated within each pattern/guideline. The forms were delivered, duly completed, either electronically or by hand before the beginning of the design tests.

5.6   Details of the Design Test

Out of the initial 45 students taking part in the experiment 39 participated in the design test: 19 in the patterns group and 20 in the guidelines group. There were three design test sessions, lasting 2 hours each. During the sessions, one more lecturer was present to assist with questions and problems that students faced during the task, taking notes while observing students and helping with the smooth process of the experiment.

To limit the possibilities of one student affecting or influencing another, computers and positions of the students were pre-arranged so that a student could only view his own screen. In that way, students were designing using their own ideas and inspiration.

The test was asking students to design a small one level deep web site about a small company hosting and creating web sites for its customers. The site contained five pages and students were required to work and design only the three pages of the site; the rest of the two pages were included in order to make the site conceptually complete and to oblige students to provide a more realistic navigation within the site. Each page of the site was based on a three-column fixed width page layout.

Furthermore in order to compare similar sites, and to avoid evaluating pages with different text and graphics resulting in dissimilar design approaches and formatting, the content, text, and photos/images were provided for each page. The use of a template and the partial model, although restricting the creativity of students, supported more consistent evaluations based on defined metrics. The metrics focussed on usability issues that patterns and guidelines dealt with.

A separate instructions sheet was given to each student. The inclusion of specific content together with the instructions given to the students invoked the use of patterns/guidelines presented during the tutorials, and allowed us to measure the impact patterns/guidelines had on their design products.

Students had to format text, pictures, specify the layout, identify and indicate links, provide a navigation scheme using interactive buttons, and in general design according to the instructions and the requirements given. In brief, students were expected to design as best as they could, in order to have the best possible presentation of the company on the Internet, taking into account the purpose and the type of the company, using the usability principles they have learned during the tutorials.

Students were advised not to use any other material apart from that provided already in the site, unless they felt compelled to. Each student had access to a small directory containing certain small images, arrows, bullets small gif files, etc.

Students were free to use their booklet of patterns and guidelines during the tasks. Also, they were allowed to ask any question about the use of tools or how to do certain things in case they had difficulties or they couldn't remember the right procedure. We wanted students to design what they envisioned and imagined and not to be affected by lack technical knowledge.

5.7   Scoring of the Students

The evaluation of the subjects' designs was conducted by independent evaluators, using a predetermined set of metrics. Each metric corresponds to one of the patterns (and the matched guideline or guidelines) that were presented to the students. This set of metrics measures the degree to which they followed design principles and advice given by the patterns/guidelines used in the tutorial. Some of our metrics are broken down into sub-components, or sub-metrics, in order to make the task of scoring easier for the evaluators.

Table 2. *Example of a metric*

Metric Name: N5_HoPaLink	Is there a home link on every page? Do they use the logo as a link to home page? Or probably any appropriate labels (e.g. 'Home')
Protocol	Review all pages and check if there is a home link on every page. The Home Page itself should count as one of the pages.
Scores	If a link to the Home page exists in every page score =4; in 2 pages score=2; in any 1 page score=1; Otherwise score=0. Max Score=4.

Each metric was accompanied by a small explanation giving details regarding scoring and how the evaluator should proceed using the metric. Table 2 depicts one metric with the specific instructions for pattern 'Home Page Link' and the matched guideline 'Enable Access to the Homepage'.

Each metric score contributes equally to the score of the student. A score from 0 to 9 shows the conformity and application of the patterns/guidelines to the site. For some metrics, a different scale was used in order to facilitate the work of the evaluators. However, at the end all scores were converted to scores in 0-9 scale.

Three independent evaluators (academics with web design experience) were used to view and assess the students' sites according to the predefined set of metrics. Each evaluator spent on average 55 minutes for each site to make an evaluation based on the set of metrics; however the actual time to administer the whole evaluation process was much longer. Most of the times the evaluator worked better if he judged all the sites together working just on one only metric and comparing each page with another one.

The default web page browser on the student's PC was MS Internet Explorer v.6.0.2. An Internet Explorer engine based type browser (Slim Browser V4.06) with multi tab functionality was used by the evaluators. Tabs allow the user to view multiple web pages in the same window and to switch between the web pages with ease and comfort without the need to open a new browser window. The evaluators could afford to open all the pages of the site at the same time or to load a particular page from all students on the same unique browser window. In that way previewing, checking, and comparing web sites and pages was straight forward and evaluation was taking less time.

After the collection of the scores there was a review of the scores with all the members of the team and some errors that were found on the scores were corrected.

6. Results of the Design Test

6.1 Analysis of the Evaluation Scores

Using the quantitative measures of the three evaluators, we statistically analyzed the performance of the two groups. Students were assessed using the metrics in 7 different dimensions-components of good design practice: Home page; Page layout and Design; Navigation; Headings, Titles and Labels; Links; Text and Typography; Lists.

Table 3. *Average percentage scores of students*

	Home Page	Page Layout & Design	Navigation	Headings, Titles & Labels	Links	Text & Typography	Lists
Guidelines	59.8	81.2	67.9	65.1	50.8	85.5	49.4
Patterns	66.4	85.0	81.5	79.1	64.3	86.4	39.8
Difference	6.6	3.8	13.6	14.0	13.5	0.9	-9.7

Table 3 shows the differences between the calculated average scores of the students, in the two groups, for each of the seven measured categories. The average scores are given as an average percentage score, where 100 denotes the maximum that could be achieved for the category. Evidently students in the patterns groups performed better overall. Their scores were higher in six out of the seven categories; in the Links category the guidelines group scored better.

The main purpose of the experiment was to assess the effectiveness of patterns and guidelines on the design habits of novice designers. To address this question we compare scores from the 2 groups reflecting the application of usability principles that were conveyed using the two formats (treatments). The dependent variable is the scores of the students. The score for each participant was obtained by adding the points for each metric. Each metric contributed equally to the score. The null hypothesis, as described in Section 3, is that there is no difference in the performance of the groups.

An independent samples t-test (2-tailed) was conducted to test the hypothesis. The patterns group (M=128.97, SD= 20.16) performed better than the guidelines group (M=116.25, SD=13.66), T(37) =2.317, P=0.0261. Since the computed P-value is less than 0.05, we can reject the null hypothesis in favour of the alternative and accept that there was a statistically significant difference between the two groups in applying the advice, knowledge and experience conveyed by patterns and guidelines.

The combined scores of the three judges (average score for the particular metric), were used for this analysis. Actually, there were few differences in the scores of the evaluators, and a t-test performed for each individual judge produces similar results, i.e. the null hypothesis is rejected.

6.2   Subjective and Objective Metrics

Our metrics can be classified as being objective or subjective. Objective metrics, for example, are those measuring the application of guidelines like 'Provide descriptive page titles', 'Allow users to go back to the top of the page', 'Repeat navigation at the bottom of the page', etc. For the objective metrics all evaluators should be able to give the same scores.

Subjective metrics are those that produce a score depending, to a certain extent, on the judgement of each evaluator. Subjective metrics provide a measure of the application for guidelines like 'Use Moderate White Space', 'Provide Feedback on Users' Location', 'Emphasize Importance', etc.

We used the subjective metrics to produce a separate comparison of the performance between the two groups of students.

Employing an independent samples t-test (2-tailed), the patterns group (M=56.89, SD=14.82) was better than the guidelines group (M=47.61, SD=9.88), T(37) =2.313, P=0.0264.

The computed P-value is less than 0.05, indicating that there was a statistically significant difference between the two groups in favour of the patterns group.

7. Summary and Further Work

We conducted an extensive study in teaching web design with the help of patterns and guidelines. We developed two equivalent sets of web patterns and web guidelines for novice users. We also developed suitable teaching material based on the sets and used them in two pilot studies and one main experimental study. The teaching material and the set of patterns and guidelines were adapted from existing patterns and guidelines. The teaching material can be used to form the basis for teaching design principles and usability to novice designers.

Both sets were simple enough for the students to understand and, what was more important the students had the means and the technical knowledge to fully employ them in order to design a real web site in electronic form using FrontPage. The performance of the students in the patterns group was better than that in the guidelines group, in all but one category, and the overall scores of the students in the patterns group was better that the students in the guidelines group. The difference in the overall scores was statistically significant.

The comparison was based on the ratings of three independent evaluators who used the predefined set of metrics to compare the designs. What is more important is that a comparison made using only the subjective metrics shows that the patterns group performed also significantly better.

All the statistical analysis of the quantitative data that was performed through t-tests and all results indicate that the use of patterns can lead to better performance for novice designers than the use of guidelines and that patterns can have a stronger impact, provided they address design issues close to the level of experience of the students.

Future analysis of the available data could also take into account the scores of the students in the pre-test experiment, so that a comparison between high performing and low performing students can be made. At the same time, analysis of the qualitative data that we have collected through questionnaires and interviews, during the experiment, will complement our quantitative analysis and will shed more light into the effectiveness of patterns and guidelines for novice designers.

We could also look into the effect of compound and simple patterns on the design habits of students. First indication is that the impact of compound patterns is less significant, suggesting that compound patterns are close to the cognitive limitation of novice designers, that is they offer too much knowledge and advice that probably do not create a clear picture of all the usability issues involved.

References

1. M. van Welie, G. van der Veer, and A. Eliëns, Patterns as Tools for User Interface Design, in: *International Workshop on Tools for Working with Guidelines*, edited by C. Farenc and J. Vanderdonckt, (Springer-Verlag, London, 2000), pp. 313-324.
2. M. Mahemoff and L.J. Johnston, Usability Pattern Languages: the "Language" Aspect, in: *Human-Computer Interaction, INTERACT '01*, edited by M. Hirose, (IOS Press, Amsterdam, 2001), pp. 350-358.

3. L. Pemberton and R.N. Griffiths, Don't Write Guidelines Write Patterns! (cited 2006-12-22); http://www.it.bton.ac.uk/staff/lp22/guidelinesdraft.html, (no date).
4. J. Nielsen, Durability of Usability Guidelines, (cited 2006-10-21); http://www.useit.com/alertbox/20050117.html (2005).
5. E.S. Chung, J.I. Hong, J. Lin, M.K. Prabaker, J.A. Landay, and A.L. Liu, Development and evaluation of emerging design patterns for ubiquitous computing, in: *Across the Spectrum: Designing Interactive Systems, DIS2004*, (ACM, New York, 2004), pp. 233-242.
6. J.A. Borchers, *A Pattern Approach to Interaction Design* (John Wiley, Chichester, UK, 2001).
7. T.S. Saponas, M.K. Prabaker, G.D. Abowd, and J.A. Landay, The impact of pre-patterns on the design of digital home applications, in: *Designing Interactive Systems, DIS 2006*, (ACM, New York, 2006), pp.189-198.
8. J. Wesson and N.L.O. Cowley, Designing with patterns: Possibilities and pitfalls, in: *Proceedings of the 2nd Workshop on Software and Usability Cross-Pollination: The Role of Usability Patterns, INTERACT 2003*, edited by M. Rauterberg, M. Menozzi and J. Wesson, (IOS Press, 2003).
9. N.L.O. Cowley and J.L. Wesson, An experiment to measure the usefulness of patterns in the interaction design process, in: *Lecture Notes in Computer Science 3585 - Human-Computer Interaction - INTERACT 2005*, edited by M.F. Costabile and F. Paternó, (Springer, 2005), pp. 1142-1145.
10. J.A. Borchers, Teaching HCI Design Patterns: Experience from Two University Courses, Position paper for *Patterns in Practice workshop at CHI 2002*, (cited 2007-01-22); http://www.hcipatterns.org/tiki-download_file.php?fileId=19, (2002).
11. A. Seffah, Learning the ropes: human-centered design skills and patterns for software engineers' education, *Interactions*, 10(**5**), 36-45 (2003).
12. R.N. Griffiths and L. Pemberton, Teaching Usability Design Through Pattern Language, (cited 2006-10-25); http://www.it.bton.ac.uk/staff/lp22/CHIpaper.html, (no date).
13. K.P. Laakso, A. Saura, and S.A. Laakso, Pattern Languages for Interaction Design, Position paper for *CHI 2000 Workshop Pattern Languages for Interaction Design*, (cited 2006-11-19); http://www.cs.helsinki.fi/u/salaakso/patterns/, (2000).
14. A. Dearden, J. Finlay, E. Allgar, and B. McManus, Using Pattern Languages in Participatory Design, in: *Proceedings of the Participatory Design Conference 2002*, edited by T. Binder, J. Gregory, and I. Wagner, (CPSR, Palo Alto, CA, 2002), pp. 104-113.
15. A. Dearden, J. Finlay, L. Allgar, and B. McManus, Evaluating pattern languages in participatory design, in: *Adjunct Proceedings of CHI 2002*, (ACM Press, New York, USA, 2002), pp. 664-665.
16. J. Finlay, E. Allgar, A. Dearden, and B. McManus, Pattern Languages in Participatory Design, in: *People and Computers XVI-Memorable Yet Invisible, Proceedings of HCI2002*, edited by X. Faulkner, J. Finlay, and F. Detienne, (Springer-Verlag, London, 2002), pp. 159–174.
17. A. Dearden and J. Finlay, Patterns Languages in HCI: A Critical Review, *Human-Computer Interaction*, 21(**1**), 40-101 (2006).
18. P. Kotzé, K. Renaud, and J. Van Biljon, *Don't do this - Pitfalls in using anti-patterns in teaching human-computer interaction principles*, Computers & Education, DOI: http://dx.doi.org/10.1016/j.compedu.2006.10.003, (2006).
19. S.J. Koyani, R.W. Bailey, and J.R. Nall, *Research-Based Web Design & Usability Guidelines* (Computer Psychology, USA, 2004).
20. D.K. Van Duyne, J. Landay, and J.I. Hong, *The Design of Sites* (Addison-Wesley, Boston, MA, 2003).
21. M. Van Welie, Patterns in Interaction Design, (cited 2006 09-14); http://www.welie.com/, (2005).

22.I. Graham, *A Pattern Language for Web Usability* (Addison-Wesley, London, 2003).

23.E. Gamma, R. Helm, R. Johnson, and J. Vlissides, *Design Patterns: Elements of Reusable Object-Oriented Software* (Addison-Wesley, Reading, MA, USA, 1994).

24.J. Bergin, Coding at the Lowest Level - Coding Patterns for Java Beginners, (cited 2006-07-15); http://pclc.pace.edu/~bergin/patterns/codingpatterns.html, (2006).

25.O. Muller, B. Haberman, and H. Averbuch, (An almost) pedagogical pattern for pattern-based problem-solving instruction, in: *Proceedings of the 9th Annual SIGCSE Conference on Innovation and Technology in Computer Science Education*, (ACM, NY, USA, 2004), pp. 102–106.

26.O. Muller, Pattern oriented instruction and the enhancement of analogical reasoning, in: *Proceedings of the 2005 International Workshop on Computing Education Research* (ACM, NY, 2005), pp. 57-67.

27.K. Koukouletsos, B. Khazaei, A. Dearden, and D.I. Tseles, Comparing patterns and guidelines in web design, in: *Proceedings of the 1st International Scientific Conference eRA2006*, (cited 2006-03-25); http://ikaros.teipir.gr/era/ab1.htm, (Tripolis, Greece, 2006).

28.P. Kotzé, K. Renaud, K. Koukouletsos, B. Khazaei, and A. Dearden, Patterns, Anti-Patterns and Guidelines–Effective Aids to Teaching HCI Principles?, in: *Inventivity: Teaching theory, design and innovation in HCI, Proceedings of HCIEd2006,* edited by E.T. Hvannberg, J.C. Read, L. Bannon, P. Kotzé, and W. Wong, Limerick, Ireland, (2006), pp. 115-120.

29.K. Koukouletsos, Evaluating the effectiveness of guidelines and patterns for web design, in: *Proceedings of HCI2005: The Bigger Picture, Volume 2,* edited by L. MacKinnon, O.W. Bertelsen, and N. Bryan-Kinns, (BCS, 2005), pp. 209-211.

Enhancing Creativity in Interaction Design: Alternative Design Brief

Corina Sas and Alan Dix

Computing Department, Lancaster University, InfoLab21, South Drive,
Lancaster, LA1 4WA, UK
{corina, dixa}@comp.lancs.ac.uk

Abstract. This paper offers a critique of the design brief as it is currently used in teaching interaction design and proposes an alternative way of developing it. Such a design brief requires the exploration of alternative application domains for an already developed technology. The paper presents a case study where such a novel type of design brief has been offered to the students taking part in a collaborative design project and discusses how it supported divergent thinking and creativity as well as helped enhancing the learning objectives.

1 Introduction

The importance of design brief on the entire design cycle cannot be overstated. This paper advocates that alternative ways of writing a design brief can support creative thinking which in turn contributes to better design outcomes. The proposed design brief encourages the exploration of new application domains for an already developed technology. Through addressing some of the limitations of the traditional design brief, it contributes to the improvement of teaching and learning interaction design. The presented case study is focused on a collaborative design project module delivered to Master students enrolled in a Human–Computer Interaction (HCI) program.

The paper starts by outlining the challenges of teaching interaction design. This is followed by an introduction of the concept of design brief together with the main limitations of its current format that has been traditionally used in interaction design education. From these limitations, an alternative way of preparing a design brief is proposed. The case study offers a detailed description of the proposed design brief together with an in depth reflection on its benefits among which the exploration of design space is particularly highlighted.

Please use the following format when citing this chapter:

Sas, C. and Dix, A., 2009, in IFIP International Federation for Information Processing, Volume 289; *Creativity and HCI: From Experience to Design in Education*; Paula Kotzé, William Wong, Joaquim Jorge, Alan Dix, Paula Alexandra Silva; (Boston: Springer), pp. 175–188.

2   Teaching Interaction Design

Interaction design is primarily a creative process which despite the efforts made to explore it, raises significant questions, i.e., the strategies involved in complex and ill-defined problems, the trade-off between conflicting design constraints, or the nature of creative insight and how it can be replicated and supported. It is this limited understanding that leads to difficulties in teaching interaction design. The challenges of teaching design can be seen throughout the entire design process, starting from problem specification, continuing with the relevant feedback that the students need to receive, and not at least relating to the assessment of design-related activities and their outcomes [1].

2.1   Challenges

This section highlights three main challenges related to teaching/learning interaction design which focus on the tension between ambiguity and structure within the problem specification, on the temporality of the relevant feedback that the students need to receive, e.g. continual/continuous feedback; and on the objectivity of design assessment, both in terms of design outcomes and design process.

Problem specification in the context of interaction design brings into attention aspects like ambiguity and structure. While educators try to provide just enough details to leave room for the exploration of the design space, students prefer a more articulated and structured problem definition [2]. This tension is generated by students' limited ability to handle less structured tasks. However, the skill to formulate problems precedes and is at least as important as the one of finding solutions. Unfortunately, in today's higher education, the emphasis is almost entirely placed on problem solving skills, while significantly less efforts have been made to ensure the acquisition of problem formulation skills [3]. From our experience of teaching interaction design, even graduate students are often less prepared for this challenge; it is a skill to be learned.

Setting the problem is needed not only during the initial stage of the design process since its iterative nature requires continuous reformulation and restructuring of the problem all along the design cycle [4, 5]. Ultimately, problem specification challenges the educator to decide what the right level of detail is.

Students' learning can hardly progress without efficient feedback. However, providing relevant feedback during the design process is a challenging endeavor which relates both to its timely quality [4] and feedback content [6]. The former refers not only to the continual feedback throughout the design process, but also to the continuous feedback during the critical phases of the design cycle. In order to provide efficient and timely design guidance, the educators need to be involved in the critical decision points along the entire design process. This is usually not a trivial task since in order to progress efficiently students need to show initiative to organize their work within and mostly *outside* the mentoring sessions [6].

The difficulty of objectively assessing the quality of design outcomes represents another challenge in teaching design which impacts also on the quality and content of the educator's feedback. This is due mainly to the difficulty of evaluating any design outcomes as being right or wrong since the design decisions that have to be made will always leave unexplored a multitude of options against which the current outcome can never be compared [6]. Of course, several prototypes can be evaluated through user trails and compared against each other but this is not enough to claim that a particular design is the best that can be produced. The evaluation of the design process (as opposed to design outcomes) is even more problematic, if one wants to go beyond the design stages and wishes to explore the considered design options and the rationale for deciding which one has been followed. The breadth and depth of the design space exploration usually goes against the limited resources of the design project. In addition, there is no current methodology that can account for the insightful conversion of a set of design constraints into affordances.

The importance that we choose to pay to the design brief is due to the fact that the design brief ultimately dictates how the design process is going to unfold. Given their significance, it is surprising how little work has focused on how design briefs should be prepared. The few attempts in this direction usually come from industrial arena and are introduced in the following section.

2.2 Professional vs. Academic Design Brief

Design briefs represent concise descriptions of a required design task. The briefs offer information on the design problem and its context, and require engagement in creative problem solving activities with the purpose of providing solutions for the design problem. The key element of the design briefs developed for educational purposes, e.g. interaction design programmes, is the provision of just enough structure which should enable a strong focus on the design process and students' reflection on it, rather than on the design outcomes.

On the other hand, the design briefs developed in business & industrial sector (professional design briefs) focus mainly on the expected outcomes of the design, while supporting the comprehensive understanding of the problem that needs to be solved [7]. Therefore, the design brief should consist of a thorough presentation of the problem, together with the expected outcomes of design, and it should answer questions such as:

- Why are we doing this project?
- Why are we doing it now?
- What specific outcomes are to be expected?
- Who are we designing for?
- Who are the key stakeholders in this project?
- What are the phases of this design project?
- How much time must be devoted to each phase?
- Who will approve the final design solution?
- What criteria will be used for this approval?
- How will the design solution be implemented?
- How will the results be measured?

The above questions could provide also a template for writing design briefs in the academic arena. In fact, some of the details offered by the answers to these questions are usually included in the narrative of a design brief. For example, below are outlined the core ideas of the briefs from the CHI Student Design Competition for the last three years:

- Design a service to promote the use of public transit (CHI 2007).
- Design a service for personal monitoring of diet, exercise and health for individuals (CHI 2006).
- Design a tool, application or service for elder companionship (CHI 2005).

These examples reflect the standard format of the design brief written for teaching/learning purposes. This consists mainly of the design problem that outlines the motivation for finding an adequate solution to address it [8, 9, 10]. Within this format, the students are given a real life topic with its own affordances and constraints and are asked to design a suitable system to address the proposed topic. While widely accepted, this type of design brief has several limitations, as identified during our experience of mentoring collaborative design projects of Master students enrolled in a HCI program.

a) Generic problems like the ones presented above are challenging since the design space could be extremely large. While students feel comfortable in exploring it, they usually lack the skills of narrowing down the problem in order to confine it to a limited range of constraints and affordances. In other words, a lot of time and effort is spent in redefining and narrowing the problem at the expense at the time needed to find alternative solutions for the identified problem. Consequently, once the problem is defined in more concrete terms, the students prefer to go ahead to refine the first acceptable option with little interest in further exploring alternative solutions.

b) Following from the above limitation, such a design brief is always at risk of providing not enough structure. In a generic problem there appears to be a challenge in providing the right level of detail.

c) The inefficient exploration of the design space can also act as a barrier for student creativity, divergent thinking and problem solving, since more time is spent in narrowing down the generic problem rather than exploring creative solutions to the design problems.

d) The time constraints that impact on any design project dictate that for a ten week-project after exploring the design space, narrowing the problem and working on the conceptual design, little time is left for prototyping the solution. Therefore, the students do not progress much in refining their ideas, and usually stop at low fidelity prototypes, e.g. paper prototypes.

e) Another limitation relates to the relevant aspect of feedback that the students need from their educators both in terms of its quality and timely characteristic.

f) The assessment of the quality of design outcomes is a major challenge in teaching design [5]. The problems relate to the rather large design space which is usually limitedly and unsystematically explored within student projects [6]. One way to address these limitations, besides a rigorous management of the time schedule, is through exploring alternative types of design briefs.

2. 3   Proposed Design Brief

We propose a design brief which requires students to find new ways of using an already developed technology. In other words, the focus is placed on finding *a problem* for a given solution rather than finding solutions for a given problems. Although this approach is currently used in industry, its role in teaching and learning design has not been explored.

The proposed design brief may sound just like technology- or business-driven design, which is normally denigrated within the HCI community. Perhaps because of this, the more positive uses of a technology focus are often missed. In a poorly conceived business-driven design which attempts to identify new markets for a particular technology, the technology on offer is foisted on to a user group without regard to its appropriateness to their needs. It is certainly true that technology should always match the user needs. However, it is not necessary that this is achieved by starting from needs and progressing to appropriate technology. In our case, we are using the technology to seek for potential design settings where such a match between needs and technology exists. It is simply the case that the order is reversed.

The following section offers a description of a case study where the new type of design brief has been offered to students taking a collaborative design project module.

3   Case Study

3.1   Study Module

The Collaborative Design Project (CDP) module is part of a Master by Research (MRes) program which represents a collaborative initiative between the departments of Psychology and Computing at Lancaster University. The overall program focuses on the development of research skills in designing and evaluating interactive systems. The program runs for a small group of students, e.g. less than a dozen, who are usually highly motivated, sometimes with couple of years of industrial experience, and with educational backgrounds in Psychology, Computer Science, Information Technology and sometimes Arts. This is a fortunate mixture which resembles some of the multidisciplinary nature of real design teams.

Within this program, the CDP focuses on collaborative design of an interactive system. It is a compulsory module which runs for 10 weeks and worth 10% of the degree. This CDP module is structured to support a constructivist approach to learning [7]. While mainly a collaborative project-based learning, e.g. students usually work in groups of three or four with mixed educational backgrounds, the CDP module presents also some elements of problem-based learning.

By the end of the module, students produce low fidelity prototypes or simulations rather than working prototypes. The assessment procedure involves three tasks: two individual reports in which students reflect on the design outcome and the collaborative nature of the design process respectively. In addition they have to prepare a website and a poster that needs to be explained to a panel of experts during group presentation.

3.2   Proposed Design Brief

We experimented with the new type of design brief in the 2005-2006 academic year. Below is an excerpt of the design brief:

> *This design project will focus on the technology developed in the "Pin and Play" project running in Computing Department (http://ubicomp.lancs.ac.uk/pin&play/overview.html). The latter focuses on developing a general architecture for constructing physical interfaces that can be ad hoc composed and adapted by their users.*
>
> *Your task is to explore alternative, innovative ways of exploiting this technology, through a set of applications, others than those already developed within this project. For this, you are expected to generate a large pool of possible applications. After their evaluation, you will select couple of them and designed them in greater details. The mains constraints are defined by the technology already developed.*
>
> *You will be working in two groups, each group involving participants with psychology and computer science background to enrich the pool of group resources. Each team will focus on a different theme, targeting two different dimensions of human activity. One group will search for applications aimed towards supporting work, e.g. probably in office environment but not only, while the other team will try to design applications supporting play, e.g. in indoor public spaces but not only. The teams will collaborate, in terms of evaluating each other's design outcomes.*

The rationale for choosing the Pin and Play technology relates to its versatility, since this technology gradually became a growing toolkit for exploring tangible interactive surfaces. A brief description of this technology is outlined below.

Pin and Play is characterized by an augmented surface, which provides data connectivity and tangible interactive artifacts that can be added to or removed from the surface. When an artifact is added, it becomes connected, acquires a digital representation and can be manipulated while it is on the surface, providing thus a link between the digital and the physical worlds. The surface provides the connectivity and the physical support to enable this.

4   Discussion

The design process entailed by the proposed brief consists of three phases. This section describes in details each phase together with its outcomes and benefits.

The Phase I involved intense collaboration between students and the researchers in the department involved in the development of Pin and Play technology. The opportunity to enter into a dialog with these researchers ensured students' access to first hand knowledge and experience. They learned to ask the right questions in order to develop a thorough understanding of the system.

Apart from engaging in a dialog with the researchers developing Pin and Play, the students also had the opportunity to play around with the system itself. This experiential component [9, 11, 12] added significant value by enriching students' knowledge of the system functionalities, constraints, affordances as well as look and feel. In addition, the tangible dimension of Pin and Play itself added value to this experience.

Through this process of inquiry and experiential learning, the students identified a large set of constraints related to system functionality. The thorough understanding of the Pin and Play system allowed students to identify a set of the system constraints which is outlined below.

- Maximum number of components that can be used simultaneously
- Component operations and delays
- Grouping components
- Mapping components to actions
- Transitioning on knobs/sliders
- Size of the fabric
- Short circuits
- Spatial awareness
- Prongs and safety
- Power requirements
- Data transfer
- Miscellaneous

The identification of constraints took place alongside with a literature review activity. For this, each group put together a list of academic papers to ensure that the most important areas to focus on are well represented, and to avoid any duplication of efforts that otherwise may occur. Subsequently, each student reviewed three papers and entered the reviews on the group website, thus making his/her work available to the other members of the group. During the literature review, students experienced a first recognition of the user needs as captured within the literature review.

Once the constraints were identified and the state-of-the-art explored, the students started to engage in the development of a large pool of ideas. Thus, by the end of week five, i.e., half way within the project cycle, each group produced around 20 conceptual designs as alternative ways in which Pin and Play technology could be used. This was an important step within the design cycle that lasted almost three weeks. The ideas were developed as conceptual designs, each with several low details paper prototypes. During this phase, the students succeeded in developing ideas that indicate a broad exploration of the design space. This could only be possible through intense divergent thinking (Fig. 1).

Indeed, brainstorming sessions were particularly encouraged at this stage, which represented the most exploratory stage of the design process. This initial phase was the least constrained one (and arguably the most creative), since the creative process being has focused on the ill-defined problem without any attempt of assessing the ideas.

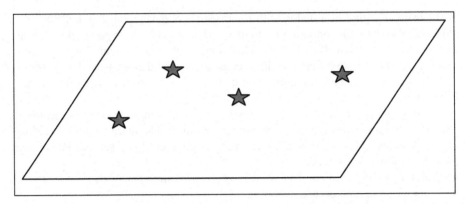

Fig. 1. *The Phase I of the design cycle involved a broad exploration of the design space. The stars represent the explored ideas in different areas of the design space*

The explored dimensions associated with the conceptual designs are outlined below. This presentation starts with the conceptual designs and prototypes developed by the group focused on identifying application domains to support *work* activities.

- Supporting collaborative tasks like information retrieval, participatory design, or ontology building.
- Supporting fluid interactions between digital and physical artifacts in applications like tangible desk or customizable mouse.
- Supporting exploration of the physicality for multiple selection tasks like order interface of assembly line-style sushi bar, or dynamic timeline wall.
- Mapping for navigating at ease around a map to be used as an educational tool, or for crime investigation.
- Supporting scheduling like Outlook/iCal assistant, and collaborative notice board.
- Supporting security like secure door entry, or tangible safe.
- Exploring graphic/sound aid in the form of photo filter tool, or garage production studio.

Below are the conceptual designs and prototypes developed by the group focused on identifying application domains to support *play, fun, learning and entertainment*.

- Simulations of real world systems like dress selector, 3D outfit, board game interface or garden design.
- Educational support like electronic circuit game, pin doctor.
- Language development like language education board, spatial sound board.
- Domestic control tools.
- Interactive games like hangman game, pin potato head or customizable pin and playball game.
- Multiplayer games like pin & fight, multiplayer etch a sketch.
- Memory based games like "PinPlay says" or safe cracker game.

To summarize, the main dimensions within the design space that have been covered are the following:

- use of Pin and Play for both individual and collaborative tasks;

- use of the fabric of Pin and Play both in the traditional two dimensions as well as in three dimensions;
- use of Pin and Play both in stationary and dynamic/mobile way; and
- use the spatial awareness which Pin and Play empowers its users with.

In this way, the main outcome of the Phase I consists of identifying system constraints, the main dimensions of the design space and the large pool of ideas exploring the design space in the forms of seven conceptual designs with three prototypes each as alternative applications for Pin and Play. The major benefit of this Phase consists of encouraging students' divergent thinking in exploring broadly the design space.

Phase II can be viewed as a breaking point between the other two phases since it requires students to stop and assess their work before moving forward with an in-depth exploration of the design space. Thus, once the conceptual designs/prototypes were developed the Phase II involved their assessment.

The main outcomes of this phase consisted of a list of criteria developed for assessing the conceptual designs and their associated prototypes. For this, each group has prepared a leaflet where one page was dedicated to each conceptual design or prototype. The criteria outlined below were proposed by the students and refined with input from the course tutor.

- Functionality.
- Information and clarity of the concept.
- Integration between the conceptual design and the user goals.
- Successful exploration of the haptic and tangible aspects of the system.
- Originality and novelty.
- Overall satisfaction.

The assessment was carried out in week 5 by a team of academic staff and researchers in the department and has led to the identification of a winner conceptual design (Fig. 2).

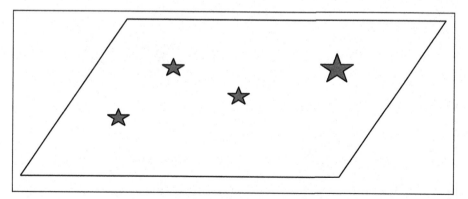

Fig. 2. *The Phase II of the design cycle enables the identification of the conceptual design that successfully meets the assessment criteria. The larger star represents the conceptual design selected among the competing ones.*

The benefits of the developed criteria consist of making the selection phase more objective which in the end also helped the assessment/marking process for this module. Through engaging students in formulating the assessment criteria they became involved in critical reflection and in a movement from the mere "I like it" to an understanding of the dimensions of the problem space. This is in itself a significant and often neglected aspect of design.

Phase III consisted in refining the selected conceptual design and its associated prototype. The main outcomes of this phase are encapsulated in students' final prototypes.

One group produced a video prototype which outlined a complete game scenario involving a doll, pins and other artifacts as physical prototypes. In the PinDoctor application which is a tangible medical game, the child plays the role of a doctor whose task is to diagnose and treat the patient: a doll made of the fabric of Pin and Play. The interactive component embedded in the game allows the doctor to play with various types of pins for performing medical tasks, e.g. injecting drugs, sampling blood. The pins inserted into the patient fabric could be consequently used to perform two functions. One is to provide diagnostic information such as temperature or heart rate (Fig. 3). The other is to provide treatment through administering medicine. The pins change their state as the game progresses and the feedback is provided by sounds from the doll and through the visual information from GUI. Particular emphasis is placed on the sequence of events, e.g. diagnosis of symptom and treatment, and the spatial location of action, e.g. if a drip is administered in the correct location.

Fig. 3. *PinDoctor physical prototype*

The other group produced a working prototype which required understanding the code behind the Pin and Play and the ability to integrate new code in the existing system. Pin & Search is a tangible collaborative tool for information retrieval aiming to offer a standard interface outputting search results from a database people wish to search from. Initially a number of keywords are entered into the system, printed on cards and associated with pins. Consequently, when a tagged pin is entered into the fabric of a collaborative board, the search starts. It can be changed as pins are added on or removed from the fabric. The search results are displayed on a screen located alongside the collaborative board, and they can be further manipulated through the use of navigation controls.

This depth in the design cycle has not been previously reached by the former cohorts of students exposed to the traditional design brief (who usually stopped at the level of paper prototyping). This outlines the benefit of this phase which enabled a thorough exploration of the design space. Such exploration has been possible due to the stronger starting point, i.e., an already developed technology rather than an abstract idea (Fig. 4).

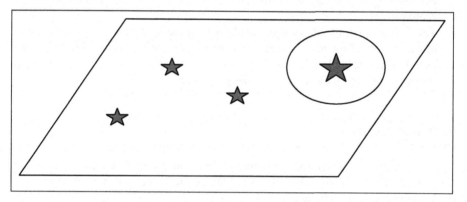

Fig. 4. *The Phase III of the design cycle enables an in-depth exploration of the design space in the area around the conceptual design selected in Phase II.*

It is indeed, the exploration of design space that represents the main advantage of this type of design project. The traditional design brief can be summarized as follows:

Generic Problem →
    Specific problem →
        Brief exploration of solutions →
            Selection of technology →
                Prototyping a solution.

The proposed design brief can be represented like:

Existing Technology →
    Understanding the technology →
        Exploration of how it can be used→
            Choosing "a problem" →
                Prototyping a solution.

Whereas the greater amount of time in the first case is spent on specifying the problem, the second case allows the greater amount of time to be spent on the exploration of alternative ways of using the technology and prototyping the chosen solution. This exploration ensures a broad coverage of the design space, whereas the work on prototyping the selected solution ensures an in-depth exploration of the design space.

To summarize, the main outcomes of this case study that enriched students learning experience consists of:

- The acquisition of a set of transferable skills for inquiring the developers about the existing technology.
- The thorough knowledge about this technology which led to a comprehensive set of constraints.
- The development of skills required to elaborate a list of criteria that supports the objective evaluation of the conceptual designs, as well as the transparent assessment of the entire module.
- The development of knowledge and skills required to produce a large number of conceptual designs, e.g. seven for each group with 2-3 sketched prototypes for each concept.
- The development of knowledge and skills required to produce a refined version of the prototype for the selected conceptual design, e.g. a video and a working prototype respectively.
- Enhanced creativity throughout the design process.

5   Conclusions

Each of the design challenges of teaching interaction design that were identified in first section are revisited below and suggestions are made into how the proposed design brief can address them.

The replacement of a generic problem with an already developed technology offers a different starting point in exploring the design space. Rather than having an abstract idea, students are faced with a tangible working system. The concreteness of an existing system is an advantage that cannot be surpassed by a design brief that is purely imagined.

The time budget can be better used for generating and assessing multiple solutions rather than stopping after the first one has been found.

This type of brief, particularly when the technology proposed has been developed in the department offers additional benefits. It allows students' access to an ongoing departmental project which enables the development of transferable skills, such as scientific inquiry, building on research expertise, and communication skills. In this way, the students benefit from more mentoring, both from the module tutor and from the research team involved in developing the existing technology. Thus, the amount of feedback that they receive along the design cycle is substantial. In other words, this type of brief enables students' access to a community of practice [11, 12], namely the one in the department.

The proposed design brief supports transparency and objectivity in assessing students' work, through facilitating students' involvement in developing assessment criteria.

The proposed brief can be seen as part of a larger family of approaches to design, those involving the ready to use technology from the very beginning of the design process. This allows for a strong experiential learning component [13] to be part of the initial exploratory phase which in turn increases the quality of the design process. However, while in this paper the ready to use technologies represents a starting point leading to new incarnations for different application domains, tasks and user needs, i.e., Pin and Play; in other situations it can be more a means to an end such as mediators facilitating fast prototyping, i.e., the phidgets developed by Saul Greenberg at University of Calgary (http://grouplab.cpsc.ucalgary.ca/phidgets).

Beside the benefits outlined above, the proposed brief has also limitations that need to be mentioned. Indeed, the proposed type of design brief is particularly relevant for innovative technologies such Pin and Play. For an existing technology such as the use of the web, there will be the danger that the students will be blinkered by previous experience of its applications. In such cases, more radical means, for example BadIdeas [14] may be needed in order to encourage divergent thinking during the exploration phase. A limitation of the evaluation process taking place in Phase II consists of its lack of objective criteria. Future work can address this limitation by including expert evaluation of the conceptual designs.

Not at least, the quality and the number of the developed conceptual designs suggest the advantage of this type of design brief both for supporting divergent thinking and for allowing a better exploration of design space both in breadth and in depth.

6   Acknowledgements

Our thanks to the MRes students 2005-2006 for their enthusiasm and hard work when faced with this new type of design brief, and to Nicolas Villar for generously sharing his time and knowledge about Pin and Play.

7   References

[1] C. Sas, Learning Approaches for Teaching Interaction Design, in: *Proceedings of HCIEd.2006-1 Inventivity,* Limerick, Ireland, 23-24 March, 2006.
[2] D. Schön, *Educating the reflective practitioner* (Jossey Bass, London, 1987).
[3] Frederiksen , N. Implications of Cognitive Theory for Instruction in Problem Solving. *Review of Educational Research,* 54(3), 363-407 (1984).
[4] C. Kehoe. *Supporting Critical Design Dialog,* Ph.D. Dissertation, Georgia Institute of Technology, 2001 (unpublished).
[5] D.A. Wroblewski, The construction of human-computer interfaces considered as a craft ,in: *Taking software design seriously,* edited by J. Karat (Academic Press, Cambridge, 1991), pp. 1-19.

[6] G. Strong, J.B. Gasen, T. Hewett, D. Hix, J. Morris, M.J. Muller, and D.G. Novick, *New Directions in HCI Education, Research, and Practice*, (Washington, DC: NSF/ARPA, 1994).

[7] P.L. Phillips, *Creating the Perfect Design Brief: How to manage design for strategic advantage* (Allworth Press, New York, 2004).

[8] B. Hartfield, T. Winograd, and J. Bennett, Learning HCI design: Mentoring project groups in a course on human-computer interaction, *SIGCSE Bulletin*, 24(1), 246-251 (1992).

[9] S. Howard, User interface design and HCI: identifying the training needs of practitioners, *SIGCHI Bulletin*, 27(3), 17-22 (1995).

[10] D. Benyon, P. Turner, and S. Turner, *Designing Interactive Systems* (Addison-Wesley, London, 2005).

[11] J. Lave and E. Wenger, *Situated Learning: Legitimate Peripheral Participation* (Cambridge University Press, Cambridge, 1991).

[12] E, Wenger, *Communities of Practice: Learning, Meaning, and Identity* (Cambridge University Press, Cambridge, 1998).

[13] J. Piaget, *The Psychology of Intelligence* (Routledge, New York, 1950).

[14] A. Dix, T. Ormerod, M. Twidale, C. Sas, P. Gomes da Silva, and L. McKnight, Why bad ideas are a good idea. *Proceedings of HCIEd.2006-1 Inventivity*, Limerick, Ireland, 23-24 March, 2006.

A Case Study - Hindrances and Success Factors in Student Projects

Marta Kristin Larusdottir

School of Computer Science, Reykjavik University,
Ofanleiti 2, 103 Reykjavik, Iceland
marta@ru.is

Abstract. Third year undergraduate students in Computer Science at Reykjavik University complete a practical project in which co-operation between the students and the industry is emphasized. The students form small groups and develop software for eighteen weeks at a company's site where they get access to all needed facilities. In this study the students were asked to state the hindrances they experienced. Data was gathered from eleven student groups both with interviews and on-line questionnaires three times during the project period. Furthermore a contact person at each company was interviewed one month after the delivery date and asked to rate the quality of the project work. Based on that rating the groups were divided in three categories, the best, the middle and the worst. The success factors characterizing the best groups were analysed. Also the customers were asked to rate what quality factors of the product they emphasized the most. The students did not experience many hindrances five weeks after the commencement of the project, but after nine weeks 73% of the groups named that understanding the requirements of the project was a hindrance. The methods of Human-Computer Interaction could be of great value for the students in these two periods, understanding the user, their tasks and the context of use. When only 4 weeks were left of the project the biggest hindrances for the groups were technical problems and lack of time. A study of the work of the best groups showed that the main success factors are: being very organized, keeping good co-operation in the group, and getting feedback from the customer and the users.

Please use the following format when citing this chapter:

Larusdottir, M.K., 2009, in IFIP International Federation for Information Processing, Volume 289; *Creativity and HCI: From Experience to Design in Education*; Paula Kotzé, William Wong, Joaquim Jorge, Alan Dix, Paula Alexandra Silva; (Boston: Springer), pp. 189–202.

1   Introduction

The curriculum for the 3 year BSc degree study in Computer Science at Reykjavik University provides as solid theoretical foundation as well as putting emphasis on practical aspects that meet the needs of Icelandic industries, business and institutions. The number of students enrolled in undergraduate studies in Computer Science has been around 300 the last two years. It is compulsory for all students to work on a 12 ECTS final project. The students have two possibilities: A practical project in which co-operation between the students and the software industry is emphasized or a research based project where the students work with a researcher at the university. Most students choose the former alternative, which is described in this paper.

The companies invite a group of students to work on a software project suggested by a contact person at the company, here called the customer, and the students get all the needed facilities at the customer's site. It is valuable for the students to be able to experience how it is to work in the software industry while still in their studies and some of them have got recruited by the company after their graduation. Such a direct co-operation with the software industry is also positive for the university. The students are working in the industry on actual projects suggested by the customer, still the projects are controlled, all having the same duration and the students deliver similar effort each so the project are of similar size. These circumstances make it possible to study how it is for practitioners to work on their first software project out in the industry, what the main hindrances are that they experience during the software development and how the customers rate the outcome.

In this paper the progress of these practical student projects is studied from the students' perspectives. We want to explore what the success factors in students project work are, when in the project period the students experience hindrances, and what these hindrances are. To measure the success of the product, customers were asked to rate the students work one month after the delivery of the product. The customers were also asked about how they rate different quality attributes for the software product.

The remainder of this paper is organized as follows: In Section 2 related works are reviewed. Section 3 presents the experimental design and how data was collected. Section 4 presents the results while in Section 5 the findings are discussed.

2   Related Work

A software product is considered to be a success if it is delivered on time, within budget, and contains all specified features or services, as defined by the Standish group in their annual Chaos Report [1]. In 1994 the reported success rate was 16.2% for software projects, in 2004 it was up to 29% [2]. In these reports, the reasons for failure and success are studied. The major success factors in 1994 [1] were: 'user involvement', 'executive management support', 'clear statement of requirements', 'proper planning' and 'realistic expectations'. The failure factors were more or less the reverse of the success factors, that is: 'lack of user input', 'incomplete or changing requirements and specifications', 'lack of executive support' and 'technology incompetence'. In the Standish group study the focus was on the customer's view of what characterizes successful projects.

Other studies have reported on the software developer's view of successes in software projects. Linberg [3] found that developer's perceptions of success are very different from the traditional definition of a project success. The developers were asked to name their most successful project: 5 out of 8 participants named a project that was over budget by 419%, over schedule by 193%, and over size estimates by 130%. The success factors they mentioned were: 'the product worked the way it was supposed to work', 'developing it was a technical challenge' and 'their team was small and high-performing'.

A recent study from Procaccino et. al. [4] reports on a survey of success factors that affect software developer's perception of project success and is based on several previous studies. The 29 success factors are divided into three groups, process-related factors, work-related factors and project-related factors. The three highest rated process-related success factors were: 'requirements are clear and understood'; 'team is sufficiently skilled' and 'customer/user and team have good relationship'. The lowest two factors in that category were: 'The team was able to negotiate changes' and 'the team does not feel pressured'. There were 5 factors in the work-related category, of which the highest two were: 'You had sense that you delivered sufficient quality' and 'You had sense of achievement' and the lowest was: 'You learned something new'. Of the nine project-related factors, the two highest factors were: 'requirements were met' and 'final system worked as intended', while the lowest factor was: 'the project was completed within budget'.

A recent study of Dannelly, et. al. [5] explored what factors students believe important to measuring the success of professional software development projects. The students were asked to assume they had graduated and were working for a company that was developing a software-based product. Because of their lack of industrial experience their opinion was based on academic training. The highest rated success factors from previous studies were gathered and the students' opinions of these were measured. Their findings generally correspond to the findings of Procaccino, et. al, [4]: the students find factors like: 'not feeling pressured', 'acquiring new skills' and 'being challenged' not important in contrary to the software developers. Both surveys showed that quality is important for students and developers as well as factors like: 'The product meets customer's needs' and 'the customer finds the product useful and easy to use'. The major difference in opinions was that the students rated the factor 'within budget' as very important were as the developers rated it rather low.

In a study from Verner, et. al. [6] Australian software practitioners were surveyed to understand what software development practices were used in their recent software projects. The authors were particularly interested to discover what project management practices are common in Australian software projects and why some projects succeed and others fail. Their results show that the success factors are: 'Skilled project manager', 'good and complete requirements', 'good schedule and estimates' and 'working long hours'.

Finally, Berntsson-Svensson, et. al. [7] give a good summary, based on eight papers, of the results of studying both project and product success factors in software projects. Based on this summary a questionnaire was made to investigate software project and product success factors in Swedish and Australian software companies. The study compared the similarities of success factors across three categories of industries: financial services, consulting industry and telecommunication industry. There are two factors that all three industry types considered as important for project success: 'complete and accurate requirements from project start' and 'having enough time for requirements elicitation'. All subjects considered 'a satisfied customer' as being the most important factor for product success.

In the context above, it can be concluded that students working on a practical project are good representatives for software developers, because they rate the success factors similar to developers [5]. Many of these studies state the success factors and failure factors in project work from the developer's perspective. In all of the above studies data is gathered after the project is delivered. In our study, however, we follow the progress of the students work, and see how the hindrances change during the software development process, to be able to understand better the success and failure factors. Also we want to measure the customer's perceived success of the work after the delivery of the product and analyze the success factors in the project work according to that rating. It can also be concluded that there are many different success factors stated in the literature, but many of the studies state that a satisfied customer is very important for product success. In our study we want to look deeper into that issue and describe what makes a customer satisfied by analysing what quality attributes our customers emphasize.

3   Materials and Methods

In this section we describe the subjects and the process and of the student projects, the purpose of the study, and the data gathering methods used.

3.1   The Subjects of the Student Projects

The subjects of the practical projects can vary a lot, two examples are: A system to register attendance during athletic lessons by GSM-phone and a web for the parents to check their kids attendance; and a system to seet passengers in a airplane to distribute the weight evenly. The students work on 'a new idea', they gather and analyze requirements, design, implement and test the software. Documentation during the whole project is emphasized. Often the projects are a part of a larger system, adding some new functionality to an existing system, for example adding a home accounting functionality to an internet bank. Most often there are actual end-users that work with the delivered systems so the students have to place emphasis on usability, although occasionally the students are making system functions with no user interface. In some cases the projects are a 'proof-of-concept', the students have to find a way to solve technical things, and occasionally the companies define the projects as prototypes to see how tasks can be solved in an easy way in the new software.

3.2   The Process of the Student Projects

The students work in groups of 2 to 4 persons. Usually each student contributes around 400 hours during the project, so the size of the projects is 800 – 1600 man-hours. All the groups follow the same process, which is as follows:

1. Contact persons from Icelandic companies send in suggestions for student projects to the final projects organizer. Usually these companies are developing software and the suggestions are for software projects that would fit into their development.
2. All incoming suggestions are made accessible to students at the same time.
3. The students form groups and ask the company they want to work with, if the project is available. When the students have got an agreement from a company for a particular project, they deliver a more detailed project description to the final project organizer.
4. An organizing committee having three members reads through the project descriptions and checks if the projects are suitable as a final project in Computer Science.
5. When the projects have been accepted, one supervisor and one censor are assigned for each group.
6. All the final projects start on the same date and are delivered on the same date, eighteen weeks later.
7. There are three checks in the project period where the students inform the supervisor, the censor and the final projects organizer on the status of the project. These check points are 4 weeks after the project started, 8 weeks after and near the end of it. The group meets the supervisor weekly. For this study there were additionally three check points were the groups were interviewed: five weeks, nine weeks and fourteen weeks after the commencement of the projects.
8. The students deliver a running system and supplying documentation at the end of the project period. After the final delivery, the students give a formal 30 minutes presentation of their projects, which is open to public.

3.3   The Purpose of the Study

The purpose of this study is to answer the following questions:

1. What are the main hindrances that the students experience during the practical project work and do they change during the project period?
2. What feedback channels do the students value the most during the project period?
3. How does the customer rate the groups work?
4. What quality attributes of the product does the customer emphasize?
5. What are the success factors to get high rating from the customer?

3.4   The Data Gathering

We gathered data by two on-line questionnaires followed by structured interviews with each student, three times during the project period. Additionally structured interviews were conducted with the customer one month after the delivery date. Eleven student groups took part in the study, 45 students in total.

3.4.1 The On-line Questionnaires for the Students

We gathered data through two on-line questionnaires one for background information of the students and another for measuring the progress of the projects. The latter was sent out two times during the project period. There were 17 questions in the background questionnaire covering background information, the student's relation with other group members, and their concerns about the project. There were 38 questions in the process questionnaire covering the students experience in the requirements analysis phase, design phase, and implementation phase.

3.4.2 The Interviews with each Student

Interviews were conducted three times, 135 interviews in total. The interviews were conducted five weeks, nine weeks and fourteen weeks after the project start. The total project duration was eighteen weeks.

At each interview there was a conductor of the interview and a note-taker. There were 20 questions covered in the first structured interview, covering the process of the project, the hindrances that the students had experienced so far, and general questions about the group work. All the interviews were audio recorded. In the second and the third interview there were 28 questions, going in more detail into the progress of the projects than in the first interview.

3.4.3 The Interviews with the Customers

We conducted 11 structured interviews with the customers. At each interview there was a conductor of the interview and a note-taker. All the interviews were audio recorded. The questionnaire covered 49 questions in total, there were 9 questions about their rating of the students work and 40 questions on the six quality attributes from ISO-9126 [8], usability, functionality, reliability, efficiency, maintainability and portability.

4 Results

In here we present our results about the main hindrances found by the students and the customers rating of the students work. This is followed by a discussion of the common factors in the student group work and finally results are presented about what quality attributes the customers emphasise.

4.1 The Main Hindrances in the Project Work

In the interviews, the students were asked about the main hindrances they had experienced in the period following the last interview. There were three periods, the first five weeks of the project, the next four weeks, and the next five weeks.

4.1.1 The 1st Period

The main hindrances that the students mentioned in the first period of the project work can be seen in Table 1.

Table 1. *The main hindrances in the 1st period of the students project work*

Hindrance	% of groups
Lack of experience in project planning	27%
Lack of time	27%
Unclear or changed requirements	18%
Unclear project description	18%

The groups named only one or two hindrances at this point and two groups did not name any. At this time the groups are starting the project work, so it is not surprising that the project plan and gathering requirements is hard for them. What is surprising is how few groups mention this.

4.1.2 The 2nd Period

The hindrances the groups named in the second period can be seen in Table 2.

Table 2. *The main hindrances in the 2nd period of the students project work*

Hindrance	% of groups
Understanding the project	73%
Technical problems	55%
Designing and implementing the database	45%
Lack of time	36%
Unclear or changed requirements	36%
Problems in the implementation	36%
Hard to describe use cases and user roles	36%

Many of the groups mentioned that fully understanding the project is a hindrance. Here they have been working on the project for nine weeks and realize now what they do not know. Also they are having all sorts of technical problems, with the development environment they are working in.

4.1.3 The 3rd Period

The main hindrances from the third period can be seen in Table 3.

Table 3. *The main hindrances in the 3rd period of the students project work*

Hindrance	% of groups
Technical problems	75%
Lack of time	75%
Designing and implementing the database	63%
Problems in the implementation	50%
Problems because of legacy systems	38%
Lack of knowledge of the version control system	38%

The students have been working on the project for fourteen weeks and have four weeks left. Here many of the groups name that they have technical problems and are lacking time to achieve what they wanted. The students are still having trouble while designing and implementing the database.

4.1.4 The Lessons Learnt

As a Human-Computer Interaction (HCI) educator I see opportunities in helping the students in the 1st period while gathering requirements. This can be done by emphasizing the methods described in the HCI literature for gathering information from the users and describe the users side of the software, for example contextual interviews, scenarios and personas. It is utterly important in this period to look at the context in which the users are working.

In the 2nd period the main hindrance was to understand the project and there the methods for understanding the user and the task will be of a great help to the students. Encouraging the students to interview the users, look at the context, analyze the users and tasks, make paper prototypes, and get feedback from the users early in the development period would for sure help the students to understand the project domain better.

In the 3rd phase the most frequent hindrances were technical problems and lack of time. There are not any particular HCI methods that could help to cope with these hindrances.

4.2   The Customers Rating of the Groups

The customers were asked to rate the students work on the scale from one to five where five is the best. The rating was supposed to reflect on both the delivered system and how professionally the group worked during the development process. The results from the customer ratings are shown in Table 4.

Table 4. *The customers rating of the groups work and delivery*

Customer rating	1	2	3	4	5
Number of groups	0	0	4	4	3

As can be seen in Table 4, three projects got the highest rating from the customer, four projects ranked as the middle ones and four ranked as worst. The projects will be labelled according to this grouping in the following as the worst, the middle and the best. When asked about the reason for the best ratings the customers stated that the groups were very organized, always delivered in the documentation as planned and delivered in a system that was put into use. For the worst groups, the customers commented that the groups did not follow the predefined requirements, did not contact the customers much and worked very isolated and unorganized.

4.3   The Highest Rated Feedback Channels

The students were also asked which feedback they valued the most. They were asked to name one feedback channel. The results are shown in Table 5 grouped by the customers rating of the students work.

Table 5. *Feedback channels that the students value the most*

Feedback during the project work	Student projects		
	Worst	Middle	Best
Customer	68%	48%	33%
User	0%	10%	22%
Supervisor	26%	39%	39%
Examiner	5%	3%	6%

These results are interesting, especially for HCI educators because the students doing the best projects name in 22% of the cases that the best feedback comes from the users, but no students doing the worst projects mentions this. So someone in the group taking care of getting feedback from the user could be one success factor in doing to do good projects.

What is also of interest here is that the groups doing the worst project say in 68% of the cases that feedback from the customer is the most important feedback channel. When looking closer at the comments from the customers on the worst groups we see that the customers complain that the students in these groups worked in isolation and did not ask the customer questions or for advices. The customers thought that the delivered system was very different from the system they had asked for and commented that if the students had been more in touch they would have done a better system. The students were probably to shy to ask for the customers comments.

4.4   The Success Factors in the Project Work

When looking into more detail at the data that was gathered in the interviews with the students some factors were common for the groups sharing the same rating from the customer. The success factors are drawn from analyzing the common factors from the groups.

4.4.1 Common Factors - the Worst Projects

The groups doing the worst projects had in common that the project management was lacking. They did not have any project plan for the whole project period, but made project plan week by week, day by day, or even did not plan at all. As a result they did not really know when the other group members would be working on the project. There was nobody taking the role of a project manager, no one kept track of things and encouraged the group members to stay focused. The groups did not work steadily during the project period, but worked in some working sessions.

The lack of facilities is one negative factor for the worst projects. The customers did not have the facilities for the students they had promised, for the entire duration of the project. This could indicate that getting a common room for the group during the whole project period preferably at the customer's site, is very important for the project's success.

4.4.2 Common Factors – the Middle Projects

The groups doing the middle ranked projects had in common that they were only missing minor things to get the highest rating. All the customers were quite satisfied with the delivered system.

The groups were somewhat organized, but they did not follow their project plan in detail. There was divided responsibility, for example someone was responsible for the documentation and another one for the programming. There was not enough communication in the group, so the person responsible for the documentation was not sure on the progress in the programming and visa versa. The groups did not have a detailed work schedule so the group members where on site when it suited them.

4.4.3 Common Factors – the Best Projects

The groups doing the best projects were very well organized. They did a project plan right in the beginning and referred to that plan during the whole project period. There was very good co-operation in the groups and these groups made a schedule for each week so all the group members would be in same place at the same time for several hours a week. The groups were very focused, so the time they were together was only used to work on the final projects. All the groups had one project manager that kept track of time spent on each task and was responsible for communicating with the customer and the supervisor.

All the groups had good co-operation with the customers and some co-operation with the users of the systems.

4.4.4 The Success Factors

To sum up the success factors we read from these results, the issues that are vital for the students to be able to do good projects, are listed here below:

- Assign the role of a project manager to one member of the group
- Have an agreed working schedule for each week so the group meets at the same time on the same place several times per week
- Register the hours spent on each task carefully and compare that to the project plan each week
- Be focused when working on the project
- Keep good co-operation in the group
- Have a shared working room for the whole group the whole project period, preferably at the customers site
- Take the initiative to ask the customer for advice
- Assign one person in the group responsible for getting feedback from users
- Put emphasis on the requirement phase to discover the essence and hindrances in the project work early in the project period.

So the recommendations we have for the students beginning their final projects are to emphasise these success factors. We tell them to be organized: assign a project manager, do a project plan and keep track of the progress of the work, decide when and how many hours a week they are going to work on the projects. We also tell them to take good care of the communication within the group, with the customer and the users. Finally we advice them to take good time for requirements gathering and use the methods thought on that.

4.5   Results on Quality Attributes

The customers were asked to rate the six quality attributes from ISO 9126 [8]: usability, functionality, reliability, efficiency, maintainability and portability on a scale 1 to 5, where 5 is the best, and point out which of the factors they regard as the most important one. Some customers could not name only one so they mentioned two. The results are shown in Table 7.

Table 7. *The most emphasized quality factors*

Quality factor	Number of customers
Functionality	3
Usability	2
Usability and Functionality	3
Usability and Reliability	1
Maintainability	1
Maintainability and Portability	1
Efficiency	0
Total	11

So there were 6 customers that mentioned that functionality was the most important or one of the most important quality factors, and there were also 6 customers that mentioned usability as the most important attribute or one of the most important attributes. Two customers mentioned maintainability, one customer mentioned reliability and one portability. Nobody mentioned efficiency as the most important quality factor. In Fig. 1, the rating for usability and functionality is shown.

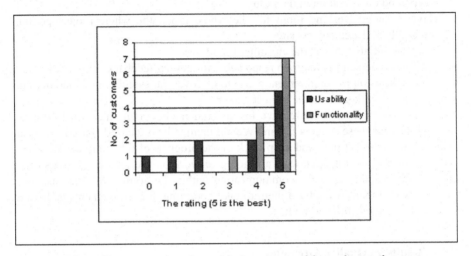

Fig. 1. *The customer's ratings of the importance of the quality attributes*

All the customers rated functionality as three or above and 7 customers gave it the highest rating. For usability the score is more mixed, seven customers say that it is very important and four give it a very low score, so there is a different pattern there, it is either very important or not important at all, while functionality is always regarded as somewhat important.

5   Discussion

The results of this study were interesting in many ways. Firstly, the students did not mention many hindrances in the project after the first four weeks. We would have imagined that at that point they would be very frustrated with not having a clear picture of the requirements of the project. However, they named a lot more hindrances later in the project. The most interesting result is that 73% of the students mentioned that they did not have a clear understanding of the requirements of the project when half of the project period had passed. It seems like the students discover how many unclear things there are when digging in the project, but do not really see all of these right in the start.

During their education it has been stressed that success factors like the ones from the Standish report from 1994 [1], for example 'clear statement of requirements', are very important. Also, developers from the Procaccino, et. al study [4], give the success factor 'requirements are clear and understood' the highest rating. In that study the developers give their rating after the project is delivered, so they know by then that this is very important. From our study we can see that the developers are already half way through the project when they discover this and would most likely benefit from emphasizing this earlier in the project. This gives HCI educators the indication that students would benefit of using the data gathering methods from the HCI literature to be able to understand the projects better right from the start.

Another interesting result of the study is that the students who received the poorest rating from the customer, thought in 68% of the cases that feedback from the customer was the most valuable one. On the other hand, the customer commented that these students did not ask for help or advices. The groups getting the highest rating from the customer did value getting feedback from different sources: the customer, user and the supervisor. This is in line with the results from Standish group [1], stating that user involvement is one of the most important success factors. The results from Procaccino et. al. [4] stating the importance of the customer and the developer having good relationship can be extended by our results, saying that both the customer and the developers have to find the relationship valuable.

The success factors that characterized the student project work in our study are very process oriented and very much in line with those stated by Verner, et. al. [6], where two of the most successful factors are: 'skilled project manager' and 'good schedule and estimates'. These student projects have very tight time schedule, only 18 weeks and a definite delivery date, there is no chance of getting some extra days, so it is not surprising that these factors lead to successful projects especially in these circumstances.

6 Acknowledgements

Our thanks to Anna Ingolfsdottir, Gudmundur Valsson, Jon Freyr Johannsson, Jonheidur Isleifsdottir and Jonina S. Larusdottir for their very valuable comments and inspiration on a draft of this paper. Also we would like to thank Yngvi Bjornsson for his proofreading and good comments on the final version.

7 References

1. Standish Group, Chaos Report, 1994, (cited December 2007),
   http://www.standishgroup.com/sample_research/chaos_1994_1.php
2. J. Johnson, *My Life Is Failure: 100 Things You Should Know to be a Successful Project Leader.* Standish Group International, West Yarmouth, MA, 2006.
3. K. L Linberg, Software Developer Perceptions about Software Project Failure: A Case Study, *Journal of Systems and Software,* **49**(2-3), pp.177-192 (1999).
4. Procaccino, J. Drew, Verner, June M. and Lorenzet, Steven J. Defining and Contributing to Software Development Success, *Communication of the ACM,* **49**(8). pp 79-83 (2006).
5. Dannelly, R. Stephen, DeNoia, Lynn, Student Opinions of Software Project Success, *Proceedings of the 45th Annual Southeast Regional Conference,* (Winston-Salem, North Carolina 2007), pp. 327-330.

6. J. M. Verner, N. Cerpa, Australian Software Development: What Software Project Management Practices Lead to Success?, in: *Australian Software Engineering Conference (ASWEC'05)*, (2005), pp. 70-77.
7. R. Berntsson-Svensson, A. Aurum, Successful Software Project and Products: An Empirical Investigation, *Proceedings of the 2006 ACM/IEEE International Symposium on Empirical Software Engineering*, 2006, pp. 144 – 153.
8. ISO/IEC TR 9126, *Software engineering – Product quality*, 19-12-2000.

Conceptual Design and Prototyping to Explore Creativity

Manuel J. Fonseca, Joaquim A. Jorge, Mário R. Gomes, Daniel Gonçalves
and Marco Vala
Department of Computer Science and Engineering,
Instituto Superior Técnico,
Technical University of Lisboa, Av. Rovisco Pais s/n,
Lisboa 1049-001, Portugal
mjf@inesc-id.pt, jaj@inesc-id.pt, mario.gomes@tagus.ist.utl.pt,
daniel.goncalves@inesc-id.pt, marco.vala@tagus.ist.utl.pt
WWW home page: http://web.ist.utl.pt/

Abstract. Many approaches to teaching HCI focus on either user requirements or prototyping. However, these two techniques do not provide enough tools for students to explore the design space in breadth at early stages of conception. Indeed, even when these two approaches are combined, students still lack tools to explore the design space and bridge the gap from requirements to prototyping. In this paper, we describe the way we teach Human Computer Interaction, stimulating students to be creative during interface design. To that end we added course materials on conceptual design and scenario based interaction, combined with the exploration of different low fidelity prototypes, which we believe increase both the usability of student-developed prototypes and foster learner creativity. To illustrate this we present some of the best examples of interactive prototypes designed and developed by students attending our HCI course in the context of Information Systems and Computer Engineering (ISCE) curriculum at the Technical University of Lisbon, Portugal. While the current approach seems to elicit positive responses and draw encouraging remarks from students, work remains to be done in emerging interface paradigms and more formal evaluation on how this approach positively affects student outcomes.

1   Introduction

Currently, many Human Computer Interaction courses in most undergraduate IT curricula all over the world, adopt the iterative method for interaction design (see Fig. 1). However, most common methodologies pose problems in the first steps in

Please use the following format when citing this chapter:

Fonseca, M.J., Jorge, J.A., Gomes, M.R., Gonçalves, D. and Vala, M., 2009, in IFIP International Federation for Information Processing, Volume 289; *Creativity and HCI: From Experience to Design in Education*; Paula Kotzé, William Wong, Joaquim Jorge, Alan Dix, Paula Alexandra Silva; (Boston: Springer), pp. 203–217.

the interaction design process. The usual approach is to go straight from task analysis to prototyping. We think that this presents problems in interface development methodology. Indeed, going directly from task analysis to paper prototyping limits student creativity, since they are forced to start thinking in terms of interaction styles and screen layout instead of focusing on solving user needs. As a consequence, both the quality and creativity of coursework suffers and students find it difficult to explore the design space.

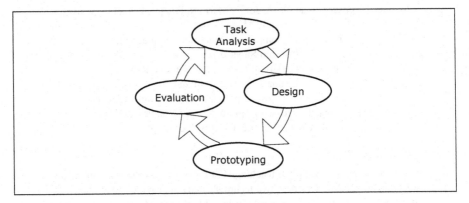

Fig. 1. *The iterative development cycle*

A summary analysis of existing courses on Human Computer Interaction reveals different approaches in communicating the HCI discipline to students. Indeed some courses structure subject matter around scenarios [9]. Other courses focus on task analysis instead [4]. A third group combines task analysis, scenarios and prototyping. However, few if any of the syllabi surveyed include conceptual design in the overall cycle of developing an interactive system.

From our experience, introducing Conceptual Models and Scenario-Based Design in the syllabus in combination with the other techniques indicated allows students to break the creativity gap from task analysis to prototyping. We added a module about conceptual modeling between task analysis and prototyping. Creating conceptual models during this phase of the interface development forces students to think about concepts and actions that their system will offer to users, instead of being worried about screen layout and color schemes as discussed in [5]. Moreover, the selection of metaphors to include in the conceptual model, stimulates students to be creative in the analogies they choose, and allows them to explore the design space more thoroughly than they would had if they started by directly sketching low-fidelity prototypes after requirements analysis. Arguably a better conceptual model when applied thoroughly may well make the final system more familiar to users, and consequently easier to learn and use.

Additionally to the conceptual design, we also explore three different scenarios in our course syllabus. First, problem scenarios describe how actually users perform tasks. Second, activity scenarios describe how users will perform tasks using the concepts of our conceptual solution. Third, interaction scenarios describe how users will interact in detail with the implemented solution. Additionally, in the most recently taught semester (Spring 2007), we also asked students to design three alternative prototypes, before they start developing the final design.

We present the Introductory HCI course which is taught to ISCE students on the third year of a five year Computer Science and Engineering undergraduate degree taught at *Instituto Superior Técnico* (IST), the school of Engineering of the Technical University of Lisbon, which is the oldest engineering school in Portugal. The course has evolved considerably over the years since its inception in 1992. The pedagogical approach described herein is the result of curricular changes started in the 2002/2003 academic year. The one-semester course is currently taught to 280+ ISCE students across the two campi of IST, spaced 30km apart. In what follows, we describe the program as currently taught at IST with special emphasis on course structure and coordination between recitation, laboratory classes and project development. To illustrate results, we show some exemplar prototypes developed as coursework by students followed by discussion, conclusions and proposals for future developments.

2   Teaching Human Computer Interaction

At the core of the subject matter of any HCI course lies the design, development and evaluation of Interactive Systems. However, not every school teaches HCI the same way. We can characterize most curricula in two broad categories. One, which we call *task-oriented*, hinges course delivery on task analysis and identifying user needs. Another, which we call *prototype-oriented*, focuses on the design of the interface proper. Its curricular structure focuses on exploring the design space through a series of prototypes. While we feel that both approaches have their advantages and disadvantages, we want to provide our students with the best of both worlds. In this section we show how we have combined the strong user focus of the first approach with the progressive refinement approach favoured by the second. To this end, we first tell students how to identify potential users and tasks that those users may want to perform on the interactive system being designed. Then, we lead them through the principles and basic guidelines required to design and develop creative solutions with usable user interfaces. Finally, we train them on evaluating interfaces at different phases of development, by applying the most suitable evaluation technique at each stage. We do this by combining recitation classes, laboratory work and group projects so that student work flows continuously in lockstep with subject matter.

In the next subsections we describe in detail the subjects of our theoretical and laboratory classes and explain how they are synchronized with the development of the course project.

2.1   Theoretical Classes

Our theoretical classes are organized around seven main chapters, which we believe are important to give students a good basis for their future work as interface designers, interface engineers or usability evaluators. These areas are organized in seven large study sections as shown in Table 1. Below we describe each section in more detail, highlighting its contribution to the goals of our HCI course.

Table 1: *Course Organization*

Unit	Subject Matter
I	Introduction to User-Centered Design
II	Know the Users and Their Tasks
III	Interactive Systems Design
IV	Evaluation
V	Documentation, Help and Interaction Devices
VI	Web Pages
VII	Toolkits

2.1.1 Introduction to User Centered Design

In this chapter, besides introducing the course and all administrative things, we try to give students an overview of the overall process of designing an interactive system, creating bridges to upcoming classes. During these classes we also try to provide students with a more comprehensive view of Interactive Systems (Appliances, Car consoles, etc), beyond desktop interfaces with windows and buttons. Additionally, we provide them an introduction to Usability Engineering and ISO Certification.

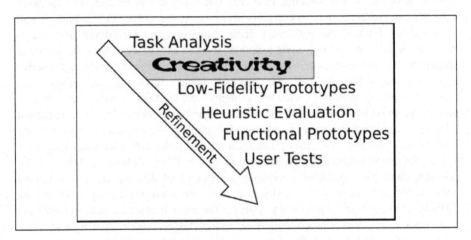

Fig. 2. *The creativity gap in Iterative Refinement*

2.1.2 Know the Users and Their Tasks

One of the most important aspects to developing an interactive system is to know who will use our system and for what. To that end we teach our students the different methods to perform task analysis, from observation to questionnaires. Later on, during the development of their project, they will have the possibility of applying these techniques to collect information about users and tasks, and answer eleven questions on task analysis [4] (Who will use the system? What tasks do users perform now? What new functionalities do they want in the future? How do users learn to perform the task? Etc.). By performing task analysis and answering these questions, students obtain a clear idea of present user requirements and collect important information relevant to the next step of their project assignments. Since we are developing interfaces for people, it is important to know how the human information processing system works. The key idea is to show to students that humans are limited in their capacity to process information, and that they must take that into account while designing user interfaces.

2.1.3 Conceptual Models

In this chapter we teach how to go from user requirements (collected during task analysis) to the development of the prototype or prototypes. We start this section by studying the conceptual model, where students learn to create solutions for user needs independent of the intended devices or interaction styles. The conceptual model includes metaphors, to create analogies of real world entities and activities, and concepts that the system will expose to users. Such concepts can either be objects, attributes or actions that can be performed on objects. Other components from include relationships between concepts and the mapping between model concepts and entities arising out of the adopted metaphor. Indeed, using metaphors forces students to seek existing solutions that can be adapted to their novel interface. By using good metaphors, students understand that their systems become easier to learn and to use, since users quickly associate new concepts provided by the system to those taken from the metaphor. For example, if we use the phone call cabinet metaphor for a drinking machine system, we can say that "buying a drink is like making a phone call. First we insert the money and then we select the desired drink (phone number)". Using conceptual models to bridge the gap from task Analysis to Interaction Design is a relatively new addition to the curriculum. Indeed, we have added Conceptual Models over the last three years after noticing that students experienced considerable difficulties in mapping user requirements to low-fidelity prototypes. This is because low-fidelity prototypes already entail many design commitments and embody sufficient decisions that students feel "locked" to a given screen layout and interface organization that they do not attempt to further explore the design space. To overcome this significant barrier to creativity, we have gradually introduced Conceptual Modeling into the design cycle, following the inspirational writing by Johnson [5]. Additionally, we are guiding the students through design space exploration by using scenarios [9]. In our revised setting, students flesh out user requirements into problem scenarios, which help them weave user requirements and specifications from task analysis into coherent stories that help them both explain and communicate the most important features their design has to provide. From problem scenarios they evolve into metaphors, concepts, relationships and activity scenarios to detail the main components of the interface but *before* committing to any detailed aspects of the interface while keeping the design at a very abstract level. We believe that this design discipline helps students flesh out the main components and structure of their approaches *before* committing to any details, be it screen or interaction design. In this way, creativity is fostered and better designs may emerge, since students are "forced" to think through their designs against the user requirements before crystallizing solutions into prototypes as was the case in the past.

2.1.4 Interactive Systems Design

After finishing studying the conceptual model, students go into the next step of interface development, which is to find solutions for the user interface that satisfies the conceptual model. Only on this phase of the process we ask students to worry about the type and "look & feel" of the user interface. To that end, we present to them the different interaction styles, going from the basic command line, menus, direct manipulation, to the more recent and futuristic interaction styles, such as, augmented reality, wearable computing or tangible interfaces. Additionally, we teach the more important guidelines about screen design, namely, spatial layout, font types, use of colors, alignment, etc. Finally, to conclude this chapter, we explain how to create low-fidelity prototypes (LFP), as a fast, simple and cheap way to develop prototypes to show to final users. We also stimulate students to create storyboards, as a mechanism to explain how tasks are performed on their systems. We would like to mention that along these years of teaching the HCI course with this methodology, students produced very creative and interesting LFP. We would also like to highlight that in this chapter we teach students to create activity scenarios (making part of the conceptual model) and interaction scenarios, as a complement to LFP and storyboards. We believe it is important to teach the conceptual model, the interaction styles, the screen design and prototyping, as unique module, because this way students understand that the same conceptual model (and correspondent activity scenario) can lead to different interface solutions, LFP and interaction scenarios.

2.1.5 Evaluation

After creating prototypes, the next step is to learn how to evaluate them. To that end, we teach three types of usability evaluation: Evaluation by usability experts (heuristic evaluation), Predictive evaluation; and Evaluation with users. We start by teaching students to become usability experts. They learn Nielsen's heuristics [12], we give a set of interfaces that respect and violate these heuristics and finally, we practice an example in class. Our goal is that by the end of the course, and after performing six heuristic evaluations to their colleagues' projects (in the laboratory classes), students are usability experts. We believe that by practicing heuristic evaluation in laboratory classes, students not only learn the Nielsen's heuristics, but also apply the evaluation to practical cases. Besides the heuristic evaluation, we also teach predictive evaluation using GOMS, CCT and KLM. Finally, students learn how to perform usability tests with users, how to write a protocol for the tests and how to summarize and analyze the collected data using the correct statistic methods.

Documentation, Help and Interaction Devices

In this chapter we teach students to write documentation for interactive systems (tutorials, user manual, reference manual, quick reference manual), as well as to develop interactive and contextual help. One of the things that we highlight is that manuals and help must teach users on how to perform tasks with the system and not describe menus or options. To conclude this chapter of the course, we talk about different input and output devices, emphasizing to students that the design of the interface is very dependent of it. An interface for a PDA (with a limited resolution) will have to satisfy some constraints that an interface for large displays will not have, and vice-versa.

2.1.6 Web Pages

Until this chapter we have been teaching design and development of user interfaces in a general sense. However, in the last years, the majority of created interfaces are web pages. So, we decided to dedicate some classes to this particular type of user interfaces. First we show students the main differences between designing "ordinary" interfaces and interfaces for the web. Then, and taking into account that anyone, independently of its knowledge and education about user interfaces, creates web pages, we discuss the "Original Top Ten Mistakes in Web Design" [10], and the most recent "Top Ten Mistakes in Web Design" [11]. These way students can compare current web design problems with original ones. Another subject very important in web design is design patterns. We teach some of the more relevant patterns, such as, the rules to create a good Home Page, e-commerce and the shopping cart. Finally, we talk about personalization of web sites, standardization, accessibility, cascading style sheets and HTML and CSS validating software.

2.1.7 Toolkits

During the development of their prototype, students create functioning "simulators" of the final interactive system, where the interface is the most important thing. However, if the prototype were supposed to evolve into a real product, the tools used to create the prototypes (Flash, HTML, Javascript, Visual Basic, etc.) might not prove to be the more appropriate choices. To overcome this, we dedicate the last chapter of our HCI course to the study of UI software architecture and Toolkits. The main goal of this section is not to teach the particulars of a given toolkit, but rather to discuss fundamentals, such as the event model, windowing system and program interaction, and callbacks. We conclude this chapter by teaching the MVC model, in order to illustrate a programming architecture that separates the semantic of the application from visualization and control.

2.2   Laboratory Classes

One of the major goals of the course is to teach students a user-centered interface design methodology. While theoretical classes lay the knowledge foundations required to accomplish that goal, we feel it is important for students to actually use that methodology in the development of an interface and, thus, learn by doing. This posed an interesting problem: given the iterative nature of user-centered design practices, and the different stages it comprises, it would not be effective to simply require students to design an interface and check the result at the end. Indeed, it is the usage of the methodology itself that concerns us, rather than the final result, as we try to impart skills that can be used at later times, in the student's professional lives, in whatever interface design challenges they might face.

The only way for us to ensure that the appropriate design methodology is being used, and that students receive timely and relevant feedback is to closely follow the entire design process. To that end we create the course's laboratory classes, synchronized with the theoretical recitations. Usually, any given subject is used in the laboratory two weeks after it has been taught in a theoretical class. This gives time for students to assimilate that subject and resolve any doubts they might have regarding it. The order in which the different subject matters are considered (described in the previous section) mimics the order in which the different interface design stages should take place, allowing each laboratory class to focus on a specific stage. We typically have eight groups of three students on each laboratory class.

At the beginning of the semester, each student group is given a project assignment (as described in the next section). The project, consisting on the design of an interface, will be developed throughout the semester by students. Each laboratory class has a set of goals to be attained. These are known beforehand by students, at least a week before class, and directly reflect an interface design stage. Namely, there are classes for:

1. Creating task analysis questionnaires.
2. Presenting the task analysis' results and a conceptual model for the interface.
3. Heuristic evaluation (HE) of a low-fidelity prototype.
4. Presenting the results of the HE
5. Heuristic evaluation of a first functional prototype.
6. Heuristic evaluation of a second functional prototype.
7. Presenting the results of the HE of the second functional prototype.
8. Presenting results from usability tests with users.

As can readily be seen from the above list, each class closely follows an iteration of the user-centered design cycle. As it would be unfeasible to develop the entire prototype in the classroom, the classes focus more on the presentation of results rather than on actual development. This allows us to provide instant feedback about their work, and correct any problems that might arise. Also, as students present their results to the entire class, they benefit from a discussion with their colleagues in which the instructor acts as moderator. This exposes them to alternative ways to solve the same problems, requires them to stand behind their choices and adequately justify them, and allows them to see other problems that might arise, so that they may avoid those pitfalls in the future.

The description of each class gives students not only the goals of what is to be accomplished in that class, but also what should be prepared beforehand. A list of work to be done and deliverables is provided with that description, on a weekly basis. Doing so has a major advantage: it imposes a constant work pace, so that the project is created in a timely and ordered fashion. Also, as each stage of the design cycle must be presented in a different class, it prevents students from skipping stages and cutting corners, enforcing the use of the appropriate design methodology. Finally, as laboratory and theoretical classes are synchronized, students will not tackle problems they are not yet ready to solve.

Students are graded in each class, based on their performance in the classroom, on the work they have prepared beforehand, and on the deliverables produced. This evaluation is accompanied by comments given by the instructor so that students may know what they could have done better. In some cases, when it is deemed reasonable both in terms of work involved and timings, students are allowed to correct the major flaws in their work, to improve their grades and to have a chance to apply the instructor recommendations.

Aside from the classes we mentioned above, there are three others, not directly related with the development of the course's project. The first two classes of the semester consist of an informal evaluation of two web sites by students and the presentation of their findings. We felt this is necessary as at that stage most students lack an awareness of interface problems (ours is an introductory HCI course). This evaluation and ensuing presentation and discussion helps motivate students and gives them an overall idea of what a properly designed interface should be like. The other class not directly involved with the project occurs before students have to present a conceptual model for the interface of their projects. We found that conceptual models are hard to grasp, as they require an abstraction power most students don't possess or seldom exercise. Thus, we spend an entire class guiding them through the construction of a conceptual model for a sample interface. This is done collaboratively. After a short exposition about conceptual models (complementing what was taught in theoretical classes) all students are asked to provide their opinions about the conceptual model that is being created. The instructor facilitates the exchange of ideas between students, and provides comments about their suggestions. Gradually, a conceptual model emerges. As all students are involved in their creation and directly face the problems and questions involved in it, they gain insights that allow them to, after the class, properly develop conceptual models for their own projects.

3   Course Project

The course project plays a very important role in the course structure. It allows students to apply the knowledge acquired in the theoretical classes to a concrete scenario as close as possible to what they will find in the future. We usually propose eight different assignments which are presented at the beginning of the semester and randomly distributed for each group.

According to our experience, the assignments should only be a couple of paragraphs describing the general goals of the project. Students should look at the problem cleanly without being guided to a particular solution. During task analysis and the design phases (of the iterative development cycle) they should gather as much information as possible about users and their tasks, and they should find solutions for the problems encountered. Indeed, shorter assignment descriptions encourage students to be more creative in the way they explore possible solutions.

We found out that students are motivated if we use a commercial-looking language in the assignments stating for example that "company x wants to hire your team to create a new product y". Most seem engaged by the prospect of doing something similar to what they would do if they work in a real company. We try to emphasize this aspect during both development and evaluation phases.

It is also very important to have several different assignments. Usually laboratory classes have eight groups and we try not to have two groups doing the same assignment. We found that by using different assignments for all groups in the same laboratory session, students tend to focus more on their work and less on the neighbors' work, which has lead to better and more creative solutions. Moreover, since each group evaluates other group projects during the laboratory classes (these are mainly heuristic evaluations performed as part of the evaluation phase of the iterative development cycle), we observed that student groups perform better as evaluators and tend to find more usability problems when they evaluate project assignments which are different from theirs.

As we mentioned before, student projects are developed throughout the semester and most of the laboratory classes include checkpoints to assess the various steps of the project. In the next sections, we provide an overview of the methodology, some examples of projects developed as coursework and comments and remarks elicited from students as well as our informal assessment based on these remarks and observations of student performance.

3.1   Methodology

The main objective of the course project is to allow students to experience the iterative development cycle. We want them to practice all the phases in the cycle and to learn they should go through the cycle several times to achieve good results.

Students start with the creation of a task analysis questionnaire which is discussed in the first laboratory class dedicated to the project. Then, they use the questionnaire to enquire target users in order to get information and compile the task analysis' results.

After task analysis, they move to the design phase. They create a conceptual model of the interface with metaphors, concepts and activity scenarios. Both the task analysis and the conceptual model are presented in the laboratory class where they receive feedback from both their colleagues and the teacher. At this stage, we clearly highlight the importance of having a good conceptual model as a baseline for the prototyping phase.

After design, they go through prototyping. Students start by designing three alternative low fidelity prototypes for the conceptual model created before. From this set of prototypes, they choose one to evolve for the functional prototype. However, most of the times, students incorporate solutions from the other two prototypes in the selected one. By doing this, the quality and creativity of the resulting prototype increases relatively to the first version. Additionally, students do storyboards and interaction scenarios, for the selected prototype, bringing all these elements to the next laboratory class where they are evaluated.

In the evaluation phase, each group does a heuristic evaluation (HE) of the low-fidelity prototype of two other groups and gets his prototype evaluated by two groups also. During the process, students not only learn and practice HE as they get useful information to make their prototypes better in the next iteration of the cycle. The results of the HE are presented and discussed in the next laboratory class and it completes the first rotation of the iteration cycle.

Students are then encouraged to go through task analysis and design phases again, and to revise their conceptual models to reflect the results of the HE. Then, they do the first functional prototype which is evaluated in the next laboratory class. In this second rotation, they consolidate what they have learned before and they get a second evaluation done by an expert in interfaces.

In the third rotation, they repeat the process again and they create the second functional prototype (a revised version of the first after getting the results of HE). The second functional prototype is evaluated once more between groups of the same laboratory class.

In the fourth and final rotation, students present their final prototypes (a revised version of the second after getting the results of HE) and they do a final evaluation with users. These usability tests and their results are presented in the last laboratory class.

Students not only learn better experiencing the iterative development design, as they get a solid methodology to use in the future. All the deliverables produced along the iterative process are compiled into a group webpage on weekly basis and at the end we can get a very rich overview of the entire process.

A final note pertains to regular presentations which students have to deliver in the laboratory sessions as part of their work. These contribute to create important soft skills such as how to make a presentation and how to present a project in development to colleagues and faculty and students regard them very positively.

3.2   Examples

In this section, we present some of the best student projects developed during the most recent course (at the time of this writing) – Spring 2006/2007.

The example from Fig. 3 illustrates a low-fidelity prototype of an interface for an intelligent system that will integrate the different types of information accessed by drivers in a car, such as, car check-up, traffic information, calendar, phone calls, radio, GPS, etc. The resulting system should allow the monitoring of information and also the integration between the different functionalities, like for instance, show the way to the person the driver is calling, or alert the user if the car is running out of oil and give him the location, the path and the phone number of the nearest garage.

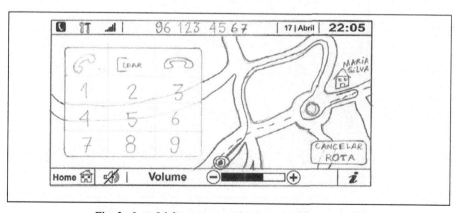

Fig. 3. *Low fidelity prototype for a car intelligent system*

The prototype illustrated in Fig. 4, succeeded very well in integrating those functionalities, was very creative and presented a good screen design and layout.

Fig. 4. *Intelligent car system prototype*

Another example taken from student work is a system to control the security systems of an house or office, from a cell phone. The future system will provide access to all the cameras in the house, the execution of actions when an intruse is detected or the definition and activation of different profiles according to the time of the day and/or the day of the week. Fig. 5 shows a low fidelity prototype of this assigment, where we can see the design of the device and two screens of the application. The main challenge of this project was the small display available to present the information to users. In the prototype presented in Fig. 6, students were able to achieve this chalenge by creating an interface with a clean screen design and very good navegation through the execution of the different tasks.

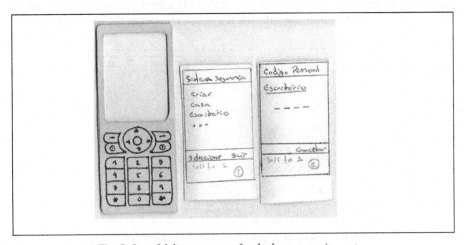

Fig. 5. *Low fidelity prototype for the home security system*

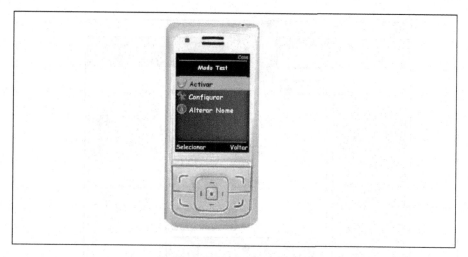

Fig. 6. *Security system prototype*

Finally, the last example presented here is a kiosk for tourist information about a city, which can provide information about monuments, restaurants, cultural events and transportation to go to those places. Moreover, it will be able to suggest a trip plan to visit the city according to user's constraints and requests, namely time and important places to visit. The big challenge in this project was the smooth integration between the information about the city, tourist relevant items and the access to services relate to them, such as, tickets for events, tickets for transportation, city maps, etc. Fig. 7 presents one of the prototypes that clearly achieve these goals by providing a system with a good screen design a good navigational and integration mechanism, which makes the performance of tasks very easy for users.

3.3   Student Comments

At the end of the course we collected feedback from students about the methodology that they were "forced" to follow during the development of the project. The majority of them complained about the quantity of work required from them week after week. However, all of them agreed that without this strict schedule and method the quality of their projects would be considerably worse and probably would not satisfy users' needs. Students also highlighted the involvement of the final users during task analysis and during the final usability tests. Finally, they understand the need for several iterations in the development of an interface, because they saw the positive evolution of their prototypes during the semester. An informal comparison with previous years' projects highlighted more creative and less uniform approaches to problems, and a more formal analysis showed that the average grade of the final prototype increased from 70% to 75%. We believe that the combination of the conceptual model design with the exploration of alternatives during the creation of the low fidelity prototype, positively influence the final quality of the prototypes.

Fig. 7. *Tourist kiosk prototype*

4   Conclusions

We have presented our approach to teaching an introductory HCI course within a
five year degree setting. While many challenges remain, it can be argued, that
Conceptual Design enables a smoother transition from gathering user requirements
to prototype user interfaces. Indeed, focusing on concepts rather than on screen- and
interaction-design details allows them to better explore project alternatives without
making early commitments to both interaction styles and screen layout. This
approach includes carefully synchronizing main course components, from recitation,
to Laboratory and Student Projects. We are happy that student response to the recent
changes in curricular content has been highly positive. Additionally, we noticed that
our introducing conceptual design in the course curriculum was accompanied by
marked improvements in the general quality, usability and creativity of student
projects. Further, informal evaluations, project quality surveys and assessment by
students show that the curricular structure presented here had a positive influence on
both learner attitude and performance. Of course, the ideal balance remains an ever
elusive target. We plan to further improve the syllabus to address emerging
interaction techniques and guidelines, introducing mobile devices and ubiquitous
computing to replace the current emphasis on Web development [2]. Finally, we plan
to conduct a more rigorous assessment on how the teaching approach and curricular
structure impact student performance, with special emphasis on project quality.

References

1. A. Dix, J. Finlay, G. D. Abowd and R. Beale, *Human-Computer Interaction*, 3rd ed. Prentice Hall, 2004.
2. D. K. van Duyne, J. A. Landay and J. I. Hong, *The Design of Sites*, Addison-Wesley, Boston, MA, 2002.
3. J. Preece, I. Rogers and H. Sharp, *Interaction Design: beyond human-computer interaction*, John Wiley & Sons, 2002
4. C. Lewis and J. Rieman, *Task-Centered User Interface Design: A Practical Introduction*, downloaded from ftp://ftp.cs.colorado.edu/pub/distribs/clewis/HCI-Design-Book/, 1994
5. J. Johnson and A. Henderson, *Conceptual Models: Begin by Designing What to Design*, Interactions, Vol. 9 (1), pp. 25-32, ACM Press, January 2002.
6. M. Rettig, *Prototyping for Tiny Fingers*, Communications of the ACM, Vol. 37 (4), pp.21-27, ACM Press, April 1994.
7. A. Marcus and E. Chan, *Designing the PDA of the Future*, Interactions, Vol. 9 (1), pp. 34-44, ACM Press, January 2002.
8. J. Nielsen, *Guerrilla HCI: Using Discount Usability Engineering to Penetrate the Intimidation Barrier*, Academic Press, 1994.
9. M. B. Rosson and J. M. Carroll, *Usability engineering: Scenario-Based Development of Human-Computer Interaction*, San Francisco, Morgan-Kaufmann 2002.
10. J. Nielsen, *Original Top Ten Mistakes in Web Design*, Jakob Nielsen's Alertbox, May 1996. (cited 2007-10-20), http://www.useit.com/alertbox/9605a.html
11. J. Nielsen, *Top Ten Mistakes in Web Design*, Jakob Nielsen's Alertbox, February 2007. (cited 2007-10-20), http://www.useit.com/alertbox/9605.html
12. J. Nielsen and R. Molich. Heuristic evaluation of user interfaces. Conference on Human Factors in Computing Systems (CHI'90), pp. 249-256. ACM Press, 1990.

CRaSh-ing into HCI

Janet C Read, Matthew Horton, Gavin Sim and Emanuela Mazzone
School of Computing, Engineering and Physical Sciences,
University of Central Lancashire,
Preston, PR1 2HE, England
{jcread, mplhorton, grsim, emazzone}@uclan.ac.uk
WWW home page: http://www.uclan.ac.uk

Abstract. This paper describes a novel classroom based project that looked at methods for sharing the contributions of students during activities in undergraduate classes. Initially intended for HCI students, the CRaSh product has wide applicability for creative use of class time and for inspiring students in their design work. The method employed was a prototype interface that allowed the sharing of digitally ink based content by uploading this content to a secure website. Encouraging shared learning, the project focuses on the creation, completion and management of worksheets for students. This paper describes the design of the prototype and explores the ethical and legal discussions associated with this sort of product.

1   Introduction

This paper describes a product that was designed to provide undergraduate students on an introductory Human Computer Interaction (HCI) course an opportunity for a new learning experience. The project was intended to increase student engagement, assist in student learning and promote lecturer reflection. As uptake in British Universities has increased, the education of a more diverse set of learners and the challenges of larger class sizes and wider participation has provoked many innovative and interesting solutions. Proposing a new solution requires imagination and enthusiasm but the evaluation of new solutions is altogether a more complex process.

We describe here the design and implementation of CRaSh and conclude with a discussion of the difficulties surrounding the evaluation of its use in context.

Please use the following format when citing this chapter:

Read, J.C., Horton, M., Sim, G. and Mazzone, E., 2009, in IFIP International Federation for Information Processing, Volume 289; *Creativity and HCI: From Experience to Design in Education*; Paula Kotzé, William Wong, Joaquim Jorge, Alan Dix, Paula Alexandra Silva; (Boston: Springer), pp. 218–227.

1.1   Costs and benefits of Technological Interventions in the Classroom

In the modern university, there are several challenges to overcome. Some of these, like teaching large groups of students from different backgrounds, are generic across all courses; others are specific to a single subject area. In HCI Education, there are several challenges, three of these are:

- The teaching of design.
- Combining theory and practice.
- Teaching skills that are useful in industry.

Often feeling rather marginalized in a computer science curriculum, the HCI lecturer seeks to encourage reflection rather than skills gathering, design rather than development, and theory rather than fact. This makes HCI relatively difficult to teach and the engagement of students can be quite low, partly as they see HCI as a 'wooly' or 'soft' choice, but also as they do not fully understand the different emphasis placed by the typical HCI lecturer.

Disseminated through the HCI Educators workshop and via other similar routes, there have been many novel ideas suggested to improve the overall student experience in the HCI classroom. These novel ideas include industry led assessment and socially responsible project work [12], participation in real research studies, peer teaching [8], readings based teaching and case studies [5]. These approaches all have merits; and in all cases, a higher level of student engagement is reported.

One of the downsides to educational initiatives is the overhead on the course tutor in the management of the novel methods. In recent years, the increase in uptake of content management systems, the need to comply with disability legislation, and the demands of a computer-centered student base have all increased the workload on lecturers and course managers. It is certainly the case that as learning and teaching becomes more individualized and less lecture room driven, the cost to the instructor is higher. One metric to be considered in technological solutions is the cost to the course manager / lecturer. It would be expected that there would be a cost at the outset in developing the application but additionally, the tutor should be able to see some payback with the product use over time.

Technological solutions for education are often seen as a 'quick fix'. In primary and secondary state education, certainly in the UK, technology is encouraged as a means to enhance student learning and increase motivation, although the extent to which this succeeds is heavily debated. Computers in the classroom, broadband access to the internet, and devices such as interactive whiteboards can be found within the majority of classrooms today but rigorous studies that examine the real value of these products are few and far between.

There are several accounts of technology enhanced learning in Higher Education and Further Education. These include the use of tablet PCs in lectures [7], the use of lecture room response systems [4], and interactive lectures using mobile systems [11]. In most of these studies, the emphasis is on the development of a novel solution; the costs ad benefits are less readily reported.

The focus on technology in HE has been on the lecture room. This is not surprising as the lecture room is a difficult place for student participation (hence ideas like tablet PCs in class), is also a place where student engagement is low (hence the ideas for interactive systems) and is a place where the lecturer is not able to easily gauge the learning experiences of the students (hence the lecture room response systems). Enhancing small group activities with technology is much less reported, however the small group space lends itself to different technological enhancements. In particular, due to the smaller potential numbers of users, more expensive, and therefore scarcer technologies can be employed.

This paper describes such a technological innovation. The CRaSh application depends on a small (circa 5) number of tablet PCs and a web server. CRaSh is intended for use in small groups of around 20 students, to support small group work.

This paper begins with a discussion of the background pedagogy and then goes on to describe the prototype application before concluding with some observations about the potential for the product and a discussion about the evaluation of technological solutions in the classroom.

1.2   Creating and Sharing in the Classroom

There are several pilot projects using tablet PCs in the classroom being carried out across several institutions. These include Notre Dame, MIT, and the University of Washington and the focus in these studies is to examine the impact of these devices as teaching tools [7], however the take up of use of tablet PCs in educational settings has not been as rapid as was earlier hoped. One reason for this is that the applications that support educational work are not present and a second is the cost of the technology. The cost of a tablet PC is far greater than that of a laptop with similar technical specifications. That said, several studies point to the positive aspects that tablet technology brings to learning situations, especially with regard to improved visibility and the possibilities for sharing the work so created [6], [14].

As an adjunct to a classroom experience, a computer; tablet or otherwise, offers a unique ability to save work that can be referenced, or referred back to, at a later date. This has been seen as a benefit by students involved in such studies [7], aligned with this, students report that the quality of lecturers notes, and the ability to create notes of their own before a class improves when computers are brought into the learning space as this allows students to spend more time listening to the lecturer [1], [7].

When technology can be connected, either to other pieces of technology, or to other output / input devices, one way in which the addition of technology into the lecture space affects learning is in the increased possibilities for interactivity between the students and also with the tutor. Several studies have shown that the use of interactivity in lectures increases engagement and motivation [9],[10]. The suggestion is that knowing work might be shared or seen by others, or knowing that it is possible to make instant responses to a lecture, encourages a level of thought and reflection above the superfluous. Aligned with this idea, one way to engage students is to let them see the work they have just completed or see the work of others within their class. It is commonly the case in early education to show ones work to the class or to read a story that has been created but, as the learners become older, this practise is much less adopted.

Several low-tech solutions exist for sharing work; one is to have the students write on overhead projector films and then present these to the class, another is to use a visualiser to directly display their written work. The problems with these methods are that after the 'show and tell' moment, the work cannot be back referenced and the time taken to show multiple answers can be excessive. An extra problem can occur when students might feel embarrassed about showing their work and would prefer to remain anonymous.

1.3   Context of the Work

The work described here was developed at the University of Central Lancashire (UCLAN) where HCI is taught as an introductory course to around 120 students each year. HCI is taught in the second year with approximately 75% of the participating students having completed a web design course in year one that introduced some introductory HCI principles.

Students on the introductory HCI course come from a wide variety of degree streams including Computer Forensics, Games, Web and Multimedia, Database Systems, Networks and Combined Honours.

The second year HCI course is based on the [3] text book and is taught in 24 1-hour lecture classes over a full academic year. The students also attend tutorials and a handful of practical sessions; tutorials and practical sessions are typically held in groups of around 20 students at a time. Generally, but not always, the tutorials are taken by PhD students or associate staff who do not deliver the core syllabus. In general, the process is that the course leader prepares an outline activity for the tutorial class, emails this out to the tutors and then goes on to prepare the next weeks work. Apart from some informal reporting back, there is currently no system in place to ensure that the tutorial classes achieved their aims

Assessment on the course is partially dictated by local regulations that stipulate that a certain percentage of the marks have to be gained from a formal examination. In addition, a department policy on limited groupwork dictates that coursework, where used, be primarily individual. This restricts the options for innovative assessment methods. In 2006/7, the assessment pattern was 50% exam, 40% a single coursework assignment and 10% practical activities.

2   CRaSh – CReate and Share

CRaSh is a prototype application that allows students to create and share notes that they create on a tablet PC. There are two similar solutions found in the literature, the first is described in [13]. This application has two interfaces, the student interface and the presenter interface, and the students respond at points, using their interface, during class teaching. The application allows the responses to be saved, thus allowing discussions about the student learning during and after the class. That said, the application focuses on interaction rather than on note taking and is designed to promote a two way dialogue, during classes, between the tutor and the students. NotePals [2] is a more similar solution. This application uses digital ink and allows the sharing of notes made on PDAs. All three of theses applications, NotePals, CRaSh and the [13] application, use two interfaces, one for the student and one for the tutor. In NotePals and CRaSh, the former is primarily designed for note taking, the latter for browsing.

In NotePals, a custom interface was created for the PDAs to make the best use of the small space on the screen, in CRaSh, customisation was provided via a tablet driven interface that, aside from the navigation buttons, allowed a large and useful writing space. The interface for the note taking aspect of CraSh can be seen in Fig. 1.

Fig 1. *The CRaSh Note Taking Interface*

As well as providing an interface for free sketching and note making, the CRaSh prototype application has an added feature by which lecturers and instructors can design worksheets ahead of time and send them to the students for completion in class. This feature makes this application different from NotePals; this is not a criticism of NotePals as the size limitations of the NotePals interface would render such an application nonsensical.

Worksheets in CRaSh are saved as pictures (in pdf format) on the tablet PCs and then sent across to the server using any available wireless networks. An option, if the wireless network is not available, is to use physical communication methods like USB memory sticks to transfer the files from the tablet PCs to a computer that is physically connected to the internet. Once the pictures from the worksheets are in the host computer, they can be uploaded to the server. It is also possible to upload directly from the tablet PC.

The second interface for CRaSh is the web interface where students log on to see the worksheets that have been created and also to download worksheets for the next class if they have not already received them. This interface involves the use of a Postgress database to store data including student details, course and group details, and uses the server side scripting language PHP in the manipulation of this data. This interface is shown in Fig. 2.

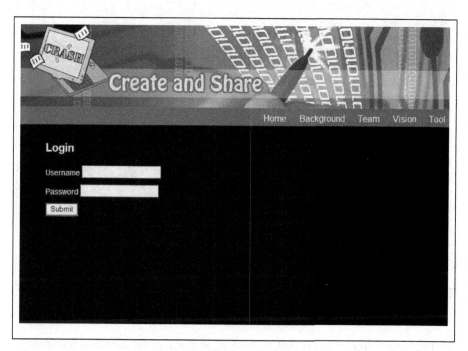

Fig 2. *The CRaSh Login Interface*

In the default option, work that is uploaded to the CRaSh website becomes visible to all others in the group. The group is defined by the lecturer and so, whereas individuals could be defined as groups and thus, a student could only see his or her own work, the normal situation is that a group will comprise as a minimum the members of the tutorial class, or maximally, all the students enrolled on the course. The lecturer (as administrator of the application) can change viewing privileges for modules (courses) that he / she manages by setting up these course groups within the admin section of the web interface. It is not possible for students to hide their work so the system is very open; when the work is viewed, it is anonymous and so, unless they know one another's writing style, students work remains anonymous with only the students who have created the piece of work knowing which is their own.

The CRaSh administrator has the option within the web interface to create new modules, add new staff members, add new students, and also add students to modules. This allows different lecturers to use the application with other modules if they wish and also to share the application with other members of staff who may also be teaching on the same module or who may have seen the application and wish to make use of it within another discipline.

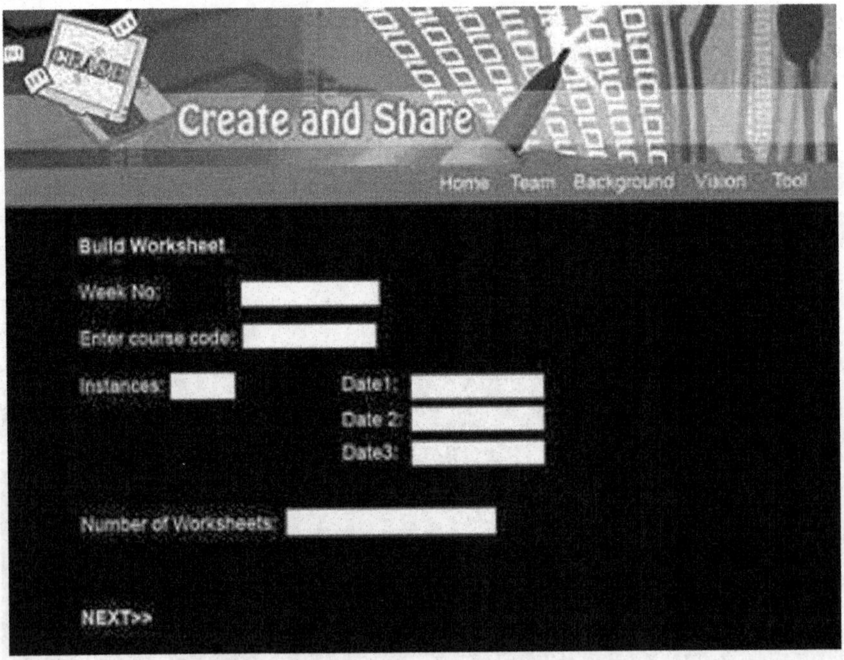

Fig 3. *The CRaSh Create Worksheet Page*

The current application is push technology in that it is the instructor who creates the worksheets at the standard PC and sends them to the students via email (or leaves them on the server to be downloaded by the students themselves). These worksheets are then uploaded to the tablet PCs by the students at the beginning of the class. This does therefore restrict the students on the tablet PCs in that they can only complete as many sheets for an individual class that they have been given. Thus, in the example shown in Fig. 1, the students know that there are only three worksheets available to them. This limitation was built in as it encourages sensible use of the tablet interface and ensures that the system does not become overloaded. Without such constraints, students have been known to cover 8 or 10 tablet pages with scribbled notes in a class session.

It is during the creation of worksheets that the necessary file organisation for the web material is created. The instructor needs to specify courses, weeks, and groups. The current application only allows a maximum of ten groups for each course/week but this would be reasonably easy to alter within the database on the server. There is also a current limit on the number of worksheets per course/week to three. The worksheet creation screen is shown in Fig. 3.

When worksheets are uploaded, the metadata, course, group, worksheet number is sent to the server and used along with the image to ensure that the image is stored in the correct place on the server. By sending the extra data with the image it ensures that the worksheets are only viewed by the students who are registered on the specific course relating to the uploaded image.

2.1   Usability of CRaSh

The CRaSh application was user tested in June 2007 with four students from the second year undergraduate HCI class. The application was found to be very easy to use and each part of the system worked without any problems. However, there were several requests from the students:

1. Students wanted the option of working in a landscape format.
2. Students wanted to be able to save (and upload) the worksheet even when they had only done one from a set of three.
3. Students wanted to be able to select pen colour from a palette.
4. Students wanted a space on the web server application to add comments to the images.

The first three of these requests have since been incorporated; the last one has not yet been implemented as there are several questions about the security and privacy aspects of this add-on that have yet to be resolved.

Two members of staff user tested the application, both had no difficulty creating worksheets and driving the application (a small instructional video was made to assist in this) but each commented on the limitations of the templates for worksheets. This limitation was noted and considered to be worth pursuing at a later date. One useful idea was to have small thumbnails of the different worksheet types available so the first time user was better able to know what to create. This has been added.

2.2   Evaluation of CRaSh

The CRaSh team was keen to test out the application with a cohort of students in real use. There are several difficulties with evaluating technology interventions and because of this a filed evaluation has not yet been completed. Initially, the intention was to have all the students in the undergraduate HCI class use the technology for six weeks, with half using it for the first six weeks, and the rest for the following six weeks. However, this was not possible as there were concerns about the accessibility of the technology for students with various learning difficulties and sensory disabilities. Because, in its present form, the application could not be made inclusive, a formal trial of it was not possible.

The authors are adapting the application so it can be used with a first year entertainment computing module in the summer of 2008. This module is less problematic as it currently has no students with sensory disabilities and, as it is a module that students have only to pass, that is, the marks accrued don't matter, an intervention study, as is needed in this case, is easier to carry out.

In a HCI classroom, it seems that CRaSh is most effective for small group work activities. In these instances, a group of two or three students would share a tablet PC whilst collaborating on a single well defined problem. The students would sketch and note their ideas on the tablet PC and later, would all be able to access the single notes and images as well as visit the offerings of their peers which would allow them an opportunity to reflect on their own work and compare their ideas with others.

3   Summary

The paper has described the CRaSh application and reflected on its use. The application provides lecturers with a facility to create worksheets that can be used very easily and has the added benefit of saving time and resources in producing paper worksheets for every student. The application also allows the lecturers to view the work that has been created providing them with a chance to see whether students have understood the subject matter taught and the questions that they have been asked.

CRaSh allows students to share their work with other members of their class. This also gives the students a chance to see whether they understood the work in the same way other members of the class did or where they may need to improve their skills at communicating information or their subject knowledge. This self discovery of learning is known to be especially useful for learners. The anonymity ensures that students do not feel threatened or identified.

With the tool being web based, the work can be viewed as soon as it is uploaded and by anyone from the class that is logged on at the time, there is no restriction to that amount of people who can view the work simultaneously. This allows for the material to be reviewed at the same time in class but also from home or from labs on normal PCs at a later date. As all the work sheets are saved, there is a useful resource created that can be reviewed at the end of the year to determine patterns of engagement and student activity. This allows staff to make changes to their teaching either by changing the way they teach a particular area due to pattern emerging showing students did not understand what they were being taught, or where they feel further work is required in certain areas of the syllabus. It also allows for a great revision guide for the students who have access to all the group work that has been done throughout the year, not only by themselves but also others for comparison and better understanding.

One attractive extension of the tool is to incorporate other digital ink technologies including digital pens and PDAs so the application is not so dependent on the tablet PCs, the web based side of the application would need little or no modification to achieve this.

Further evaluations of the tool will be carried out by students and staff to show the benefits the tool has brought to the groups that have used it.

Acknowledgments

We would like to acknowledge Microsoft and the ICS subject centre of the HE Academy that provided funding for this project.

References

1. Berque, D., et al., The design of an interface for student note annotation in a networked electronic classroom. Journal of Network and Computer Applications, 2000. **23**: p. 77 - 91.
1. Davis, R., et al. NotePals: Lightweight note sharing by the group, for the group. in CHI '99. 1999. Pittsburgh: ACM Press.
2. Dix, A., et al., *Human-Computer Interaction.* 3rd ed. 2004, Harlow: Pearson.
2. Draper, S.W. and M.I. Brown, *Increasing interactivity in lectures using an electronic voting system.* Journal of Computer Assisted Learning, 2004. **20**(1): p. 81 - 94.
3. McCrickard, D.S., C.M. Chewar, and J. Somerwell. *Design, Science, and Engineering Topics? Teaching HCI with a Unified Method.* in *SIGCSE'04.* 2004. Norfolk, Virginia: ACM Press.
4. McFall, R., et al. A Demonstration of a Collaborative Electronic Textbook Application on the Tablet PC. in World Conference on Educational Multimedia, Hypermedia and Telecommunications. 2004: AACE.
3. Mock, K., *Teaching with Tablet PC's.* Journal of Computer Science in Colleges, 2004. **20**(2): p. 17 - 27.
5. Plimmer, B. and R. Amor. *Peer Teaching Extends HCI Learning.* in *ITiCSE'06.* 2006. Bologna, Italy: ACM Press.
6. Rodger, S.H. An interactive lecture approach to teaching computer science'. in Proceedings of the twenty-sixth SIGCSE technical symposium on Computer science education. 1995. Nashville.
4. Roth, W.M., et al., Differential participation during science conversations: The interaction of focal artefacts, social configurations, and physical arrangements'. Journal of the Learning Sciences, 1999. **8**: p. 293 - 347.
7. Scheele, N., et al. Mobile Devices in Interactive Lectures'. in World Conference on Educational Multimedia Hypermedia and Telecommunications. 2004. Lugano.
8. Shneiderman, B., et al. Making a Difference: Integrating Socially Relevant Projects into HCI Teaching. in CHI 2006. 2006. Montreal, Canada: ACM Press.
9. Simon, B., et al. Preliminary Experiences with a Tablet PC Based System to Support Learning in Computer Science Courses. in ITiCSE'04. 2004. Leeds, UK: ACM Press.
10. Thomas, M., A. King, and T. Cetinguc. My First Year with a Tablet PC: Has Literacy Found a Means to Ubiquitous Computing at Last? in SITE. 2004: AACE.